Advance praise f
Create Your Own TV Series

"Recently, I wrote and produced my first Internet series and, quite frankly, I wish I had read Ross Brown's book before I started."
—Bill Rosenthal, creator of the web series *Greetings From Home*, writer *Nurse Jackie*

"A must-read for anyone trying to break in on the Internet."
—Fred Rubin, Professor, UCLA School of Theater, Film and Television

"Outstanding guidance, advice, and inspiration for anyone who wants to make a web series."
—Joel Surnow, Emmy winning co-creator and executive producer of *24*

"Ross Brown has taken his indelible knowledge and experience from the world of network TV and crammed it into the new and fast-paced industry of Internet content. Having studied how the web series has taken hold, gone viral, and continues to change the landscape of entertainment, Ross imparts his own wisdom in comedy writing, series structure, idea creation, and character building. This is a book for anyone who has ever wanted to make a web series— and for anyone who already has. I'm excited to learn how to correct my mistakes from the first time around."
—Christine Lakin, creator and star of the award-winning web series *Lovin' Lakin* and co-host of *Internet Icon*

"Ross Brown's enormously informative and entertaining book is enriched by his insider chops as a network series showrunner, and by his years of inspiring students in university television courses. This book is clearly a must-read for anyone interested in creating a do-it-yourself web series. But in a larger sense, it also presents the tools for establishing the enduring concept, core characters, and story engines required of *any* television series, regardless of length, making it an invaluable resource for anyone aspiring to a small screen career."
—Brad Buckner, consulting producer, *Supernatural*

"At a time when many in the entertainment industry still struggle to see the viability and inevitability of web-based entertainment as a major player, new media producers are blessed to have an advocate and teacher in the form of veteran producer, Ross Brown. Even though there are no hard and fast rules in this burgeoning medium, he offers sage advice to those needing guidance on the subject of how to create and produce a high-quality web series."
—Courtney Zito, CEO, Hollywood Girl Pictures

"As a video creator looking to produce content for online audiences, I've found this book to be indispensable. *Create Your Own TV Series for the Internet* provides just the right amount of information to get you started and make you feel like you know what you're doing in these uncharted waters. It's the perfect book at the perfect time!"

—Trevor Mayes, writer/director, *My Demon Girlfriend*

"This is the best and most thorough resource for anyone who has an interest in creating a web TV series. . . . As an experienced screenwriter and filmmaker, I cannot think of an area not covered in this timely volume. Highest recommendation."

—Robin Simmons, filmmaker

"Ross Brown knows creating stories from the bottom up. This book comes at a crucial time and shows you the way to create stories online for all audiences. All creators and storytellers should read this book now and for the future."

—Dave Watson, editor, *Movies Matter*

"Whether you're an emerging digital creator, a seasoned filmmaker looking to migrate to the web, or a media educator looking for new and innovative ways to engage your students, *Create Your Own TV Series for the Internet* is an essential read."

—Steinar Ellingsen, Director of Education, Melbourne Webfest

"Know who should read this book? Directors, sure. But also *every television writer in the world*. As a TV writer, much of your job is standing on set helping a director bring your script to life. This book is the bring-your-script-to-life toolbox, complete with instruction manual, that many writers never get to have."

—Chad Gervich, TV writer (*Dog With a Blog, After Lately,* and *Cupcake Wars*) and author (*How To Manage Your Agent* and *Small Screen, Big Picture*)

"With so much stuff out there, it's all too easy to get lost in the noise. This book gives you the tools and techniques to lift your content out of the fighting pack and put it in front of viewers. . . . Ross Brown has written *the* indispensable guide to creating a successful web series."

—Robert Grant, screenwriter and author of *Writing the Science Fiction Film*

Create Your Own

TV SERIES

for **THE INTERNET**

ROSS BROWN

SECOND EDITION

MICHAEL WIESE PRODUCTIONS

Copyright 2014 by Ross Brown

All rights reserved. No part of this book may be reproduced in any form or by any means without permission in writing from the author, except for the inclusion of brief quotations in a review.

Published by Michael Wiese Productions
12400 Ventura Blvd. #1111
Studio City, CA 91604
(818) 379-8799, (818) 986-3408 (FAX)
mw@mwp.com
www.mwp.com

Cover design by MWP
Interior design by Concord Editorial
Printed by McNaughton & Gunn
Manufactured in the United States of America

Library of Congress Cataloging-in-Publication Data

Brown, Ross, 1954–
  [Byte-sized television]
  Create your own TV series for the internet / Ross Brown. — Second edition.
      pages cm
  Originally published as: Byte-sized television: create your own TV series for the internet.
    ISBN 978-1-61593-168-2 (pbk.)
  1. Television authorship. 2. Internet television. I. Title.
  PN1992.7.B76 2014
  808'.066791—dc23

                        2013033457

Printed on recycled paper

CONTENTS

ACKNOWLEDGMENTS

First thanks go to my colleagues at the Dodge College of Film and Media Arts at Chapman University. In particular I would like to thank dean Bob Bassett and Media Arts Division chair Janell Shearer for their support and guidance of both my teaching and the writing of this book. I would also like to thank professor James Gardner for suggesting that I write this book and professor Gil Bettman for introducing me to my publishers, Ken Lee and Michael Wiese.

I'm also immensely grateful to my students, particularly those who have taken my Byte-Sized Television courses. You inspire me with your creativity, challenge me with your questions, force me to think deeply, and remind me every day that life is about learning.

Thanks also to my writing colleagues, who have generously shared so many insights about craft with me over the years, especially Bruce Watson, Bob Colleary, Neil Landau, and Deborah Brevoort.

Eternal gratitude and love to my daughters, Alexis and Rachel, for their support, encouragement, and the joy they bring to my life. And most of all, my deepest gratitude and love to my wife, Wendy, for the infinite gifts you've given me over the years: love, encouragement, wisdom, space, passion, compassion, joy, heart, and laughter.

HOW TO USE THIS BOOK

This book is intended for a wide range of users, including

- Aspiring filmmakers
- University film, video, or other media instructors and students
- Middle or high school video instructors and students
- Experienced filmmakers new to the web series genre
- Experienced film craftsmen (e.g., cinematographers, editors, grips, electricians) who want to expand their creative horizons and showcase their skills and talents beyond their current craft area
- Actors hoping to promote their careers and expand their creative opportunities by creating their own showcase web series
- Businesses interested in creating branded content or advertainment-oriented web series

Each group will find a wealth of valuable guidance in the book, but they may approach it slightly differently based on their needs and background. Here are some suggestions for each group on how to use this book:

- **Aspiring filmmakers:** If you are brand new to video production and have never written a script, used a video camera, or edited video footage, you should use this book in conjunction with one or more books on video production and postproduction. This book will help you conceive your series, develop your characters, write a pilot script, and plan the key elements necessary for production, such as casting, finding locations, and making a shot list and shooting schedule, and will guide you through the creative choices and process of editing. This book will also help you market your show and yourself. What you will need to consult other books about are the nuts and bolts of using the camera, sound, and editing equipment. Appendix 2 of this book contains lists of suggested books to help you with technical instruction in these areas.

- **University film, video, and media instructors:** If you teach at the college level, this book is organized not just as a textbook but as a kit for teaching your course. At the end of each chapter there is a "For Teachers" page with suggested assignments and techniques for reinforcing that chapter's concepts. Appendix 3 contains the syllabi and a week-by-week breakdown of the two Byte-Sized Television courses that I teach at Chapman University's Dodge College of Film and Media Arts. During the first semester each student pitches a concept and characters, then writes a script for a 3- to 5-minute web series pilot. I select two of the scripts to be shot and edited (assigning crew positions such as director, producer, director of photography, and editor to the students whose scripts were not selected for production). Then in Semester 2, the students write, shoot, and edit three additional episodes of each series based on the pilot.

- **Middle and high school teachers:** Just like university instructors, you can also use the assignments and tips contained in the "For Teachers" page at the end of each chapter and the schedule and week-by-week breakdown in my syllabi. In addition, for your students completely new to writing for the screen, Appendix 1 contains a simple and effective tutorial on screenplay format.

- **Experienced filmmakers:** If you're an experienced writer, you can use the chapters on writing less as instruction and more as a stimulant to your creative process. What may be new and more useful to you are the sections on preproduction, production, postproduction, and marketing. Similarly, if you are a pro at production, you can skim that section and focus more on learning about writing — character, structure, dialogue, and so on.

- **Actors:** This book can open your eyes to the writing, production, and postproduction processes in a big way. Learning the other parts of the filmmaking process will make you a better actor and can reveal to you other talents you have and lead to work opportunities in the film business you hadn't previously considered.

- **Businesses looking to create branded content:** Though it may be tempting to skip ahead to Chapter Fourteen (which is devoted specifically to business uses of web series), I urge you to read the other material as well. The principles of effective storytelling and the creation of memorable characters apply not only to fictional comedies and dramas but to the stories businesses want to tell about themselves and their brands.

Finally, I hope everyone has FUN. Use the book to expand your imagination. Use it to increase your creativity. Use it to motivate the part of you that is dying to express yourself but doesn't quite know how to get started.

WHY A SECOND EDITION?

The first edition of this book came out in February 2011, and it has been a great success. I measure success not only by the number of copies sold but also by the ways in which the book is helping those who've read it. It has been adopted as a text in web series classes at major film schools across the country (Chapman University, Loyola Marymount University, and Emerson College, to name a few) and around the world, including film schools in South Africa, Singapore, and China. The instructors have been uniformly enthusiastic about the book and how it has helped their students make better web series.

Independent filmmakers have been equally generous with their praise. At book signings and panels where I've appeared in Los Angeles, Chicago, Marseille, and elsewhere, I've been overwhelmed and gratified by the number of people who've come up to me to say, "Thank you for writing this book. It's just what I needed to help me make my web series." And one of my proudest moments came when my writing and teaching colleague Bill Rosenthal, a writer and producer with over 20 years of top-line credits on shows for ABC, NBC, and HBO who recently wrote and produced the web series *Greetings from Home* for a major new media company, read the book and said, "I wish I'd read this before I made my show."

That's some high praise, having a seasoned pro say he learned a lot from your book.

So if the first edition was so great, why bother with a second edition? The simple answer is that in the world of the Internet and Internet TV, a few years is a very long time. Things move at light speed, are constantly changing and evolving. And so I felt it was vital for me to update the book to keep it as current as possible and as useful as possible for readers. So the new material in this book includes

- Updated examples from new web series to illustrate key concepts
- Fresh information on the proliferation of new festivals devoted to web series
- A new section on marketing not only your series but yourself
- A new section on animated web series
- A brand-new chapter on business uses of web series, a rapidly growing area of opportunity for businesses and creators alike
- A brand-new set of interviews with creators who have advanced their careers by making web series, professionals who are finding new creative and financial opportunities in the web series world, and the founder of the LAWEBFEST, the world's first festival devoted entirely to web series

All this new material is in addition to the tips, guidance, and instruction already present in the first edition. So if you are new to this book, welcome. Enjoy the book, and I hope it helps you make great web series. And if you're a fan of the first edition, welcome back, and thank you for your continued interest. I hope this new edition helps you make even better web series than the ones you've already made.

PREFACE

Every writer, producer, network, studio, and cable channel in Hollywood is spending thousands of hours and millions of dollars trying to figure out how to connect with the YouTube audience and make a hit web series. But it's a solid bet that the next breakout short-form hit will come not from Hollywood but from the mind of someone outside the established media power structure — someone like you.

That's not to say this trailblazer will necessarily be a rank amateur. Maybe he'll be a writer who's been trying to break into network television but hasn't succeeded yet. Or maybe she'll be writing for another medium that Hollywood or the Internet suddenly discovers (can you say Diablo Cody?). Or maybe it will be a veteran writer who has been churning out bland sitcoms for decades, someone seen as over the hill, someone who throws caution to the wind and creates something totally new and original because the traditional doors to employment are now slammed in his face (can you say Marc Cherry, creator of *Desperate Housewives*?). Or maybe it will be someone now in film school, or even in high school, who came of age during the digital era, thinks visually, and intuitively knows what her peers crave in the way of short video entertainment, in part because watching short videos is a normal part of her daily experience.

The point is that everybody knows there is a huge, game-changing, hit web series lurking on the horizon, but nobody knows where it will come from. They know only that sooner or later, there will be a breakthrough smash hit in the Internet TV realm, so it might as well come from YOU.

Webisodes are the Wild West of Hollywood, a vast expanse of territory with unlimited potential just begging to be explored and mined. The territory is open to anyone with a dream and the moxie to follow that dream.

You may strike oil or find gold, or you may end up with a handful of dust. Either way, the journey will be exciting and rewarding for its own sake. It will challenge you, expand your creative horizons, and open your eyes and mind to all kinds of new skills you never knew you had lurking inside.

But before you head out on this quest to create your own Internet TV series, you need a few vital supplies: some basic equipment and know-how, a workable series premise, a pilot script, a shooting budget, and shot list — in short, you need a plan.

This book is designed to help you draw up that plan, step by step. You are HERE. Somewhere on the Internet is a place for a television series created by YOU. This book is the map that can lead you from where you are now — a person with a lot of creative ideas in his head but no clear idea how to turn those buzzing ideas into reality — to THERE, the creator of your own unique and exciting TV series designed for the Web.

I know it can be done because my students at the Dodge College of Film and Media Arts at Chapman University have been creating innovative, entertaining web series since 2007. You know it can be done because you've surfed the Net, seen the good, the bad, and the ugly out there, and said, "I can do better than that."

You're absolutely right. You can do better than most of what's out there. And you don't need a million-dollar budget or a Hollywood studio full of equipment to do it. Anyone with a digital camera and an ordinary computer has all the equipment he needs right now to make a web series.

What you probably don't have is exposure to the thought process involved in taking a raw idea for a short-form TV show and shaping that vague notion into a clear premise, defined characters, a story to introduce those characters in an engaging way, and the professional know-how to take that story through production and postproduction and end up with a polished and marketable pilot episode.

Make no mistake: It won't be easy. You can't just slap together some half-baked notion, grab a camera, and point it randomly at things that strike you as interesting or funny. That's just video masturbation. All you end up with, as Mike Judge suggests in his film *Idiocracy*, is a show called *Ow! My Balls!*

You may also need some help understanding the best way to market your web TV series — that is, the best way to let the audience know what you've created and get them interested in watching your new TV show. Simply posting something on YouTube is not enough. The Internet is a cacophony of voices screaming, "Watch me! Watch me!" You have to find ways to make your voice, and your web series, stand out from the crowd. A great series concept and superior execution are only good first steps. But to get the eyeballs to your show, you'll need to apply a little Web 2.0 marketing savvy, which is what Chapter Thirteen is all about: promoting your series AND yourself.

But if you have a sincere desire to create high-quality humor or drama in an episodic form for the Internet and to commit the time and energy necessary for marketing your work, then read on. As my students have taught me over and over again, there is an unlimited and untapped supply of fresh, compelling ideas out there begging to find their way to the screen. This book will help you to tap into that vast reservoir of creativity and give your ideas form and professional quality. It's the ultimate win–win situation: You get a shot at creating a hit TV show for the Internet, and we, the millions of daily consumers of short-form Internet videos, get a shot at watching something more compelling than *Ow! My Balls!*

For the sake of all our days and nights, read on and create something fantastic for all of us to watch.

1   WHAT IS A WEBISODE?

Simply put, a webisode is an episode of a television series designed for distribution over the Internet. It can be comedy like *Boys Will Be Girls* or its companion series, *Girls Will Be Boys*, or compelling drama like *The Bannen Way*. It can be live action or animated (see John Woo's *Seven Brothers*), fiction or reality-based (see *Start Something*, a social media documentary series presented by the Big Brothers Big Sisters organization). It can be a high-budget, intricately filmed sci-fi extravaganza with dazzling special effects like *Sanctuary*, which cost $4.3 million or approximately $32,000 per minute, one of the most ambitious projects to date designed for direct release over the Internet (which later became a cable TV series on the Syfy channel). Or it can be as low-tech as a static webcam shot in front of a convenient and free background like your own bedroom. It can be made purely for entertainment purposes, or it can be branded entertainment or "advertainment," like dozens of web series now produced by Fortune 500 companies including Kraft, Toyota, and Anheuser-Busch who hope that a little entertainment will go a long way toward getting you to buy their cream cheese, Camrys, and Bud. And the length can be whatever you choose, from a quick joke (check out the incredibly clever 5-second films on YouTube) to however long you can hold the audience's attention.

The key word is *series*. A webisode (or web episode) is an individual installment of an ongoing premise with recurring characters. A single, stand-alone short video — say of the hilarious things your cat did after she lapped up your Jack Daniels on the rocks — is NOT a webisode. Neither is that brilliant spoof of *Sex and the City* you shot at your grandmother's retirement home — unless you shot a series of short *Sex and the City* spoofs

1

with grandma and her horny pals, in which case we should take the Jack Daniels away from you and your grandma and give it back to your cat.

A BRIEF HISTORY OF SHORT EPISODIC VIDEO ON THE WEB

In the Mel Brooks movie *History of the World Part I*, Moses (played by Brooks) descends from a mountaintop lugging three stone tablets chiseled with 15 commandments from God — until Moses trips and drops one of the holy tablets, shattering it beyond recognition. Having promised 15 commandments, he covers by swiftly declaring, "I bring you ten, *ten* commandments." Five sacred commandments smashed into a pile of rubble just like that. Who knows what wisdom was lost? Maybe the missing commandments said things like "Thou shalt not wear spandex after age 40" or "Covet not thy neighbor's iPad2, for he is a tech dunce and uses it only to play Spider Solitaire." Your guess is as good as mine. But whatever moral pearls turned to dust in that moment, I'm pretty sure one of the lost commandments was not "Thou shalt make TV shows only in increments of 30 or 60 minutes."

Since the dawn of the television age in the 1940s, broadcasters have been prisoners of the clock, confined to airing shows on the hour and half hour so viewers would know when and where to find them. But the digital revolution and the Internet have changed all that. More and more, television and visual entertainment in general are part of an on-demand world rather than an on-the-hour one. Audiences can now watch what they want when they want, which, in turn, means that shows no longer have to be packaged in 30- or 60-minute installments.

It's a revolution that has fed on itself. Free from the tyranny of the 30/60 paradigm, short-form video content in all shapes and sizes has exploded on the Web. Maybe a show is 2 minutes and 37 seconds long one time, maybe it runs 6 minutes and 41 seconds the next. Each episode can be however long it deserves to be.

Audiences, in turn, have responded by changing their viewing habits. Where you used to need at least half an hour to watch your favorite comedy, now you might be able to catch two or three episodes of it in less than 10 minutes. Office workers now schedule video breaks rather than coffee breaks, boosting their energy and outlook by guzzling down a few short comedy videos for free instead of a double espresso caramel latte for 5 bucks. Or maybe you choose to watch a few webisodes on the bus or the train on your smartphone or tablet.

Never before have viewers had so many choices. And never before have creators had so much latitude on the length and type of content they can make.

In truth, short-form episodic film series have been around since well before the days of television, some even coming during the silent movie era. Charlie Chaplin, Harold Lloyd, and Buster Keaton all created one-reelers, popular early predecessors to today's web series shot on film and exhibited in theaters across the country right alongside the newsreel and the feature presentation. In the animated realm, the Looney Tunes shorts come to mind. But the equipment and processing necessary to make even a 2-minute film back then were so expensive that only professionals could afford to make these shorts. And even if an amateur had the funds and imagination to produce a clever short film, distribution was controlled by the major Hollywood studios, which also owned the theaters and had no intention of allowing the competition to cut into their lucrative monopoly.

The advent of lightweight and affordable video cameras by the early 1980s made it possible for millions to shoot their own videos. But most of these home videos were unedited, handheld footage of family vacations or children's birthday parties, usually narrated by your dad or Uncle Johnny: "Here we are at little Billy's second birthday party. Here's Billy eating cake. Here he is opening his presents. And here's little Billy pulling down his pants and relieving himself in the garden." As much as you (and, years later, big Billy) wish Dad had done a little judicious editing, that equipment was still bulky and prohibitively expensive during the first home video era. And distribution venues remained unavailable to those outside the media power elite.

The digital and Internet revolution of the 1990s changed all this. Suddenly, you didn't need a $100,000 flatbed machine to edit your video.

Your average home computer could handle the task. Video cameras were cheaper than ever, required no more technical expertise than a flashlight, and were increasingly capable of producing a high-quality video image. Best of all, high-speed broad-band connections meant that inexpensive and easy distribution on the Web was just a mouse-click away for millions of amateur video enthusiasts.

However, there was still one small problem for amateur video makers dying to show the world their wares: How would the audience know where to find your video on the Internet?

Enter YouTube. Founded by Steve Chen, Chad Hurley, and Jawed Karim, three former employees of the Silicon Valley firm PayPal, the website had a simple but powerful concept: Users could post and view any type of video, professional or amateur, on this one-stop shopping site. It was like one giant short-video multiplex, and anyone in the world could hop from theater to theater for free, without ever leaving the comfort of their own laptop.

The first YouTube video was posted on April 23, 2005. It was called "Me at the Zoo" — no explanation of content necessary — and ran all of nineteen seconds. You can view it at *www.youtube.com/watch?v=jNQXAC9IVRw*. By November, the site had 200,000 viewers watching 2 million short videos per day, even though the site was still in its experimental beta phase.

December 15, 2005 marked YouTube's official debut. Within a month users were watching an astonishing 25 million videos per day. By July 2006, that number topped 100 million, with 65,000 new videos being uploaded daily. As of early 2013, YouTube had a mind-boggling 800 million unique users per month watching more than 4 billion hours of video during each month.

Though much of the early content was either clips from ordinary broadcast and cable television or amateur silliness like teenagers lip-syncing to pop songs, the popularity of the site and promise of a ready audience opened the Internet floodgates for well-crafted content in episodic form. Among the early webisode hits launched on YouTube was *lonelygirl15*, a serialized webcam confessional of a lonely teenage girl. Though the series was presented as if the title character made the videos herself, it was soon revealed that *lonelygirl15* was not an authentic teenage video diary but a carefully scripted show starring an actress named Jessica Rose created by aspiring filmmakers who saw this new Internet venue as a way to make a name for themselves in the film business. Despite the deception and the fact that the public soon knew it was all professionally scripted, the series remained popular on YouTube and led to the creation of another series in a similar webcam diary format called *KateModern*.

Another early web series success was *Sam Has 7 Friends*, created by a group that called themselves Big Fantastic. These aspiring video makers saw the world of short-form Internet TV not as a stepping stone to other film opportunities but an art form to be mastered in and of itself. *Sam Has 7 Friends* premiered on YouTube, Revver, iTunes, and its own website on August 28, 2006. It hooked viewers with the simple slogan, "Samantha Breslow has 7 friends. On December 15, 2006, one of them will kill her." Each of the 80 episodes brought Samantha one day closer to death. It was compelling Internet television, a serialized thriller with new material and clues made available a bit at a time day by day, and its audience grew steadily as word spread.

Suddenly, amateur and professional content exploded across the Web. The webisode revolution was on, and it was televised over the Internet. YouTube had become the fourth most popular Internet site in the world and an integral part of the public's daily vocabulary, like Google or texting. Those under 30, especially, were so comfortable with capturing, editing, and posting video online that millions now thought they could create videos as easily as they could send e-mail.

The public hunger to consume short video was not lost on the professional world. If millions of eyeballs were leaving broadcast television in favor of short video on the Internet, then Hollywood, the networks, and the rest of the global media establishment wanted to find a way to recapture those valuable eyeballs.

Global media giant Sony Pictures Entertainment jumped in, creating a site called Grouper (later known as Crackle) that billed itself as "a multiplatform video entertainment network and studio that distributes the hottest emerging talent on the Web and beyond." By 2013 the site featured original web series right alongside much of Sony's library of traditional sitcoms, dramas, and feature films, a testament to the growing reality that today's audience, especially the younger part of it, makes fewer distinctions between movies, TV, and the Internet. If something is entertaining and compelling, they'll watch it. If not, they won't.

Disney launched Stage 9 Digital Media, a division dedicated to generating original online-only content. It debuted with a series called *Squeegees*, about window washers, created by a Los Angeles group known as Handsome Donkey.

Traditional broadcast networks like ABC, CBS, and NBC, which at first cursed Internet video as the enemy (just as the major movie studios had cursed broadcast television as the enemy in the early days of TV), quickly realized Internet video was here to stay, and they needed to be part of it. They made full episodes of their shows available online and soon discovered that rather than decreasing their overall audience, Internet availability of series expanded their reach. They also created original short-form webisodes for shows like *The Office* and *24*.

Established filmmakers loved the creative spirit of Internet video and dove into the webisode pool as well (though they stuck to using their real names instead of cool monikers like Big Fantastic and Handsome Donkey). Oscar-winning directors Joel and Ethan Coen (*No Country for Old Men*, *Fargo*, *The Big Lebowski*) committed to produce short features for 60Frames, a company run by former UTA Online head Brent Weinstein with an ambitious production slate. *Charlie's Angels* director McG was hired by Warner Bros. to create a series called *Sorority Forever* for The WB. Will Ferrell and other established stars contribute Internet videos to a site called Funny or Die. Successful writer, producer, and director Jerry Zucker (*Airplane!*, *The Naked Gun* movie series, *Ghost*) went so far as to form a new company, National Banana, with a soundstage and postproduction facilities and staff dedicated to creating online content.

Though A-list players were storming the Internet video world in droves, Hollywood also recognized that this new form demanded a new reservoir of creative inspiration and energy. Major Hollywood talent agencies like Creative Artists Agency and UTA formed divisions dedicated to finding new Internet talent, both in front of and behind the camera. These new agency divisions also sought to develop online opportunities for established mainstream clients who wanted to work in this exciting new realm.

Suddenly, once-obscure guerilla video artists like the Big Fantastic were in hot demand. Well-financed media mogul Michael Eisner, former CEO of the Walt Disney company, hired Big Fantastic to create a web series called *Prom Queen*, which became a major hit racking up over 20 million views in short order. Eisner then upped the ante and hired Big Fantastic to shoot 50 two-minute episodes of *Foreign Body*, a medical thriller tied to the launch of a book by the same name by best-selling author Robin Cook.

Today, nearly every major media player has made at least some commitment to create original web content ranging from low-budget experimentation all the way to Netflix financing two seasons of the hour-long drama *House of Cards*, starring Kevin Spacey and Robin Wright and released directly via the Internet.

For advertisers, who had long relied on television to provide the precious eyeballs they needed, the new Internet video culture presented a variety of problems. Not only were fewer people watching network television, but those who did were armed with digital video recorders and other devices that allowed them to skip the commercials. Advertisers quickly realized they needed to take the lemons they'd been handed and somehow make lemonade. Rather than merely placing the same old ads in this new entertainment arena, advertisers seized the opportunity and made new short-form content of their own that married their sales message to entertainment. Consumer giant Unilever promoted its new spray bottle version of I Can't Believe It's Not Butter through webisodes of a series called *Sprays of Her Life*, a parody of soap operas with the slogan, "Romance. Passion. Deception. Vegetables. Watch things heat up when the refrigerator lights go down!" Anheuser-Busch ponied up $30 million to create Bud.tv, a video site that promoted brands like Budweiser not only through product ads but by hosting original, nonadvertising entertainment content aimed at their target audience produced by Internet-eager talent like Matt Damon and Ben Affleck.

In the old network television advertising paradigm, advertisers looked for shows whose audience included the advertiser's target consumer group and bought 30-second spots on the show, hoping against the odds that the audience would stick around for the commercial message instead of muting the set, raiding the fridge, or taking a bathroom break. But in this new, short-form Internet video world, advertisers could design the entertainment to appeal to their consumers and embed their advertising message seamlessly into the entertainment itself.

Suddenly the Internet was no longer the arch enemy of Fortune 500 advertisers; it was their new best friend. Advertisers were making entertaining commercials hoping they'd go viral on the Internet. Take, for instance, the wonderfully entertaining Old Spice deodorant commercials featuring hunky actor Isaiah Mustafa as "The Man Your Man Could Smell Like." The first ones were made for traditional, pay-for-your-ad-time TV. Then Procter & Gamble had a better idea. People loved the commercials, so why not make more just for the Internet! Along with re-viewings of the original TV ads, these Old Spice spots have now received nearly 100 million views on YouTube, and the spots have been forwarded over and over again via social media like Facebook, all without Procter & Gamble spending a dime for airtime.

It's a brave new world for everyone, Hollywood hotshots and newcomers alike. We all sense that something big is coming, and coming soon. Nobody knows exactly what the Internet video future will look like, but everyone wants to be a part of it.

WHAT'S OUT THERE NOW, AMATEUR AND PROFESSIONAL

Trying to catalog every web series on the Net is a bit like trying to count the popcorn kernels in the big bin at the multiplex. You'll never get the job done because fresh new nuggets pop out of the machine faster than you can count. Seventy-two hours of video are uploaded to YouTube *every minute*. Before I finish typing this sentence, someone, somewhere, will post a new Internet-based TV series. On the Internet, time is measured not in months or years but in nanoseconds. Even when you bring two people together who are professional experts in the web video field, it's likely that each will know about dozens of high-quality web series the other has never heard of.

Daunting as the task may be, as an aspiring content creator it's vital that you survey the territory to get a basic sense of the existing landscape and scope of offerings. Start with the video segments of Internet giants such as YouTube, Yahoo! Video, AOL Video, MSN Video, and Facebook. Then explore sites featuring proprietary, professionally created content like Crackle and Funny or Die. Finally, surf a variety of video hosting sites that feature user-generated content, like Vimeo. You'll have to wade through a sludge pile of things that don't appeal to you, but you'll also be inspired by some of what you see and find some favorite new short-form shows.

Here is a list of some of the leading video-sharing websites:

- **YouTube.** The numbers say it all: 72 hours of video uploaded every minute, billions of videos viewed per day, 800 million unique viewers per month, billions of videos per week monetized locally.
- **Metacafe.** A top site that bills itself as having "more exclusive, original and curated premium video content than any other entertainment site."
- **Google Video.** They own YouTube, the 800-pound gorilla, but Google Video adds another 400 pounds of video chest-beating power.
- **Dailymotion.** The site attracts 106 million unique monthly visitors by offering advanced technology and high-quality video to users and content creators alike.
- **Yahoo! Video.** In addition to the usual boatload of amateur videos, the site includes Yahoo! Originals, high-quality, professionally created content.
- **Blip.** Their mission is to help people discover the best in original web series and to help web series producers make a sustainable living; they distribute videos on websites including YouTube, Facebook, and iTunes and to home TV sets via Roku, Google TV, Verizon FiOS, and others. Blip shares all ad revenue with producers on a 50/50 basis.
- **Vimeo.** *Wired* magazine calls it "the thinking person's YouTube." With a fresh batch of tech improvements and countless accolades from the tech press, Vimeo is a premiere destination for content creators.

Another way to educate yourself about the world of web series is to check out the work of those considered to be the best in the field by their peers. Here is a list of nominees for the 2013 Streamy Awards, which touts itself as "the first and most prestigious awards ceremony devoted to honoring excellence in original web television programming and those who create it."

Best Drama Series

Lauren

Anyone but Me

The Booth at the End

Runaways

Halo 4: Forward unto Dawn

Best Comedy Series

Burning Love

The Lizzie Bennet Diaries

Smosh

MyMusic

PrisonPals

Best Action or Sci-Fi Series

H+ The Digital Series

Drone

Halo 4: Forward unto Dawn

Bite Me

Clutch

Best Animated Series

Electric City

Dinosaur Office

Dick Figures

Oishi High School Battle

Red vs. Blue

Best Writing: Comedy

Felicia Day, *The Guild*

Peter Shukoff aka Nice Peter, Lloyd Ahlquist aka EpicLLOYD, *Epic Rap Battles of History*

Spencer Grove, *The Annoying Orange*
Bernie Su, *The Lizzie Bennet Diaries*
Benny Fine, Rafi Fine, and Team, *MyMusic*

Best Writing: Drama

Christopher Kubasik, *The Booth at the End*
Susan Miller and Tina Cesa Ward, *Anyone but Me*
Todd and Aaron Helbing, *Halo 4: Forward unto Dawn*
Vlad Baranovsky and Yuri Baranovsky, *Leap Year*
Tony Valenzuela, *Black Box TV*

Best Direction

Mike Diva, *Mike Diva Presents*
Benny Fine and Rafi Fine, *MyMusic*
Jon Avnet, *Jan*
Drew Daywalt, *Black Box TV*
Stewart Hendler, *H+ The Digital Series*

Best Ensemble Cast

Burning Love
Cybergeddon
Epic Meal Time
The Lizzie Bennet Diaries
Video Game High School

Best Male Performance: Drama

Xander Berkeley, *The Booth at the End*
Ben Samuel, *Battleground*
Jackson Rathbone, *Aim High*
Olivier Martinez, *Cybergeddon*
Tom Green, *Halo 4: Forward unto Dawn*

Best Female Performance: Drama

Rachael Hip-Flores, *Anyone but Me*
Troian Bellisario, *Lauren*

Alison Haislip, *Battleground*
Anna Popplewell, *Halo 4: Forward unto Dawn*
Missy Peregrym, *Cybergeddon*

Nonfiction or Reality Series

Kids React
K-Town
Shaytards
Ultimate Surprises
California On

Best Branded Entertainment Series

Chasing with Steve Aoki
CliffsNotes Films
Cybergeddon
Leap Year
Stories of Inclusive Innovation

Best First-Person Series

The Flog
iJustine
The Philip DeFranco Show
Ryan Higa
Daily Grace

Best News and Culture Series

The Philip DeFranco Show
SourceFed
Larry King Now
The Young Turks
Vice News

Best Production Design

Kasra Farahani, *Halo 4: Forward unto Dawn*
Rachel Myers, *Video Game High School*

Andres Cubillan, *H+ The Digital Series*
Lindsey Stirling, *Lindsey Stirling*
Greg Aronowitz and Alynne Schripsema, *MyMusic*

Best Cinematography

Sean Stiegemeier, *Drone*
Nick Schrunk, *Red Bull Moments*
Brett Pawlak, *H+ The Digital Series*
Brett Pawlak, *Halo 4: Forward unto Dawn*
Benjamin Kantor, *Husbands*

Best Male Performance: Comedy

Ken Marino, *Burning Love*
Amir Blumenfeld, *Jake and Amir*
Jeff Lewis, *The Jeff Lewis 5 Minute Comedy Hour*
Brad Bell, *Husbands*
Ryan Welsh, *Bite Me*

Best Female Performance: Comedy

Hannah Hart, *My Drunk Kitchen*
Kristen Bell, *Burning Love*
Alessandra Torresani, *Husbands*
Ashley Clements, *The Lizzie Bennet Diaries*
Julia Cho, *The Lizzie Bennet Diaries*

Best DIY or How-To Series

Do It, Gurl
FPSRussia
Lauren Conrad's Crafty Creations
Masterclass
Common Man Cocktails

Best Music Series

Epic Rap Battles of History
AOL Sessions

Songify This; *Songify the News*
Decoded
VEVO Go Shows

Best International Series

Live in Chelsea
Travel Story
MxM: Mexico around the World
Visto Bueno
PrisonPals

Best Editing

Nathan Zellner, *Red vs. Blue*
Blake Calhoun, *Continuum*
Michael Louis Hill, *Halo 4: Forward unto Dawn*
Butcher Editorial, David Henegar, Ray Daniels, *Daybreak*
Benny Fine, Rafi Fine, and Team, *MyMusic*

Best Visual Effects

Oliver Hotz and Matthew A. Rubin, *Drone*
Clayton D'Mello and John Godfrey, *Bite Me*
David Ebner, *10,000 Days*
William Hyler, *MyMusic*
Tim Kendall, *Book Club*

You could also check out the websites of festivals like LAWEBFEST or the New York Television Festival to see the work they have chosen to honor.

WHY CREATE FOR THE NET?

The reasons to create series for the Internet, as opposed to creating for other film or video outlets, are nearly as varied as the Internet itself. But the reasons are all linked, in a sense, by one word: *opportunity*.

First and foremost, the Internet offers *creative opportunity*. Broadcast and cable television are limited by all sorts of factors. By necessity, they must appeal to a broad audience. Even if you could get a meeting with the head of a major broadcast network like CBS, she wouldn't consider buying your idea unless she thought it would appeal to at least 10 million people, most of whom already watch CBS. The mandate to appeal to the widest possible audience is often why so much network television is bland or derivative. Cable has more freedom but is still restricted by the tastes of their core audience, the channel's branding choices, potential advertiser objections, and government regulations, on and on. The Internet, on the other hand, allows you to create the kind of content *you* would want to watch and seek out an audience with similar taste. Whereas 2 million regular viewers would be considered a flop on a broadcast network, it would be a phenomenon on the Internet. Take, for example, the acclaimed Internet series *Quarterlife*. The groundbreaking series attracted a loyal audience on the Net and drew financial support from major advertisers like Toyota and Pepsi. But NBC gave the broadcast version of the series exactly one airing before yanking it and tossing it on the network TV reject pile.

Another form of creative opportunity that web series offer is the opportunity to create new forms of cross-platform storytelling. Take, for instance, the outstanding *H+* from Warner Digital and executive producer Bryan Singer (director of *X-Men*). It consists of 48 four- to five-minute segments that collectively tell the story of the events before, during, and after an international calamity. Because the story jumps back and forth in time, it allowed the producers to assemble and reassemble the segments in different sequences for different platforms: one configuration on the Internet, another when the segments are grouped together to make a miniseries in foreign markets, and so on.

The Internet also offers *financial opportunity*. Most sites match advertisers with content and share the revenue stream generated by popular videos and web series with creators. Among the biggest success stories is Ray William Johnson, whose YouTube videos posted under the name RayWJ have attracted 1.5 billion views, netting him, according to the *Wall Street Journal,* a million dollars from YouTube's ad revenue sharing plan and the sale of his merchandise. Although it is highly unlikely you'll reach RayWJ's millionaire status, it is entirely possible to take in enough ad money to pay for the ongoing production of your series. Moreover, video makers are invited to post their work at no charge, as opposed to most film and video festivals that charge an entry fee.

Another huge plus for webisodes is that they provide *career opportunity*. Many students in universities, community colleges, high schools, and even junior high schools are bursting with creative ideas and video talent. They are ready, willing, and able to make films today. But rare is the film studio or traditional media business willing to take a chance on unproven talent. The aspiring filmmaker, even one with a degree from a prestigious film school, usually finds he must start at the bottom, fetching coffee and running errands. It can easily be 10 years or more before you've paid your dues and earned the opportunity to do what you set out to do in the first place: make films. On the Internet, however, all that matters is your work. You create your series, make your webisodes, post them, and let the audience decide whether you're ready to direct.

Career opportunities also abound for working film and video professionals who want to stretch their creative boundaries. Maybe you're an assistant director, grip, gaffer, editor, or other worker in the film or television business who yearns to tell stories of your own but who will never be taken seriously as a potential writer or director because the industry has pigeonholed you as "crew" rather than "creative." The Internet makes it possible for you to sidestep the narrow-minded gatekeepers of Hollywood by investing your time and energy in making your own film rather than toiling thanklessly on someone else's vision. When you read the interviews with creators in Chapter Fifteen you'll find three vivid examples of actors who created their own web series to promote their performing careers, only to find that it also opened up opportunities for them behind the camera (see Chapter Fifteen interviews with Courtney Zito, Jen Dawson, and Christine Lakin).

Creative people in a variety of artistic pursuits are discovering the enormous power of the Internet to provide what might be called *exposure opportunity*. The Groundlings, a legendary Los Angeles improvisational theater troupe that has helped launch the careers of Lisa Kudrow, Will Ferrell, the late Phil Hartman, and others, has spent decades performing in their 99-seat theater. But after they shot the spoof *David Blaine Street*

Magic in the alley behind their theater and posted it on YouTube, the video racked up 18 million plays. That's the power of the Internet. If the Groundlings performed the sketch in their theater to sold-out audiences every night, it would take 181,818 performances or more than 6,000 years to reach an audience of 18 million. On the Internet, it happened in a matter of months and scored the group a contract to provide 50 webisodes for Sony's Crackle site.

For screenwriters, the Internet offers what might be called *craft improvement opportunity*. The chance to see your work on screen, rather than just churning out spec scripts and never seeing them get made, helps developing writers get better — a lot better. It helps developing writers learn how to be more economical with story and dialogue, how to use the visual more fully, and how to truly write for the screen instead of merely for the page. Similarly, actors who have created their own web series all rave about how spending hour after hour in the editing room watching themselves (with their producer and director hat on) has informed and improved their acting tremendously.

On the Internet, with dozens of hosting sites open to all, there are no gatekeepers to tell you why you can't do what you know you can and virtually no limits to the size of the audience you can reach if your work goes viral and becomes a phenomenon. If you make a great web series (and you market it well; see Chapter Thirteen), the audience will find it. To paraphrase the mysterious voice in the corn field in the film *Field of Dreams*, "If you build it, they will come."

In short, the Internet provides unlimited opportunity for anyone with the desire to create video content. In fact, the hunger for content is so voracious that the Internet is not just opening the doors of opportunity; it's begging you to come in and make yourself at home. But you need a bit more than desire and an idea. You need the fortitude to follow through on that idea. And you need the craft and skills to turn that vague idea into a high-quality, polished pilot ready for digital distribution across the World Wide Web. Many have inspiration, but few have craft and know-how. That's what the following chapters are about: helping you acquire those tools.

Are you ready? Good. Let's begin.

FOR TEACHERS

If you taught creative writing, you'd surely insist that your students study the techniques of the masters as a foundation for their own creative work. Music, art, and film instructors also require their students to study outstanding works in the field, past and present. Short video is no different. Those who seek to be top creators should begin by studying the best work already done in the form. As an assignment in conjunction with Chapter One of this book, ask your students to watch three episodes of a current web series and write a short paper (two or three pages) analyzing the series.

For this analysis to be of depth and value, the student should not just casually surf the Net and stare blankly at a few videos but must think and write critically about the work she views. At Goddard College, where I obtained my MFA in creative writing, we were required to write weekly annotations, two- to three-page analyses of works of fiction, narrowly focused on a specific, noteworthy area of craft such as how the main character was introduced, or image motifs, or use of location as a character. The idea was to train us, as readers, to examine in detail the underlying techniques used by the writer in constructing the work.

For short-form Internet series, students could focus on aspects of craft such as compelling main characters, or economy of storytelling, or techniques used to maximize audience engagement. The students could also be asked to parse basic elements such as number of characters, genre, production value (low, average, or high), or length of episodes.

To help students understand the type of analysis and specifics you're looking for, you might try an in-class analytical exercise first. Screen an episode or two of a web series, or maybe a pilot of a web series, then ask the students to say what the strengths and weaknesses of the series are. Force them to be more precise than "It's funny" or "I just like it." Force them to articulate and analyze the underlying architecture of what they've watched.

This assignment should be given not just during Week One but regularly throughout the semester. Students of music study other musicians as a regular part of their ongoing training. Aspiring webisode artists should be equally committed to the study of their form.

2 THE SERIES CONCEPT

In early 2007, when I first began teaching courses on making short-form TV series for the Internet, I was hard-pressed to find even a handful of examples to screen for my students. The early prototypes like *lonelygirl15* and *Sam Has 7 Friends* were around, but not much else. Now, at last count, there are approximately 187 gazillion web series to choose from, roughly one web series for every 18- to 30-year-old in the world currently cruising a bar looking for Mr. or Ms. Right, or at least Mr. or Ms. Right Now. Unfortunately, despite the abundance of web series and barflies, precious few are worth your time. In most cases, you can tell within seconds that your best move is to move on.

In the case of web series, there are two basic reasons why so many are so bad. Reason One: flawed concept. Reason Two: flawed execution. This chapter aims to prevent you from falling into the pit of despair and failure that awaits you if, no matter how slick your execution is, you start out with a flawed concept.

What makes a good web series premise? Although there is no formula for success, it makes sense to study what's been done and take note of what has worked and what has flopped. As Mark Twain once said, "History doesn't repeat itself, but it rhymes." So let's start by taking a look at some really bad rhymes and try not to repeat them.

FATALLY FLAWED SERIES CONCEPTS

I once asked a former ABC comedy development executive, who spent 5 years hearing thousands of concept pitches from writers, what was the single worst idea for a series that a writer ever brought in. She cocked her head, gave it a few seconds of serious consideration — perhaps trying to choose between hundreds of equally bad ideas — then nodded confidently and said, "Talking drapes." I responded the only way I could: "Talking drapes? What the?" She said yes, a writer — not a newbie or one who had lost his mind, all evidence to the contrary, but a writer with a solid resume filled with major TV and feature film credits — came in and pitched a series about a man who buys a spooky fixer-upper of a house and soon discovers that the drapes are inhabited by a wise-cracking spirit that speaks to him in one-liners.

Like most writers, I relish all opportunities to mock the competition, so I repeated the talking drapes story to a friend who actually knew the writer who had pitched it. My friend called the writer and said, "You actually pitched a series to ABC about talking drapes?" The talking drapes writer shot back indignantly, "Look, that could have worked."

When it comes to creativity and art, there's no predicting what can or will work. And sometimes even the most unlikely notion, in the hands of gifted writers, directors, and performers, becomes successful, possibly even critically acclaimed. (Think *Seinfeld*, a show that proudly claimed to be about "nothing.") But some ideas are just so wrong that they deserve to be thrown under the bus like disgraced politicians.

The most common mistake in formulating a pitch for a web series is thinking something is a series when it's really just a one-shot (or three-shot at best) idea. As the word *series* implies, your idea must contain characters and a premise that can be mined for subsequent episodes over and over again. So if you attempt to make a series called *Zippy and Skippy*, about the hilarious things that occur when you smear peanut butter on your golden retriever Zippy's genitals and he tries to lick it off, you may end up with a humorous 60 seconds of video, but you won't have a series pilot. Why not? Because there's no Episode 2. You've exhausted all the stories that the Skippy on Zippy premise can sustain. And no, smearing chunky instead of creamy or switching to cream cheese on the cat's privates wouldn't count as different stories any more than changing from Little Red to Little Blue Riding Hood would.

A good series concept must have legs — that is, the ability to be used for lots and lots of episodic stories based on that premise, regardless of whether the episodes are 60 minutes or 60 seconds long. The one exception to this rule is if you are doing, in essence, a soap opera or serialized version of a long story. In that case, your series will consist of one long, extended story that is broken up into chapters, each chapter being an episode. But if you go the serialized route, you should probably take a few minutes and jot down what you think the first dozen or so installments might cover, rather than just writing a pilot, then seeing your story run out of gas after Episode 3.

To illustrate the difference between a concept with legs and one without, let me once again cite an example from half-hour network television that most people will be familiar with: *Seinfeld*. The central premise of *Seinfeld* (despite its claim to be about "nothing") is that of four neurotic, dysfunctional friends in New York City and the neurotic, dysfunctional adventures they get into dealing with the everyday minutiae of life — things like coping with your parents, the travails of dating, and the endless parade of bizarre New York characters they encounter, like the Close Talker or the Soup Nazi. Clearly, dozens of episodes or "installments" can be written based on Jerry, Elaine, Kramer, and George and this basic premise. NBC aired 180 of them over the show's 9-year run, and they continue to rerun in syndication worldwide.

But let's say, for the sake of illustration, that instead of focusing on Jerry and the gang, you decided that the Soup Nazi is the funniest character in all of New York City and therefore should be the center of the your show. Big mistake. As funny as the Soup Nazi was in one episode, his character and that premise — all the wacky people who come into his soup emporium — does not provide a good central premise for a series. Why not? Because there is basically only one story or episode that would be repeated over and over: The customer comes in, and the Soup Nazi cops an attitude and shouts, "You, no soup, two weeks!" There won't be stories for Episodes 2, 3, 4, or 44. All you can do is write Episode 1, 1A, 1B, 1C, ad infinitum. And nobody will stick around for any of the subsequent episodes because after they watch your pilot, their reaction to each of the others will be, "I've already seen this."

Another common mistake in choosing a premise is making it so personal and obscure that the only audience that can possibly be in on the joke is you. Even though one of the oldest adages about writing is to write what you know, if what you know is impossible for anyone else to understand or relate to, then what you write may have a potential audience of exactly one.

Let's say you work at a plumbing supply store. Better yet, let's say you work as a regional sales rep for a wholesale plumbing supply distributor that sells to the major hardware and big-box home improvement stores in the Mid-Atlantic states. You've done this for 20 years, have had a ton of laughs along the way with all the weird characters who have been your customers, and feel certain there's a great Internet comedy with hundreds of hilarious episodes based on your daily work life. You've even got a great title: *Flushed!* Practically writes itself.

Unfortunately, *Flushed!* will probably go right down the drain because to understand most of the humor you and your fellow plumbing parts pals have shared, you need to be in the plumbing supply business, or at least be familiar with the names of all the major parts of a toilet. As hilarious as you think it is when Ernie from Ernie's Hardware of Baltimore says, "Whatever floats your float rod," or when Del from Home Depot of Dover, Delaware responds to your question about restocking his ballcock supply with a pithy, "That's what she said," you, Ernie, and Del may be the only ones laughing. Your series premise doesn't have to appeal to everyone. But the comedy or drama must be accessible beyond your immediate circle of friends and coworkers if you hope to attract an audience of any significant size.

BE BOLD, FRESH, AND ORIGINAL

The above warning notwithstanding, you must also avoid the opposite temptation — namely to be so "universal" in appeal that all you are doing is recycling pale imitations of old concepts that have been successful. Today's Internet video consumer has literally millions of options to choose from. If you want to grab his attention, you must begin with a concept that makes him say, "Oooh, that sounds interesting." Clones and knock-offs don't do that. "It's like *Cheers*, but instead of a bar, it's set in a Laundromat" won't make anyone grab anything but his head.

So what has worked? Let's take a look at a few successful Internet series and analyze what made each premise attractive. To make sure we're focusing on premise rather than other factors, we'll exclude series made by known Hollywood players like Ed Zwick and Marshall Herskovitz (*Quarterlife*) or that include recognizable on-camera talent, like *Dr. Horrible's Sing-Along Blog*, starring Neil Patrick Harris. Because of their star power either in front of or behind the camera, these series get press coverage to help promote the show and draw an initial supply of viewers. Most of you won't have access to that sort of publicity machine and will therefore have to come up with a concept that makes the video surfers of the world say, "I've gotta check that out."

The Guild (*www.watchtheguild.com*)

Before Felicia Day became an Internet goddess, she was a fairly anonymous actress. She'd had some modest success, including a recurring part as Vi in the final season of the cult TV series *Buffy the Vampire Slayer*, but she grew tired of waiting for the phone to ring, hoping some unknown producer or director would deign to offer her a part. So she took matters into her own hands and created a TV series for herself. A longtime video game addict (she's a level 66 gnome warlock and a level 63 priest in *World of Warcraft* according to *www.geeksaresexy.net*), Day decided to write what she knew best and created *The Guild*, a comedy web series about online gamers and their relationships with each other both on and off line. In the pilot episode, Day's character, Codex (her online gamer name), is fired by her therapist for refusing to admit she has an addiction to video games. Things get even worse for Codex when fellow gamer Zabu shows up at her apartment, convinced that because Codex "winkied" him online, she's hot for his bod, and they're destined to be an item.

What makes this a good web series premise? First and foremost, it appeals to an audience that spends a huge amount of time online, namely online video gamers. Whereas humor about plumbing supplies and toilet parts would be met with blank stares by the cyber-geek crowd, this group totally gets what a "winkie" is. And they totally OMG get how addicted you can get to video games LOL, and how your fellow addicts become your BFFs and perhaps more (#stalkers), whether you like it or not.

Day originally wrote *The Guild* as a half-hour pilot but was told the subject matter was "too niche" for network or cable TV. Probably true. But it's perfect for the web series world because that's where the natural audience for a series about online gamers is.

Day partnered with Kim Evey, who had co-produced the successful web series *Gorgeous Tiny Chicken Machine Show*. Day and Evey self-financed the first three episodes of *The Guild*. The episodes were successful in that they attracted a sizable and loyal audience, but Day and Evey ran out of money to continue the show. Then they got a brilliant idea. Why not see whether the fans of the show would pay for more episodes? They put a PayPal button up on the existing episodes and solicited contributions, and lo and behold the viewers sent in the money. Not get-rich-quick-and-retire-to-Tahiti money, mind you. But enough money to finance production for the rest of Season One.

There can be no better proof that you are doing something right than to have an audience that has been receiving something for free voluntarily send you money so you can keep doing it. And in the end, both the audience and Day were rewarded further. *The Guild*'s grassroots success became a story covered by the national media, one that caught the attention of Microsoft, who agreed to sponsor the show for Season Two (and later more) and to put it on its newly launched Xbox Independent Video Channel online.

The bottom line is this: Know your potential audience. If your audience is online, then your premise should appeal to some group of people who spend a fair amount of time online. They don't have to be gamers or Facebook addicts or other online junkies necessarily, but the show you create should appeal in tone, subject matter, style, or some other way to those who spend a significant amount of time online.

The following are a few examples of what I would consider to be appropriate premises for online series.

Script Cops and Gaytown

Script Cops is a stylistically spot-on parody of the TV show *Cops* where we ride along with the men in blue as they bust lowlifes for bad script writing. Made in 2007, the series has gotten renewed life thanks to a reissue sponsored by the popular screenwriting software Final Draft. Episodes include a virtual SWAT team assault on a group of students for making a film stuffed with clichés. (A serious-as-a-heart-attack cop tells the wanna-be filmmakers, "Do you realize 83% of all student films begin with a shot of an alarm clock?")

Gaytown is about a closeted heterosexual man in a predominantly gay world trying to do straight guy things without being outed. Our hero yearns to play basketball (with the girls) because all the "normal" boys just do ballet and will beat the living snot out of you with their designer shoes if they find out you're a hetero "pervert." In the pilot our straight hero gets busted by undercover gay cops for secretly meeting other heteros in a public toilet to play fantasy football.

The concepts couldn't be more different. So why have I grouped them together? Because they share one essential quality: You can explain the premise and give people a sense of where the humor will come from in only a few words. Making the premise easy to understand — and easy to explain — is essential for a short-form series. If each episode is to run about 3 minutes, it had better not take 4 minutes just to explain the basic idea. The online entertainment audience has a notoriously short attention span. If you want to grab their attention, you must do it quickly. Even if the execution of your series will have subtleties, complexities, and nuances, make sure the basic concept can be conveyed simply, quickly, and clearly. With *Gaytown* and *Script Cops*, the titles themselves come close to explaining each show's premise.

Some other examples of simple, clear premises follow.

Black Version (from 60frames.com, now on YouTube)

This series consists of parodies of famous movie scenes, such as the "black version" of the fake orgasm scene in *When Harry Met Sally*, where the woman's passion talk during her simulated orgasm is so wildly over the top (including cuts where she's suddenly wearing a blond wig) and yet the black man still believes it was real and walks away even more cocky about his sexual prowess.

The Ed Hardy Boyz (www.funnyordie.com)

This is a basic mystery premise like Andy Hardy, except the "detectives" are two "dese, dem, and dose" Jersey goofballs who wear Ed Hardy clothing and try to solve mysteries while hitting on any available woman with lines like, "Excuse me, do youse two play for an Anaheim baseball team because you're both angels."

What the Buck?! (www.youtube.com)

Imagine if Jack from *Will & Grace* had his own online celebrity dish program. Michael Buckley took $6 worth of fabric for a backdrop, a pair of work lights from Home Depot, a video camera, and his catty approach to celebrity dish and turned it into 2008's most popular entertainment program on YouTube with more than 100 million views.

Hot for Words (YouTube or www.hotforwords.com)

Okay, here's the premise: An Eastern European philologist explains the etymology (linguistic history) of words such as *scrumtrilescent* and *pulchritudinous*. Sounds like a complete snooze, you say? Perhaps I left out one crucial detail. Here is your *Hot for Words* host and instructor (facing page).

Has your passion for philology and etymology just taken a gigantic leap? No, it's not porn, but Marina Orlova, who holds degrees in teaching of Russian language and world literature and teaching of English language specializing in philology, definitely has the kind of classroom presence that holds students' attention — at least male students who aren't residents of Gaytown. She launched *Hot for Words* on YouTube in mid-2007 and within a year racked up more than 150 million views. Her success caught the attention

Marina Orlova. Photo by Justin Price.

of cable TV news mogul Bill O'Reilly, who booked her for multiple guest appearances and tutorials, and she was voted fifth sexiest woman on the Web by G4 TV (which makes one wonder just who the heck are the top four).

A picture is worth a thousand words, and when you check out Marina Orlova's site, you get to learn the thousand words as well. Those of you hoping to learn a new word a day will be thrilled to learn that Marina has a wall calendar.

The point is that Marina Orlova really does have a passion for language and words. But she found a way to package that passion to capture an audience. Her premise is simple to understand, is easy to sell visually (online video is, after all, visual), and has the entire unabridged dictionary as a source for potential future episodes.

And by the way, *pulchritudinous*, as Orlova explains in coy detail, means beautiful, sexy, hot, gorgeous, alluring — she goes on for a while with the synonyms, each one delivered with the subtext "you want me and you know it." How in the world did Marina ever find the word *pulchritudinous*, I wonder?

SO WHERE'S THE DRAMA?

Good question. Although there is no law saying that all Internet TV series must be comedies or reality series, most fall into one of those two categories. The reason, I suspect, is that drama is a much trickier proposition when the average length of an episode is only 3 to 5 minutes. It's difficult to build the elements crucial to drama, like suspense, tension, and character arc, in that restricted amount of time. In theory, you can just take a longer drama, like a 1-hour network drama series or a feature-length thriller, and break it into smaller parts. But the reality is, it's a huge challenge to re-establish dramatic elements and the heightened emotions that drama demands for every episode. It would a bit like having to stop your car every block or two, turn off the engine, then pop the hood and break out the jumper cables to get it going again. The journey takes more effort than it's worth.

That said, there have been some successful (that is, well done and critically acclaimed) short-form dramas on the Net, like *Quarterlife* or *Anyone but Me*, both of which featured episodes closer to 8 minutes in length. There have also been some noteworthy examples of high budget dramas like *H+*, *Sanctuary*, and *The Bannen Way*, which were made for the Web but were also designed, if the episodes were edited together consecutively, as feature films or miniseries. If drama is your thing, or you have a premise for a drama in mind that you think can really work on the Internet, have at it. But be aware of the challenges of sustaining audience involvement. One way to address this issue is to shoot lots of episodes before posting any —at least six. That way, the audience can get hooked on the premise, characters, and story lines by watching an entire season, instead of watching the pilot, being intrigued, but having to wait another month for Episode 2, then another month for Episode 3, and so on.

YOU NEED A KILLER TITLE

Although it is technically not part of the premise of your series, coming up with a killer title is just as important to the success of your web series as devising a solid premise. Your title is the first thing that gets a potential viewer to either click through and view or click away and move on. Your goal is a title that both *tells* and *sells* — in other words, a title that both clearly communicates what your series is about and makes the audience say, "Yes, I want to see that." Remember, the Internet video revolution means potential viewers have literally millions of video entertainment products to choose from. Your title has to grab their attention and make web video surfers stop, click, and check it out.

For my money, here are some strong titles that tell me what the show will be about before I even see it and make me want to sample an episode or two:

- *Boys Will Be Girls*
- *We Need Girlfriends*
- *5-Second Films*

Each of these titles gives me a pretty good idea what the show might be about and hints at the type of humor the show will have — the hook that gets me to check it out. A title can also be effective if it's not exactly clear but is so bizarre that it makes people want to click through just to see what the heck it is. Although it turned out to be a series I didn't care for, *Gorgeous Tiny Chicken Machine Show* was certainly a compelling enough title that I had to click through and see what it was all about. *The Ninety Year-Old Hooker*, on the other hand, is a title for a nonexistent show that, though perfectly clear, may not be the right bait to lure predominantly young Internet video audiences.

FOR TEACHERS

Students can benefit from two types of premise assignments: analytical and creative. The analytical work can provide context and illumination in preparation for the students' own creative work.

For the analytical assignment, they can write a short analysis of two or three web series and why their premise is effective, or why it isn't. As in the previous chapter, the key to success in this assignment is specificity.

A simple thumbs up or thumbs down is useless. What is of value is developing the students' ability to critically examine the inner architecture of the video series they see on the Web.

For the creative, they can pitch a premise for an original web series that they will write a pilot script for later in the semester. I usually ask my students to come in with two series ideas, one fully developed, the other less so. *Fully developed* means they can explain the premise, define the main series characters, and give a sense of the tone, style, and type of stories the series will present.

I require my students to write the idea down on paper and also be prepared to pitch it orally. The verbal pitch is the standard method of television and film, and so even shy writers must learn a bit of salesmanship and some oral presentation skills if they are to succeed in this world. But requiring them to put their pitch on paper as well forces them to examine it more closely than if they just wing it with a verbal pitch, one they might cook up 3 minutes before class if they aren't required to put something on paper as well.

3 CREATING COMPELLING CHARACTERS

Your title may be the tempting appetizer that lures viewers into sampling your series, but your characters are the primary ingredient that keeps them coming back for meal after meal. Quick, name some of the most memorable network TV series of all time. Here's my off-the-top-of-my-head list:

- *I Love Lucy*
- *The Mary Tyler Moore Show*
- *All in the Family*
- *Happy Days*
- *The Simpsons*
- *Law & Order*

The first two have the main character's name right in the title of the show. Why? Because that character is the main reason people watched the series week after week. In fact, people usually referred to these two landmark series simply by the character's name, as in "Did you see the *Lucy* where she works in the chocolate factory?"

What about the next two? No character names in those titles. Still, what's the first thing that comes to mind when I say *All in the Family*? Archie Bunker, of course. Yes, the series had brilliant writing and embraced groundbreaking, provocative subject matter like impotence, menopause, and racism. But it was the phenomenal popularity of Archie Bunker (and

Edith, the Meathead, and Archie's "little girl," Gloria) that was the primary driver of the series' long-lasting popularity.

Same goes for *Happy Days*, the nostalgic half-hour comedy about suburban middle-class life in the 1950s. Ask anyone to say the first thing that comes to mind when you mention the show *Happy Days*, I'd lay odds that 95 out of 100 people would instantly say it's the Fonz, and then 80 of those 95 would pretend to comb back their ducktail hairstyle and say, "Ayyyyy!" just like the Fonz. Ironically, the Fonz wasn't supposed to be the star of *Happy Days*. In the pilot, he was a minor character who had half a dozen lines. But the audience loved the Fonz, as played by Henry Winkler, and the Fonz launched *Happy Days* to the top of the ratings heap. How powerful a character was the Fonz? In the months after the show aired an episode where he got a library card for the first time, over a million kids nationwide went to their local library and signed up for their first library card — so they could be just like the Fonz. That's a powerful character.

It's no accident that CBS and ABC paid Carroll O'Connor and Henry Winkler record sums to continue playing Archie and the Fonz year after year. The networks knew that without those characters (and the actors playing those characters), the audience would tune out.

Even with shows like *The Simpsons* and *Law & Order*, ensembles with many characters and either brilliant humor or riveting story lines, the characters drive the popularity and long-term audience appeal of the shows. People love *The Simpsons* because of the great characters, both the main ones like Bart and Homer and the peripheral ones like Apu or Krusty the Klown. And as for the *Law & Order* franchise, I suspect the audience chooses which particular series to watch (*Special Victims Unit*, *Criminal Intent*, or the original) based on which set of characters they like rather than what sort of crimes are dealt with.

The importance of character cannot be overstated. There have been zillions of medical shows, cop shows, and family sitcoms on television over the years. But the shows that succeeded — and that continue to bring audiences back to watch them even 50 years later in reruns worldwide — are the ones where the characters made a powerful and lasting impression on the audience. You might say that it's just a function of the actor and his or her popularity, but you would be wrong. Bill Cosby has had several TV series, but only when he played Dr. Heathcliff Huxtable, beleaguered but affable father of five, did he achieve megastar status. Same thing for Mary Tyler Moore. Even today, more than 30 years after the series' final installment, most people remember her fondly as Mary Richards. But almost no one remembers her, fondly or otherwise, as Annie McGuire (the title character of her 1988 ABC series that disappeared faster than the fifth runner-up on *American Idol*).

Yes, you need great actors, and we'll talk quite a bit about how to find them in Chapter Nine. But actors need great characters in order to do great work. And audiences need great characters in order to return to a series episode after episode. Here's Blake Snyder, in his screenwriting book *Save the Cat!*, explaining the overriding importance of character, or who your story is about:

> The "who" is our way in. We, the audience, zero in on and project onto the "who" whether it's an epic motion picture or a commercial for Tide detergent. The "who" gives us someone to identify with... because it's easier to communicate an idea when someone is standing there experiencing it for us. And whether we're watching *Lawrence of Arabia* as Lawrence tries to figure out how to attack Acaba... or a Tylenol commercial in which a busy Soccer Mom wonders when her headache will go away, the principle of involving us in the story is the same.

Characters, especially your main character, are what compel people to come back to your little video party week after week. And Snyder is quite right: It matters not whether we're talking about *Die Hard* or an Old Spice commercial. The characters, John McClane in *Die Hard* and The Man Your Man Could Smell Like in the Old Spice ads, are what bring the audience back for installment after installment.

Think of your main character as the host of your party — or, more accurately, your series of parties. He greets the guests at the door, sets the tone for the experience. The audience's decision about whether to return for the next installment of your particular party is based largely on how they feel about the host. Is he someone they want to hang out with again and again? Or is he a tiresome bore who makes them say, "Screw the free guacamole, we're outta here!"

CHARACTER ESSENTIALS

Okay, you get it. You need to have great characters. But what makes for a great character? Broad strokes? Fine details? Larger-than-life traits? Probably all the above. But I think a good place to start is by saying that all truly great characters have to *resonate* with us. That is, they must strike us as real — not ordinary or trite but familiar in a way that makes us say, "That's just like my boss" or "I knew a guy in high school just like that."

For all of Archie Bunker's flaws, he rings true to us. We've all got a blowhard uncle like Archie. Or a neighbor. Or maybe even a small, unappealing part of ourselves. Norman Lear, who developed *All in the Family* for American television (it was based on a British show called *Till Death Us Do Part*) once called Archie Bunker "basically a horse's ass." But Lear also remarked that Archie was "the bigger-than-life epitome of something that's in all of us, like it or not." In other words, the character resonates.

Because of their much shorter episode length, web series cannot create characters in as much depth as a 30- or 60-minute network TV show or a 2-hour feature film, but the principles of character are no less relevant. The characters in your short-form series, especially the main character, must resonate with the audience. Take *The Guild* as an example. Microsoft bought the show for its Xbox online channel because it knows the channel's natural audience — online game fanatics — will instantly relate to *The Guild*'s characters, a bunch of online game fanatics. The audience gets the show's characters, like Codex and Zaboo. They know their world and understand their video-obsessed behavior and gamer lingo. And because they know (and like) these people, they want to attend their party — the episodes of *The Guild* — time after time, season after season.

Does this mean the only people who can enjoy *The Guild* are online gaming addicts? Absolutely not, any more than the only people who enjoy *All in the Family* are bigots and fools. For a character to resonate, or be relatable, he doesn't have to be "just like you." He only has to be recognizable, meaning he might be like you, or he might be like someone you know or have somehow encountered in your life.

The next essential element of all great series characters is that *we can instantly imagine those characters in dozens of juicy situations* — juicy in either a comedic or a dramatic way, depending on the tone of the series. Let's return to the Soup Nazi from *Seinfeld* once again. Great character for an episode or two — fabulous guest star or peripheral character. Terrific spice but not a good main ingredient. As hilarious and memorable as the Soup Nazi was for that classic episode, he's not a good choice for a regular, every-week series character and definitely NOT the lead character you can base an entire series around. Where do you take the Soup Nazi other than his restaurant to get stories? What other situations can you put him in? I suppose you could send him on a date, or meet his family — maybe there's a Soup Nazi Sr. or Grandma Soup Nazi, and we not only see where the Soup Nazi came from but gain a measure of sympathy for him as an improved version of his predecessors. But when you boil it down, every episode becomes nothing more than repetition after repetition of the same basic gag: "You, no second date, two months!"

For a series regular, a character you see in every episode of a series, to be truly useful that character must have depth and dimension. In other words, he or she must be a human character, not a two-dimensional caricature. If Archie Bunker had merely been a malaprop-spouting bigot, *All in the Family* would never have lasted as long as it did. It would have been a one-joke pony. But Archie was a multidimensional human being, a man born and raised in one time railing against the rapidly changing world around him. A man stuck in one time fighting against change stimulates dozens of situations and ideas. A mere bigot? Not so many.

The third vital element of all good series characters is *specifics*. The devil is always in the details. If I say "car," you probably get a picture in your head, but it's blurry and out of focus until I get more specific. For instance, if I say "sports car" or "SUV," the picture in your head is sharper and a lot more specific. Better still would be "red Ferrari" or "black Hummer." Now we know precisely what we're talking about, and we have a much clearer sense of the "character" we're talking about than we did when we simply said "car."

Specifics are what make a character. If I ask you who your main character is, and you say, "She's a waitress," you really haven't told me much, and you certainly haven't sketched any details that make me want to watch a series about "a waitress." You need more specifics. Waitress at an elite eatery in New York City or a greasy spoon in Buttscratch, Oklahoma? Is she 22 or 52? Is this Madison Kemp's first day at TGI Friday's, a job she only plans to keep until she sells the novel (or Internet video series) she's been working on since high school? Or does today mark 30 years at the Buttscratch Eat 'n Gas for Nadine, and the chef celebrates the occasion by putting a candle in a sausage patty and leading the regulars in a hearty chorus of "Happy Anniversary"? They're both waitresses, but Madison and Nadine are two entirely different characters, which means the stories you tell about them, and how they react and behave in the situations those stories present, will be vastly different. It's all about the details.

In *The Guild*, all the characters are online gaming freaks. But aside from that shared video addiction, they are all distinct individuals. Here is a partial character breakdown for *The Guild* from its Wikipedia page:

Knights of Good

- **Codex** (real name Cyd Sherman) is the Priest. Codex is shy and non-confrontational, tending to panic under stress. Outside the game she is a concert violinist (and former child prodigy), unemployed after setting fire to her boyfriend's cello. She is an addicted gamer who tries at first to control the time she spends online but fails. For this reason, her therapist drops her. At the beginning of the series she is quite reclusive, with no real-life friends; she is often self-conscious and awkward around men. Codex is portrayed by creator Felicia Day.
- **Zaboo** (real name Sujan Balakrishnan Goldberg) is the Warlock. Zaboo describes himself as a "HinJew," having a Hindu mother and Jewish father. He shows great skill with computers; for example, his stalking of Codex included obtaining (presumably through

the Internet) the floor plan of her apartment and all her past residences. His obsessive attitude toward Codex reflects his mother's smothering. When talking, Zaboo often uses "-'d" after some key word or expression, self-commenting on what he just said (e.g., "bladder'd," "testosterone'd"). While Zaboo doesn't appear to have a profession, he admits having attended college for 4 years (to which his mother drove him every day). Zaboo is portrayed by Sandeep Parikh, Indian American writer, director, actor, and producer of comedy and founder of Effinfunny.

- **Bladezz** (real name Simon Kemplar) is the Rogue. He is a high school student who spends most of his time outside school in his mom's garage playing the game. He is rude to the other male guild members, and he hits on the female guild members and makes lewd sexual jokes and comments. He is worried about being sent to military school, and to save up for college his mom forced him into modeling; he uses the name "Finn Smulders" to keep it a secret from everyone. In Seasons Four and Five, he becomes an Internet meme. Bladezz is by nature a rogue and tends to sneak around, betraying, lying, stealing, and causing mayhem. Bladezz is portrayed by Vincent Caso.

- **Vork** (real name Herman Holden) is the guild leader and Warrior. He enjoys managing the guild and budgeting, and he believes only in rules and logic. He lives frugally (and illegally) on his late grandfather's Social Security checks and is a certified notary public. When he became guild leader he "cut the fats of life," including electric power; he steals his senile neighbor's Wi-Fi (and shed) and keeps his food cold by buying ice with food stamps. In the penultimate episode of Season Three he reveals that he can speak fluent Korean; in Season Four, he speaks Hindi to Zaboo's mother and claims to know all languages. Vork comes to believe that shared hatred of him is what keeps the guild together. In Season Four, his desire to own a guild hall leads him to manipulate an in-game exchange market, nearly causing him to be banned from the game. Vork is portrayed by Jeff Lewis, an accomplished character actor and comedian.

- **Clara** (real name Clara Beane) is the Frost Mage. Clara is a stay-at-home wife and mother, college partier, and ex-cheerleader. Her three children are all young, with the youngest still breastfeeding, and she is shown to be an irresponsible mother; though proud of her children, she tends to put gaming before her family and sometimes tries to mix the two, such as by recruiting her husband, "Mr. Wiggly," to the guild. She uses her real name as her avatar name because her kids saw her old name, "Mominatrix." She comes off as ditzy, scatterbrained, and eccentric, with occasional bursts of insight. In the fifth season she proves herself to be a capable mother when she stops Zaboo from going mad with power and lack of sleep. Clara is portrayed by Robin Thorsen.
- **Tinkerballa** (real name April Lou) is the Ranger. Tink distances herself from the guild, trying not to let them know anything about her personal life; she even keeps her real name a secret from her fellow guildies, introducing herself as Tinkerballa. Her real name isn't revealed until the fifth season. In reality, Tink is adopted and has two sisters. She also has been lying to her parents about being a pre-med student, when she has actually switched courses for a degree in costume design. She is shown to have a huge video game addiction, always having an alternate game in hand when not playing the guild's game, even when raiding. She is cold and manipulative, and she uses men to get what she wants, including Bladezz, who deletes Tink's character to avenge himself after she uses him. Following this, and Vork's refusal to punish Bladezz, she leaves the Knights of Good and joins the Axis of Anarchy but later finds them too "douchey" even for her (she even says that she went on a date with Fawkes to join). She rejoins the Knights of Good during an in-game showdown with the Axis of Anarchy when they call her "Tainterballa," and she allows her avatar to be killed off intentionally to give Codex a shot at victory for the guild. Tink is revealed to be possibly the most social of the group, although she is incredibly grounded in the online world. In Season Five, Codex reunites Tink with her family at the gaming con. Tink is portrayed by Amy Okuda.

Granted, this wealth of details was developed over six seasons of episodes. But the fundamentals of each character were there from Season One on. When you create your characters, be as specific as you can. BUT — and this is absolutely crucial — you must also make sure that the specifics you lay out about your character are relevant and telling, that they reveal important things about who your character is on the inside. A laundry list of random details about someone is useless unless those details reveal something significant about who that character is, how she might behave or react to the world around her. Saying your main character Susie's least favorite color is blue and she has a pet parrot are specifics, but they're not terribly revealing or important. They don't tell us much about Susie or the kind of person she is. However, if Susie hates blue, the parrot is blue, and the parrot used to belong to her hypercritical mother who loved blue, and now the parrot mocks and criticizes Susie's every move just like mom used to do, *that's significant*.

CHARACTERIZATION

Character is something internal — the essence of who a person is. So how do you take this internal thing — a person's essence — and communicate that essence to your audience? Through characterization.

Characterization is simply the techniques by which you communicate internal character to us. It is the externalization or dramatization of the internal. And there's great news, boys and girls. When you get right down to it, there are really only three ways for you to convey or reveal who the characters in your series are: what they say (*dialogue*), what they do (*action*), and the *environment* they create, like their clothes, car, job, and living situation.

Forget about writing for the moment and think about real life. When you meet someone new, how do you decide what kind of person they are? By taking careful note of exactly the details stated earlier. Each of us is kind of like The Terminator, with an involuntary mental computer that constantly processes data about the world and people around us. You walk into a Starbucks and spot a woman at a nearby table. The computer kicks in: She's in her 30s, dressed in designer casual clothes, texting on her iPhone with one hand while she alternately sips a chai latte and shares her oat bran muffin with a toddler girl named Chloe in a stroller. Two cars are parked out front: a nearly new Toyota hybrid SUV and a mud-caked 40-year-old VW van with flowers painted on it. Which car is hers? You can make a pretty good guess because you already know — or think you know — her "character." You know who she is and how she thinks, and you can probably predict what kind of car she'd buy.

You walk out of Starbucks, and on the sidewalk out front is a guy in his early sixties, long graying hair and a beard, playing a beat-up old guitar with a peace sign painted on it. He's singing songs like Bob Dylan's "Blowin' in the Wind" and Barry McGuire's "Eve of Destruction." Based on these clues, your mental computer says, "Hippie refugee from the 1960s." Now you have a pretty good idea who owns the VW van. And you probably can make all kinds of other character assessments. Republican or Democrat? Neither — probably Green Party. Or maybe he didn't vote at all *because that's how The Man controls you, man, and we've all got to fight the power.*

In a sense, the process of creating your characters is an inversion of the process you use to figure out who people are in the real world. As a writer, you will first decide who you want your characters to be, then your task is finding the ways to communicate that "who" to your audience. Let's return to the 60Frames web series *Be a Celebutante*. The main characters are two rich, spoiled, less than intelligent party sluts whose only interests are money, self-indulgence, and hooking up — and helping you learn how to live the same charmed and fulfilling lifestyle. The pilot, which runs all of 95 seconds, is chock-full of character clues. Two hotties in bathing suits and fur shawls lounge by a private pool (*environment*). They introduce themselves as "the Douche (pronounced "doo-shay") sisters, heiresses to the douche fortune" (*dialogue*). They are drinking and dispensing smug advice on how to make extra money (*action*). Dannah and Danielle's ideas include:

                    DANNAH
        If you really want to rake in the
        dough…

                    DANIELLE
        Or make money…

                    DANNAH
        You should "accidentally" make a sex
        tape.

CUT TO FOOTAGE OF THE DOUCHE SISTERS IN BED WITH A MAN,
CLEARLY AWARE OF THE CREW AS THEY "ACCIDENTALLY" MAKE A
SEX TAPE.

                    DANNAH
        Yeah, when our "accidental" sex
        tape "accidentally" leaked onto the
        Internet, we "accidentally" made five
        million dollars.

                    DANIELLE
        Oopsies…

You get the idea. Everything your characters say, do, wear, drive, eat, or come in contact with should tell us something about who they are as a person. Once the audience picks up on who they are (and hopefully finds them amusing or interesting enough to follow around for 6 or 12 or 100 episodes), the audience also begins to anticipate the juicy situations you might put them in.

YOUR OVERALL CHARACTER LANDSCAPE

Characters do not exist in a vacuum. They exist to serve the overall premise, and they exist in concert with each other. It's not enough for each individual character to be cool or interesting in his own right. They must work together, as a team, with the whole being greater than the sum of the parts. Each character should serve a specific function within your series, and that function should be unique. You wouldn't want a rock band with five lead singers but no drummer or bass player. Instead of Hootie & the Blowfish, you'd end up with Hootie, Hootie, Hootie, Hootie, & Hootie. Even Hootie's mom wouldn't want to see that act. The premise is *band*. The characters must form a complete team or group, one with stars *and* supporting players.

I think of this overall character composition as the *character landscape*. Your series landscape needs balance and variety. Each character should cover a different "instrument," a distinct function or sound within your overall composition. Take *The Guild* once again. Yes, they are all online gaming freaks. But aside from that, they are different types of people: a mom so addicted to video games that she virtually ignores her three young children (Clara); a young woman so afraid of revealing any real details about her personal life that when asked what she does for a living, she gives the plot line to *Ugly Betty* (Tinkerballa); and even, starting in Season Two, Codex's hottie neighbor who has absolutely no interest in video games at all (Wade). Characters with distinct differences are crucial to the success of your series because character differences are what lead to *conflict*, the essence of all comedy and drama and, therefore, the life-giving reservoir of stories for your pilot and your series.

LEADING CHARACTERS VS. SUPPORTING CHARACTERS

All series have both. As stated before, no good group can be composed of all Hooties (leading character) or all Blowfish (supporting characters). But why is Hootie (or Mick Jagger or Bono) the leading character? What makes him more important? Surprisingly, the answer is pretty much the same for both music video and series television. *Your lead character is the center of gravity for your group.*

In a music video, the camera focuses on the lead singer more than anyone else. And when the camera isn't on the main character, what we see is seen mostly through his eyes. In a television series, we experience most of the action through the lead character's eyes. In *Gaytown*, the lead character is the straight person who is desperately trying to avoid detection and persecution. We follow the action of *Gaytown* from his POV, as opposed to, say, the perspective of a morals cop trying to track down the "perverted heterosexuals." We experience the world of *The Guild* primarily through the eyes of Codex. In *Seinfeld*, Jerry is the lead character, the primary prism through which the story is filtered.

So what makes these characters leads as opposed to supporting players? What makes these characters capable of anchoring a series? For one, as quirky and troubled as Jerry and Codex are, they are, from most of the audience's perspective, the most "normal" person in the universe of the series. Yes, Jerry on *Seinfeld* is a neurotic mess. But compared to George or Elaine or Kramer he's a rock. Same goes for Codex. She's so warped even her therapist abandons her. But compared to Zaboo or Tinkerballa, she's a solid citizen. So one job description of your leading or main character might be "sane person in an insane world." (Note: The rock band analogy breaks down here. There is no rule that says the lead singer of a rock band must be the sanest or most normal. He is free to have as many substance abuse and legal problems as he chooses. In fact, in the world of rock and roll, the more messed up you are, the higher your profile.)

DRAWING ON REAL LIFE

So where do characters come from? Do they just pop into your imagination randomly? Of course not. Creative inspiration, despite the mystery that often surrounds that concept, is usually quite methodical. "Inspiration" comes because you work at it. William Faulkner once said, "I only write when I feel like it. Fortunately, I feel like it every day at 9 a.m." A successful and prolific TV writer and producer once described the main job qualification of the writer as "butt in chair."

Your characters will come to you because you work at it — conscientiously, purposefully, by design. To begin with, you've got your premise. Let's say it's *Seinfeld*, where the premise is that a stand-up comic observes and comments on the small insanities of life, and he lives in the capital of insanity, New York City. That's the roots of the world that series creators Jerry Seinfeld and Larry David began with. So their task, then, in developing that premise is to figure out who we surround Jerry with. Rather than randomly spitballing a few zany characters off the top of their heads, Seinfeld and David did something incredibly logical: They were writing about the world they knew, so they chose real-life characters they knew (or fictitious versions of them) to be the supporting players. Believe it or not, Kramer is actually based on a real person that Larry David knew in New York, Kenny Kramer. If you are so inclined, you can visit the real Kramer's website, *www.kennykramer.com*, and take his personal tour of New York City. George is based on Larry David himself. Not each and every detail; George isn't a writer. But emotionally, and in the neurotic way his mind functions (in other words, his essence or character), George is based on Larry David.

Real life is always the richest resource for fiction. Not a stereotyped version of real life but keenly observed, specific details of real-life people. When Felicia Day developed the character landscape for *The Guild*, she didn't have to just imagine a bunch of characters. She could draw on the types of people she knew among her *World of Warcraft*–playing friends and other online gaming acquaintances.

Drawing on real life is what allows you to be specific rather than generic. Let's say you wanted to create a boss character for a workplace series you were creating. TV series have had countless boss characters, and your temptation might be to merely imitate one of those. Bad idea. Your character would come off as exactly what it is: a pale imitation of somebody else's character. If, instead, you drew on real life — your own boss (you have a day job, surely) — well, then you've got a much better chance of creating a real character, an individual that seems like a flesh and blood human being, rather than a cardboard cutout. And even if your own real-life boss doesn't fit the bill, surely someone you know has a boss he's described in brutal detail who would fit the bill. For instance, my brother-in-law once had a new boss come in on Day One and tell everyone that his goal was to make sure that by Christmas time, the competition's children all had one less gift under the tree. Terrible, disgusting, repulsive boss. But great character — and memorable dialogue you'd never come up with on your own in a million years.

GROWING YOUR CHARACTERS

The characters in your pilot are not intended to be a finished product. They are a work in progress. They must be, or you will have nowhere to go in future episodes and future seasons. For your series to continue to grow and thrive, your characters must do the same. Although much of this will be a voyage of discovery for you, and you will find ways for your characters to grow as you write and shoot more and more episodes and spend time with those characters, you should at least have some plans for how your characters will grow when you conceive your original series and character blueprint.

Character growth in a television series can be a tricky thing. On one hand, the characters have to be consistent from week to week. Frasier must always be Frasier, from his first appearance in Season Three of *Cheers* right through to his last appearance in Season Eleven of his own series a full 20 years later. The same holds true for Codex, the Douche sisters, and Fiona Wallace, the inappropriate therapist and lead character in Lisa Kudrow's wonderful online comedy *Web Therapy*. But *consistent* should not be confused with *static*. *Consistent* means the character's core and essence — her attitudes and predominant ways of dealing with the world — remain the same. But the circumstances and challenges of her onscreen life must evolve. Otherwise, the series will become repetitive and stale.

Think about the characters on the long-running network series *Friends*. Ross, Rachel, Chandler, Monica, Phoebe, and Joey were recognizably the same characters from beginning to end. And yet their circumstances changed and evolved: new jobs, relationships, small increments of personal growth fueled by changes in the external circumstances around these characters.

That's how growth happens for series characters. Though they are essentially the same from episode to episode (consistent), they evolve in response to significant changes in their external world. This is why on network TV, as a series gets on in years, so many shows introduce new characters, new romances, or other major changes in the characters' lives such as getting married or having children. It's a way to keep the characters — and the series — from stagnating and losing the audience.

So even though the main focus of your efforts (and this book) should be devoted to the pilot and the initial conceptualization of your series and characters, you should also have, in the back of your mind, at least some initial ideas about how the characters might grow or face new, life-changing challenges. Because web series are still in their infancy, there aren't as many web series to cite as examples on this front. But take *The Guild* again, in its sixth season as I write this. Season Two saw the introduction of Wade, Codex's hot, nongamer neighbor. The introduction of an outsider to the gamer-obsessed world of Codex — especially a hot guy and potential love interest — puts more pressure on her character. In the series pilot, Codex gets dumped by her therapist for failing to acknowledge her video addiction. This new character potentially reawakens that challenge — but in a more compelling way because it comes from a hot guy.

One good way of thinking ahead about your characters' potential growth is to think in terms of season-long arcs. Characters A and B will butt heads all season long during Season One, but friction turns to sexual heat and they tumble into bed at the end of the last episode of Season One. Now Season Two can begin with a whole new energy and set of problems for your characters.

One note of caution on series growth: Don't be tempted to jump the shark. The phrase "jump the shark" refers to the writers of a show using a preposterous gimmick in order to expand the boundaries of a character or the series. The origin of the phrase dates back to the series *Happy Days*. The Fonz, their breakout character, had performed minor miracles for five seasons, elbowing the dormant jukebox back to life and so on. But the "miracles" kept getting bigger, and bigger, and bigger. So in attempt to make the Fonz ever more heroic, they did an episode where the Fonz, wearing a swimsuit and his trademark leather jacket as he waterskied, jumped over a confined shark tank to prove his bravery. It was, to say the least, a ridiculous scene. The show had crossed the line from playful fantasy to the utterly absurd and unbelievable. Despite this moment of weakness, the show remained hugely popular and lasted another 6 years. But the phrase "jump the shark" has come to mean the moment when a show becomes so gimmicky that the only humane thing to do is to cancel it and put the audience out of its misery. So yes, by all means, give your characters new challenges. Stretch them, grow them, make them deal with fresh and unexpected new curveballs. But do not jump the shark. Do not reach so far, in your desire to be fresh and new, that you catapult your series right out of its own reality.

FOR TEACHERS

As in the previous chapter, on premise, students can benefit from both analytical and creative assignments on character.

For the analytical, have the students examine a current web series and dissect its characters and character landscape. They need to do more than merely summarize externals. They must identify the internal essence of each character and then define how these characters create conflict and story potential by virtue of their conflicting or complementary character traits.

The same depth of thinking should transfer over to their creative presentation of the characters in their proposed series. They must define not just each character's individual qualities but also how they work together — how each one plays off the other to create a rich and useful character landscape for the series. What type of story possibilities will there be between Characters A and B? Character A and Character C? What about when B and D are together: What dynamics will that present?

4 CREATING THE WORLD OF YOUR SERIES

When you create a television series, you are not just coming up with a premise and a bunch of characters to populate that premise. You are creating an entire world, a coherent universe with its own rules, reality, and gravity. That reality can be whatever you want it to be. It can be relatively ordinary, like our own, America in the 21st century. Or it can be something entirely of your own making, an undiscovered planet with its own unique and bizarre reality. This bizarre reality can even be right here, hidden in plain sight in the contemporary United States of America. Take the movie *Men in Black*, for instance, set in modern-day New York City but with a less than commonly accepted reality to its world, namely that aliens live among us and there is a government agency that patrols and monitors these beings. Or you can speculate what reality might be like in the future, as the digital series *H+* does when it posits a future where we all have Internet access implanted directly into our brains. The "reality" and rules of the world you create for your series can be whatever you want. But — and this is a really big but, and I'm talking humongous megabooty — that reality must be consistent and true to itself at all times.

LAYING OUT THE RULES

The rules of your series world can be plain and simple (e.g., it's ordinary, modern-day New York City exactly as we know it), they can be based on commonly accepted reality (as in *Gaytown*, where the rules are that gay is the overwhelmingly dominant lifestyle, and the gay powers that be police and punish heterosexual behavior, so straights live closeted and imperiled lives), or they can be a complex set of special rules that define the operation and behavior of a special world, as in the movie *The Matrix*. But whatever the reality of your series, it must be consistent from episode to episode, and you must clearly define these rules for the audience early on in the series. Think about the movie *Men in Black* again. In the very first scene, they show you that aliens exist among us on this planet, that there is a special government agency that monitors these creatures, and that the knowledge that aliens live among us is such a closely guarded secret that even law enforcement officials (other than MIB) are kept in the dark. How are they and the rest of the population kept in the dark about this? The filmmakers show you, right in Scene 1. Just after the non-MIB officers witness alien behavior, an MIB agent cleanses their memories with a device called a neurolizer. The major rules of the *Men in Black* world are all laid out for the audience, right there in Scene 1. A few other particulars are knit in along the way, but the fundamentals are clearly defined up front. This allows the audience to enjoy everything that follows without saying, "Wait a minute, how come there are aliens but nobody knows about them?" If the audience starts asking those kinds of questions or becomes confused by the rules of your world, they are taken out of that world and can no longer enjoy it. Audiences are perfectly willing to suspend disbelief, to follow you into whatever universe you choose to create, no matter how wild and imaginative. In fact, they love it when you take them someplace they've never been before; just check out the box office stats for *Avatar*. But you have to give them a proper sense of gravity in your world by supplying them with a clear understanding of how that world operates.

Another note about rules: Special rules don't always have to be about aliens or altered states of reality. Your world might be perfectly realistic — say the world of online gamers of *The Guild* or the world of online therapy of *Web Therapy*. But these worlds require an explanation of the rules just as much as *Men in Black* and *Gaytown* do. Why? Because not everybody knows how online gaming or web-based therapy sessions work. So you have to explain the basics of these worlds to your audience — not by sending them a list of rules or laying them out in a crawl at the top of your pilot but by dramatizing and illustrating how these worlds work right in the body of your story.

So if the characters in *The Guild* are connected online via their game world and are also connected by telephone and speak to each other over headsets while they interact online simultaneously, you need to show that. Same goes for *Web Therapy*. The therapist (Fiona Wallace, played by Lisa Kudrow) and her clients are not in the same room. They conduct their sessions via webcam, each in his or her own separate environment. You've got to show this early on for the audience to understand and enjoy your universe. This doesn't mean that you couldn't ever do an episode of *Web Therapy* where a client shows up at Fiona's office or house. It just means that you have to establish what the status quo of this world is on a normal day in order for the audience to understand that in this particular world, showing up to see the therapist face to face is a departure from the norm.

REALITY VS. BELIEVABILITY

Whether it's a novel, movie, or Internet television series, fiction doesn't have to be 100% real in a literal sense. Of course, it is made up by definition. But that doesn't mean that anything goes. Fiction does have to be believable. The audience has to be able to go with the flow of the reality you create. If that flow is interrupted by the audience having a "wait a minute, that's just not possible" moment, then you've lost them. You have violated the unspoken agreement between creator and audience: that they will follow you anywhere as long as the place you take them has a coherent reality to it. This world doesn't have to be factually authentic; it just has to *feel* authentic. It has to ring true on an emotional level.

"Wait a minute" moments happen for two basic reasons. Reason One: The fantasy you've created is just so far-fetched or implausible that the audience is unable to suspend disbelief and accept your fictional universe. Reason Two: The rules seem inconsistent, or you suddenly or conveniently "forget" about one of the rules you've established in order to take the plot a certain way.

Let's say you wanted to do a satire on presidential politics and our dysfunctional political process. To do this, you create a series where the American public, sick of both the Republicans and the Democrats, rejects both major candidates and overwhelmingly elects a family-sized jar of Claussen dill pickles as president of the United States. You can see the hilarious scenes in your head. CNN reporters on election night show the vote tally with slides of the candidates: Barack Obama 8%, Sarah Palin 5%, the jar of pickles 87%. A record crowd of 4 million gathers near the Capitol steps to watch the historic swearing-in of the brine-soaked veggies as leader of the free world. In the Situation Room, the Joint Chiefs of Staff solemnly ask the Pickle-Jar-in-Chief whether they should invade Pakistan and wait with bated breath as the jar just sits there at the head of the table. All hilarious in your mind. And it might even be worth a 2-minute, one-time sketch on *Saturday Night Live* or *The Daily Show*, or it might provide the basis for a very funny YouTube faux news story. But I suspect if you tried this premise as the basis for an ongoing series, the audience would reject it as just flat-out impossible to believe. No matter how dimwitted you feel the American electorate might be, it's just not believable that they'd actually choose a jar of pickles to lead the free world. And no matter how clueless you feel (fill in the name of the candidate you hate the most) might be, most voters would still choose an actual human being over an inanimate object.

Reason Two for "wait a minute" moments: You violate the rules of your world as you have defined them, which is equally deadly. To illustrate, let me use the feature film *The Firm*. The world of the film is that of a Memphis law firm with a special practice: They're the Mob's law firm. Promising young lawyers (who look a lot like Tom Cruise) are brought into the firm as if it's just an ordinary, legitimate practice, they're given a taste of the good life of posh homes and fancy cars, and then they're told the truth about who they work for and informed that if they try to leave or talk to the Feds, they and their loved ones will be killed. The senior partners and their henchmen watch your every move: They bug your house and car, they even keep track of how and when you use the copy machine. Midway through the film, Young Tom is taken on a business trip to the Cayman Islands by senior partner Gene Hackman. Cruise shows up at Hackman's firm-owned condo to go to dinner. Hackman, still getting dressed in the bedroom, tells Cruise to help himself to some snacks and says that the key to the snack cabinet is on the key ring on the kitchen counter. Cruise picks up the keys and opens the wrong closet, and lo and behold, staring him in the face are boxes and boxes of secret firm billing records, all conveniently labeled Shit That Could Send Us to Prison 1984–88. That's just not consistent with the reality they had set up, and it took me right out of the movie. The movie asks me to believe that the mob — which conducts surveillance of everything right down to your underwear — keeps its secret, incriminating records in a closet with no armed guard and no video cameras, and the key to the closet is on the same ring as the key to the honor bar. Please.

BUILDING ON THE REALITY YOU CREATE

Just as you will want your series characters to grow and evolve, you may also want to grow and evolve the overall world you create in your series. Expanding your series universe is often a key to keeping a long-running series fresh and vital. Sometimes this expansion is merely a matter of adding a new character or two. But series evolution can also mean expanding or modifying the rules or parameters of your series universe.

Let's use the classic network sitcom *Cheers* as an example. For the first 5 years of the series, one of the rules was that Sam was the boss. It was his bar. But going into year six, with the departure of the Diane character, played by Shelley Long, the show's producers knew they needed to add a new female antagonist to play against Sam. And they didn't want this new character to have the exact same relationship to Sam as Diane did. That would be a backwards step for the show, not growth. So they solved their problem not only by adding a new, attractive woman to the cast but by altering the series rule that Sam was in charge. When Season 6 began, Kirstie Alley joined the cast as Rebecca Howe. And she was Sam's boss, hired to manage the bar by the company Sam had sold it to. This new dynamic gave the series fresh stories and angles to explore. It meant

Sam had to answer to a woman, perhaps for the first time in his life. It added jeopardy to Sam's situation, which added fresh comedy and drama.

Adding fresh angles to your series can and should be a part of your long-range planning for it. You don't even have to know what all of them will be. Nobody knows exactly what will happen in Episode 10 or 27 or 57 when they write a pilot, not even the creators of highly serialized material like *Sam Has 7 Friends* or the Fox network thriller *24*. TV series, and the characters in them, somehow have a life of their own. Each script you write and episode you shoot will spawn new ideas in your mind about where to take them and how to grow the show. Being open to these new ideas is crucial to keeping your show fresh and vital. Again, you can't suddenly make a change so radical that it feels like a wholesale violation of the rules of gravity you've created. But you can and should be open to the natural evolution that comes from working with a premise and characters over time, and you must strive to introduce new wrinkles from time to time. Introducing new elements and dynamics makes your series universe seem more believable and alive. In real life, unexpected new obstacles are a daily occurrence. Change happens, and that's a good thing. The same should be true for the fictional world you create because if it's exactly the same episode after episode, your audience will click elsewhere and make the big change themselves, effectively canceling your series.

WHAT IF I WANT TO MAKE AN ANIMATED WEB SERIES?

Great idea! Some of the best short series on the Web are animated. Animation opens up a wealth of creative freedoms. You can write scenes for any location that strikes your fancy, without physical or financial limitations. Want to write a show about slackers who go around the world defacing timeless monuments like the Great Wall of China or the Egyptian pyramids? No sweat! Animation gives you license to do that without flying a cast and crew halfway around the world or trying to convince the Chinese and Egyptian governments to shut down their tourist industry for a day while you film a scene demonstrating the ABCs of vandalizing their sacred property. Might be just a wee bit tough to get a permit for that.

Even beyond its ability to bypass logistical limitations, animation also expands other creative possibilities. In animation, it's not only acceptable to stretch reality, it's expected. After all, if something is 100% realistic, why bother to animate? You exaggerate in animation. Take things to absurd extremes in order to make a point. Ironically, by making things less than realistic, you have greater ability to illustrate and dramatize how things really are. By telling some lies, you get to paint a greater truth. This is one of the core principles of satire, a popular genre among animated shows.

Satire's stock in trade is exaggeration for effect — dual effect, actually. On one hand, satire stretches reality, like a funhouse mirror, for comedic purposes. But unlike the funhouse mirror, the distortion presented by animation isn't there just for humor. It also circles back around on itself and simultaneously makes a crystal clear point about its subject matter. By exaggerating our human flaws and foibles, satire holds a true and honest mirror up to our inner selves.

Because of this duality, satire has the latitude to say things in ways that realistic drama or comedy never could. Take *The Simpsons*, for instance. If you took the same characters and scripts and made them as a live action series, it wouldn't be believable or enjoyable. Imagine seeing a flesh-and-blood version of Homer chasing his 10-year-old son around with a knife as if he were going to stab him. Not funny. But because Homer and Bart are animated, we are free to laugh. Why? Because we don't have to worry about anyone really getting hurt. Animated characters shed no real blood. We know that what we're seeing is a distortion, there to make a point about how out of scale some fathers' reactions and threats are.

Same thing goes for the Looney Tunes cartoons. The Road Runner goes "beep beep" and taunts Wile E. Coyote into chasing him across the mesa and off a cliff. Wile E. hovers in space for a moment, a comic exaggeration of the moment we all experience when we know we've made a dumb mistake, can't undo it, and can only wait to suffer the consequences. Then Wile E. plummets a thousand feet, lands in a heap, gets conked on the head by a boulder, and sees stars. But he gets right back up, dusts himself off, and lives to fight (and lose) another day. All in good fun. I laughed my head off at this stuff when I was a kid. My grandkids do the same today. But if you saw a real coyote plummet a thousand feet and then get crushed by a real boulder... not good. Not funny.

It's important to point out that the freedoms of animation are not limitless. Yes, you can go anywhere you want. Of course you'll be exaggerating behavior. But most of the other storytelling rules covered in the book so far — about having a distinct series concept, appealing characters, clear and well-structured story, and so on — all still apply. Creative freedom does NOT mean you are free to do whatever, willy-nilly. Shows like *Family Guy* and *South Park* may seem like free-form animated improvisation, but trust me, they are not. They are just as carefully planned and structured as any other scripted series.

Another caveat about animation. You'll need to learn the tools of the trade, software programs for either 2-D or 3-D animation. They vary greatly in complexity, from simple enough for a 4-year-old (so they claim) to sophisticated enough for Academy Award–winning pros. Among the simpler programs, you might try Spore Creature Creator, Muvizi, or Animation-ish. All are modestly priced.

For a more adult-oriented product still aimed at beginners, you might try Smith Micro's *Anime Studio*. There are two versions: the Debut version is $49.99, the Pro version runs $199.99. Both are available as 30-day trials.

If you have the expertise and money to buy professional animation software, you probably don't need me to describe the relative capabilities of Maya vs. Softimage in handling Bézier curves or inverse kinematics. For starters, if you know what those terms mean, you're already ahead of me. But if you're a beginner at animation and want to take the next step, there are a wealth of professional 2-D and 3-D programs out there for you to aspire to. Just type "best animation software" into your search engine and shop away.

ANIMATED WEB SERIES: WHAT'S OUT THERE NOW

Just as with live action, the breadth and variety of animated web series material is astonishing. You can find everything from crude, zero-budget animated pieces done with free software tools to big-budget, sophisticated projects from Hollywood A-listers, like John Woo's *Seven Brothers* or Tom Hanks' *Electric City*, which streams on Yahoo and received a 2013 Streamy Award nomination for Best Animated Web Series. Other nominees are *Dinosaur Office, Dick Figures, Oishi High School Battle*, and *Red vs. Blue*. Just as with scripted series, you should absolutely surf the Net and check out the animated competition before you dive in.

FOR TEACHERS

Though it is highly doubtful that your students will be any more accurate in predicting exactly how their series will develop than we professionals are, it is still valuable to make them think about where their series *could* go in the future. It will help them conceive of their premise and characters as dynamic and alive rather than fixed and static.

As an exercise, have your students write a one-paragraph pitch for potential Episodes 10, 20, and 30. In addition to the plot for each episode, they should explain how that particular episode and story will help to grow one or more of the characters and make the series more fertile and rich to explore.

You might also consider having them examine an existing full-length series or web series and analyze what techniques the creators used to expand the series over time. The same assignments can apply to students planning to do an animated project. They should watch and analyze the best of what's out there. Tone and character specificity are especially important for these students. In a course I teach where students write a spec script for an existing TV show, less observant students who are fans of animated shows like *South Park* and *Family Guy* are often under the mistaken impression that "they just, you know, kind do a lot of random things and throw them together." Not so. While each show takes detours and risks, they also have well-structured stories. Make sure your students understand that a few off-the-wall jokes do not mean that a show is a totally free-form, anything-goes proposition.

5 THE PILOT STORY

Okay, so now you've studied the landscape of Internet TV shows and know it inside and out, and you have a dynamite premise for your own short-form series that has a compelling hook and legs like Angelina Jolie in 5-inch heels. You've got a great lead character and wonderful supporting characters, and know more about the tone and rules of your series idea than Lindsay Lohan knows about rehab. Time to sit down and write the pilot script, right?

Wrong! You're still missing one vital element before you can write the script. To paraphrase an old commercial about baby boomers heading toward retirement, *you, my friend, you need a plan*. And when it comes to planning a script, the basic plan or blueprint you need is the story or outline for your pilot episode.

"Haven't I already done that?" you might be asking. No, you have not. Coming up with a premise and characters for a series is not the same as planning the story for the pilot. The premise and characters tell us what the series will be like on an ongoing basis; they define the shape of the series week after week. That's why you have to develop them first. But now the task is to figure out how you will specifically introduce that premise and those characters in one episode: the first episode or pilot for your series.

CREATING A PILOT STORY THAT TELLS AND SELLS

Just like the title of your series, your pilot story must *tell* and *sell*. It must tell your audience what the show is about and make them want to watch more episodes. It must also introduce your regular series characters, serve as a template for all future episodes, define the tone and style of your series (which you will consistently adhere to in all future episodes), and tell its own unique, self-contained story that both promises dozens of stories to come and is satisfying and interesting in and of itself.

The biggest rookie mistake my students make when pitching their pilot story is constructing it to introduce the premise and characters — but nothing else. The story sets the basic gears of the concept in motion, sets up the premise, but doesn't illustrate what a typical future episode will be like. The pilot episode must do both. Is that a lot to ask? You bet. But you're creating an entire world, and that takes time, effort, and skill.

PREMISE PILOT VS. EPISODE 10 PILOT

The first decision you need to make in devising your pilot story is whether you are going to do a "premise pilot" or an "Episode 10" pilot. A premise pilot is one where the plot and action of the pilot episode are necessary to create the basic series situation, not just for the audience but for the characters in the series. If the premise of your series is best explained by showing those characters at the moment they are thrown into an entirely new life situation, then that calls for a premise pilot. An Episode 10 pilot is one where the basic situation of the series is already in place for the characters, and we, the audience, have just chosen this particular moment to drop in on their lives. The events of the pilot are not a drastic change in circumstances for the characters. We merely pick up their story in progress.

An example of a premise pilot from network television would be the 1990s ABC hit *Step by Step*, a show about a blended family where the parents love each other but the kids do constant battle. The creators chose to begin the series by showing the two families as they get together during the pilot, as opposed to having them already living as one family. Why? Because having the situation be new to everyone increased the conflict and number of stories that could be told within the basic premise. It also made it easier to write exposition and backstory. Because the characters themselves were new to each other and the situation, we got to learn about it right alongside them rather than them having to "casually" say things that they already knew just so we, the audience, could catch up with the information.

Seinfeld, on the other hand, chose to introduce the series with an Episode 10 pilot. Why? Because that show required that the characters already know each other well in order to tell the kind of stories they wanted to in the tone they envisioned. The series was built on the concept that these four people had a history together. If Jerry, George, Elaine, and Kramer were just meeting each other for the first time in the pilot, it would have been impossible to tell stories based on casual intimacy and long-term knowledge of each other's foibles and shortcomings.

There is one other type of pilot story: a hybrid of the premise pilot and Episode 10 approaches. In a hybrid pilot story, most of the characters are already living the lives and relationships they will continue to live in the series, but one or two new characters or elements are introduced to the existing world. The pilot for the classic NBC sitcom *Cheers* used this technique. Sam Malone, the womanizing owner of the bar, was already there, as were Carla the sharp-tongued waitress, Sam's former major league baseball mentor Coach (who had taken one too many fastballs to the head), and bar regulars Norm and Cliff. But the pilot introduced one major new character: snooty intellectual Diane, who shows up at the bar expecting to marry her college professor, only to be dumped, humiliated, and left in the bar without a love life or a future, whereupon Sam offers her a job at the bar, sparking the unspoken but unmistakable promise of romantic tension and eventual consummation between the two of them.

Another great example of a successful hybrid pilot is *Modern Family*. The three "pods" of the overall family are already in place when we fade in: Phil and Claire and their nuclear family; Claire's father, Jay, and his second wife, Gloria, and her son, Manny; and Jay's son, Mitchell, who is in a committed gay relationship living with Cameron. What's new, and what drives a central story line for the pilot, is the fact that Mitchell and Cameron have adopted a Vietnamese girl, Lily, and have not yet told the rest of the family. This was a very effective way to introduce the extended family because it naturally set up myriad conflicts and attitudes and provided a natural and believable way to bring the entire family together for the climactic scene where they all find out and react to what Mitchell and Cameron have done.

If the premise you devise calls for most of the characters having an established relationship, but you'd like one or two new elements to be introduced to your characters' world to shake things up, then a hybrid approach might be best for your pilot story.

Choosing which type of pilot story to pursue comes down to one basic question: Which form best serves my particular premise?

YOU'VE ONLY GOT A FEW MINUTES, SO BE ECONOMICAL

Because pilots have to accomplish so much — introduce all the characters and the basic situation, tell a satisfying story, set up future episodes, and so on — they can be quite daunting to write, even more so when you are creating a short-form series and only have a few minutes to tell, sell, and entertain. How can you possibly write one little 5-minute script that does all that? First of all, start with a premise that is easy to understand and simple to convey, with a small enough set of core characters that they can fit comfortably into the limited space of the short-form Internet format. However, if what you have in mind is a set of stories about a planet 500 years in the future where humans do battle with 11 distinct and previously unknown forms of life, and each of these life forms will have some characters who are good guys, some who are villains, and some who shift back and forth, bringing the total number of core characters to between 60 and 70, and in addition to being a science fiction vehicle, it also contains seven intersecting love stories, as well as flashbacks and flash forwards to other planets in other periods of time — well, perhaps this premise would be better served by a form other than the 5-minute web series, perhaps a 500-page graphic novel or twelve-part HBO miniseries.

But let's assume for the moment that you haven't lost your mind and have developed an appropriately compact premise with one to five core characters. Even then, you've got a lot on your plate in devising a successful and entertaining pilot. If you hope to accomplish everything you must in just a few minutes, you will need to be economical. So the first question you should ask yourself is, "Does the audience need to know about all five of these characters in the very first episode, or can I hold off introducing one or more of them until Episode 2?" In the world of half-hour and 1-hour shows, it's generally a rule that you have to use every series regular in every single episode, including the pilot. But web TV doesn't have to be a slave to the old rules. If you've got two main characters and three supporting ones, and the heart of your show is the two main characters and their interaction, maybe your show will be better served introducing the two main characters and perhaps one supporting character in the pilot, then introducing the other two recurring characters in Episodes 2 and 3, or even later.

The next task on the road to economy is devising a pilot that tells us the most important things we need to know about the central characters and their situation in the most efficient and memorable way possible. Notice I didn't say that it tells us *everything* about the characters and situation. You can't possibly tell the audience everything they will want or need to know. If you could, you wouldn't have any more stories to tell or episodes to write, and it would be the end of your series. But you do need to tell us the fundamental, crucial things we need to know in order to understand who and what your show is about. You may know 50 things about your main character's traits and background. But which two or three are the MOST important for us to know, the MOST central to establishing the essence of who that character is and the basic premise of your series? To return to the case of *Cheers*, the most important things for us to know about Sam and Diane were that he was a womanizing ex-jock and recovering alcoholic who ran the bar and she was a smug intellectual who had just been dumped by another smug intellectual. That's all the audience needs to know from the pilot in order to say, "Oooh, and they're attracted to each other! What's gonna happen when they get together?"

Once you've decided which characters must be introduced and what we must know about them, your job is figuring out how to introduce them in the most memorable way possible. What can they say or do to instantly burn an indelible image of those characters in the mind of the audience?

CREATING MEMORABLE CHARACTER INTRODUCTIONS

One of the best character introductions I know is the opening scene of the film *All That Jazz*, where we meet the film's main character, Broadway director and choreographer Joe Gideon. Gideon's defining traits are that he is a workaholic on a collision course with death through glib self-destruction. The film opens with his morning routine: hung over, popping speed, showering with a cigarette still dangling from his lips. He looks in the mirror, puts on a false face of joy, and exclaims, "It's showtime!" In a matter of seconds, we know the most important things we need to about Joe Gideon and his life of cheery self-destruction.

It doesn't have to be the first scene in your pilot, but you should strive to create a story that contains vivid moments for each of your core characters that unforgettably tell us exactly who they are. It might be an action or image (such as smoking the cigarette in the shower) or it could be dialogue. Think of Clint Eastwood as Dirty Harry, hovering over a criminal thinking about reaching for his gun, Harry's finger poised on the trigger of his .44 Magnum as he growls, "Go ahead, make my day." Or here's an example from real life. My brother-in-law worked in the radio business in the San Francisco area. Several years ago, he and several of his fellow general managers of stations in the area were called in to meet the regional vice president, their new boss. The vice president said, "My goal is to make sure that by the time Christmas rolls around, the competition's children all have one less gift under the tree." You really don't need to see or hear much else to get who this guy is: a soulless corporate drone who gets his jollies by bringing unhappiness to somebody's else's children.

That's the kind of high-impact, memorable character introduction you should strive for in your pilot — indelible snapshots that capture the essence of each character. Watch the pilot episode of *Be a Celebutante*. You'll know in less than 30 seconds exactly who these rich, shallow, spoiled women are. Same goes for *The Ed Hardy Boyz* — clear and instant creation of vivid main characters.

STORY STRUCTURE: BEGINNING–MIDDLE–END

Endless volumes have been written dissecting the "hidden secrets" of story structure. The more academic and wordy of these tomes seem to suggest that telling a story is as complex a task as building a nuclear reactor, requiring decades of study, a team of internationally trained physicists, and a secret stash of uranium-235. I don't want to suggest that any idiot can tell a story; storytelling at its best is an art. But the basics of story structure are as simple as this: Every story has a beginning, a middle, and an end, and each of these parts has a specific set of functions it must fulfill.

Though that last sentence may seem entirely self-evident — *of course* every story has a beginning, a middle, and an end — it's really quite a useful tool, but only if you remember to include the second part of the sentence: Each of these parts has a specific set of functions it must fulfill.

We'll start, naturally, with the *beginning*. The beginning of all stories, including short-form web pilots, has three main jobs. Job One is to introduce the main characters. If the script for your webisode pilot is six pages long but we don't meet your main character until page 4, then you don't have a properly structured beginning to your story. In that example, we don't even know who the story is about until it's almost over. Mistake. Big mistake. Start over and rethink the story structure. The beginning is roughly the first 20% to 30% of your story. You have to let us know who the main character of your story is during that time.

If Job One of the beginning of your story can be described as *who,* then Job Two might be described as *what*: What is the basic situation for your main character, and what happens early in your story to upset the status quo, giving your main character a new problem or situation he must respond to and act on? Let's return to the pilot episode of *The Guild*. Right off the bat we meet Codex (*who*), a young woman whose therapist fires her because she has an online gaming addiction she refuses to acknowledge (the status quo part of *what* plus a bit of a new problem). Soon thereafter, fellow online gamer Zabu shows up at Codex's apartment, convinced they are destined for each other. That's the central problem of the pilot story: This guy has invaded her space and is now pursuing her like a lovesick techno-geek stalker. Simple, clear, economical, and efficient — a good, solid structure for a beginning.

The final component of a strong beginning — Job Three — is that "world of the story" stuff we talked about. In order for the audience to fully understand the main character and her central problem, you must also let the audience know what world they are dealing with. Ordinary? Gaming addicts? Spoiled celebrity heiresses? Aliens with supernatural powers? That, too, is a crucial part of the *what*.

At this point you may find yourself thinking, "How the hell am I supposed to get all that into the first page and a half of a five-page script?" It can seem an impossible mountain to climb. But the key in the short-form webisode world is boiling the story and situation down to its essence and not getting bogged down in a million details or side journeys that, interesting as they may be, are better suited to a longer storytelling form. Think about the ultra-short story form commonly known as jokes. "Guy walks into a bar" — five words and already I know *who* and the first part of *what*, the basic situation. "Guy walks into a bar with a duck on his head" — now I know the full story of *what*, this guy's main problem. All in a matter of seconds. Yes, I know, you want to tell a real story, not some lame joke. Fair enough. But you're also not writing *War and Peace*, or even *Harold & Kumar Go to White Castle*. If you can't think of a way to economically introduce the main character of your web series and his central problem in two pages, then think some more. If you rack your brains for days and come to the conclusion that it will take at least 10 pages to introduce even the most rudimentary version of the who and what of your series, then your premise isn't suitable to the short-form Internet format. Use the idea for something else — a 30- or 60-minute network pilot spec, or even a feature film — and work on coming up with another idea that does fit the extreme demands for economy of this compact story form.

The basic function of the middle can be boiled down to two words: *complications* and *escalations*. Your beginning has introduced your main character, her normal world, and the new problem she must contend with. The middle is all about dealing with that problem. Your main character, like all of us, will naturally try the simplest, easiest way to solve that problem (Codex asks Zabu to leave). But of course that first, easy solution won't work for your hero, so she'll have to try harder. That's the essence of the middle: making things even more difficult and more complicated for your main character. Things have to get worse for your hero during the middle. If the new problem your hero encounters in the beginning section of your pilot story is that his mother-in-law, whom he despises, is coming to stay for a month, the next problem can't be that the shirt he wanted to wear isn't clean. That's not an escalation, a bigger problem, it's a backward step to a smaller problem — unless the shirt was a gift from the mother-in-law and she expects him to wear it and he must now either wear it crumpled and dirty (and get shit for that) or not wear it (even more shit). If the beginning introduces a hateful mother-in-law coming to visit for a month, then the middle must escalate or complicate things — she decides to move in forever, say, or your central couple finds out that his mother has decided to come stay with them for a month as well.

Let's use one of the stories from the *Modern Family* pilot as an example of escalations and complications. The beginning is simple enough: Cameron and Mitchell have adopted a little Vietnamese girl and are bringing her home. But Mitchell begins to worry whether they are up to the task — can they comfort her? have they painted her room too "gay"? — so Cameron calls Mitchell on his anxieties and asks what's *really* worrying him. Mitchell reveals that he hasn't told his family about the baby yet. Cameron is supportive — says he understands how Mitchell's family can be judgmental — then reveals that that is exactly why he has invited them all over that very evening for dinner, so they can tell them about the baby. Escalation! Now the problem has gone from merely caring for the baby to dealing with Mitchell's entire extended family. Further escalation comes when they arrive, Mitchell tells them he has some big news, and their guesses become a series of insulting and inappropriate statements, including Jay saying that Cam and Mitchell adopting a baby would be a terrible idea. Further escalation!

You might at this point find yourself saying, "But I'm not exactly telling a narrative story, I'm doing humor, so it's just a bunch of funny things that happen to my main character." You still need to have a beginning, middle, and end to your pilot (and your episodes), and there must be an escalation or build to the middle. In the case of broad comedy, that escalation or build means the humorous situations your character finds himself in must get progressively funnier or more outrageous. If not — if you start with your funniest bit and things get less funny from there — your audience will tune out and click away in dissatisfaction. This doesn't mean you start with something weak. It means you need to start strong and get even stronger.

Here's an example from the feature film world of how escalation is crucial to comedy. In the movie *American Pie*, there is a scene where the main teen boy's father decides to talk to him about sex. The father is determined to have this discussion despite the fact that his son would rather die than talk to Dad about sex. Things get worse when Dad breaks out a series of magazines to aid the discussion. The magazines the father pulls out of his brown bag are — in this order — *Playboy*, *Hustler*, and a magazine called *Shaved*. That's escalation. The magazines get progressively raunchier. Each is a distinct step up in how uncomfortable it makes the son. If Dad had started with *Penthouse*, then *Hustler* would be more of a duplication than an escalation, and the scene would have no comic build to it.

So, comedy or drama, narrative or sketch, you will have a beginning that introduces your central character and his problem and a middle that elevates and heightens that problem. By the end of the middle — or the beginning of the end, if you prefer — that escalation will reach a *crisis and climax*. This is the make-or-break point of your pilot episode, where the main characters must sink or swim. In the *Cheers* pilot, it's Sam's job offer to Diane. Will she swallow her pride and take this waitress job that is, in her mind, degradingly beneath her? If she does take it, is it because she really has nowhere else to turn or because she's attracted to Sam? In action stories, this crisis and climax is usually "the big shootout." It's the race to blow up the Death Star in *Star Wars* or pistols at 20 paces at high noon in a western. In a romantic comedy in series format, it's the moment when our two heroes commit to being with each other (see *Cheers* again) or are locked into being with each other against their will so that we can enjoy their love–hate antics going forward. In a broad comedy, this is the big joke — the funniest bit in the whole episode. It doesn't always work this way; sometimes audiences pick something from the middle as their favorite joke. But this final joke or bit had better be in the top three.

The final portion of the *end* — after your crisis and climax — is the *resolution*. How does your story end? Where do you leave the characters? And what problems do you leave them with? In self-contained stories, such as a novel or feature film, this resolution usually leaves us with the feeling that problems have been solved and a new status quo is in place. It's a return to calm. This is often the case in ordinary episodes of TV and Internet series as well. But a pilot is a different animal. It must leave the audience with both a sense of satisfaction with this one episode (your pilot) and a sense that this is merely the beginning, a sense that many more stories about these characters in this situation have yet to be told. Sam and Diane will be working together, so now what? Zabu just won't get out of Codex's apartment, so now what? It may seem a contradiction, but a well-crafted pilot ends with the sense that things have only just begun. Once again, think of the *Modern Family* pilot. After Jay says what a terrible idea adopting a baby would be, Cameron (not knowing what Jay has said) enters dramatically and presents Lily to the entire family. Jay apologizes, says he's no poster boy for great parenting, then is asked whether he wants to hold his new grandchild. His response — "Sure, bring the little potsticker over here" — is not only a funny joke, it's a perfect resolution. On one hand, he is perfectly accepting of his gay son and partner adopting a child. On the other hand, his utterly clueless racial insensitivity — calling this Asian tot a "little potsticker" — promises that there will be all sorts of problems and stories to come.

Bottom line: You must leave your audience begging for more. Like another type of climax and aftermath, you want your partner (in this case, the audience) to be utterly, blissfully satisfied — and eager as hell to do it all over again and again and again.

PUTTING IT ON PAPER: WRITING AN OUTLINE

One of the main differences between professionals and amateurs in the film and video world is that professionals don't skip steps. Professionals know there is discipline and value in each step along the way: developing the concept and characters first, then writing an outline for the story, then writing a draft of the script. Amateurs are so excited by their raw ideas, so enthralled by their possibilities, and so eager to fulfill the dream of seeing these ideas on the screen that they often jump right from the moment of inspiration to grabbing a camera, rounding up some props and actors, and shooting it right then and there. This is a recipe for failure. It's usually about as successful as getting the inspiration *I want a steak* and simply grabbing the nearest hunk of raw red meat and chomping into it. Raw meat isn't a steak. It has to be properly prepared first — seasoned, then cooked — in order for it to achieve its full steak potential.

The same goes for your series idea and pilot for it. The raw ingredients — the premise and characters and rough idea for the story — must be carefully, methodically prepared before they are served. If you skip any part of the process, including putting your story outline down on paper in prose form before you fire up your screenplay formatting software (more on that in the next chapter), you run the risk of ruining a perfectly good raw ingredient: your story idea. The reason is that your mind can play tricks on you. In your mind, that flash of inspiration for your series and pilot feels like a vivid, complete rendering of the idea. You can *see it* already, unspooling in sound and image on the flat-screen monitor in your mind. I believe you. Happens to me all the time. That's how you get excited about creating — that unpredictable, elusive moment when the idea for something first pops into your head. But experience has taught me that this moment, thrilling as it is, is only a first step. If I go from raw idea and just start typing a script, no matter how vivid that idea seemed in my head, I always crash and burn very quickly. You have to be disciplined and put the story outline on paper first. Because when you force yourself to put the story on paper, you start seeing all the holes in your idea that the leprechaun of creation in your brain, manic magician that he is, managed to gloss over in his fevered excitement. This can be a discouraging moment. The leprechaun is shouting, "This is great, it'll be great, let's shoot it!" But a calmer voice, perhaps one that resembles one of your high school teachers, usually the one in charge of training the hall monitors, is gently urging you to look before you leap. Most of us would rather be leprechauns than hall monitors. But the hall monitor part of us, geeky party pooper that he may seem to be, is doing us a favor. He's saying, "slow down, think this through, and make this story the best it can be." So write it down — tell your story to yourself in prose form, on paper, scene by scene. Then read it over and pretend you are seeing it for the first time. I know — that's impossible. But try. Evaluate it as if it were someone else telling you a story. Is the premise of the series clear, based on the outline you read? Are the characters sharply and clearly defined? Does the story have a clear beginning, middle, and end? With a clear central problem that escalates to a crisis, climax, and resolution? And finally, when you get to the end of the story, does it leave you wanting to see more episodes? If the answer to any of these questions is "no" — or even something tepid like "kind of" — then do not pass Go. Do not begin writing your script, thinking you'll fix it as you go along. Take the time to consider how you can turn that "no" or "kind of" into a resounding "absolutely" right now, here, in the outline phase.

PITCH IT OUT LOUD TO A FRIEND OR THREE

Now that you feel you have a solid story outline, there is one more checkpoint to pass through before you write the actual script: You need to try out your idea on a few people. The best way to do this is to pitch your series idea and pilot story to them — out loud. This provides several benefits. First, when you tell someone else your idea and story, it will quickly become obvious to you whether it makes sense or not outside your own head. Either they get it or they don't. If the people you pitch to all have blank stares on their faces or looks of utter confusion, then you need to rework either your concept or your pilot story. They're not getting it. Or if they're smiling and following along, clearly enjoying it, then go blank in one particular scene, you need to examine what's wrong with that scene.

Next, after you pitch to them, ask them what they think. This does not mean you are turning over creative control of your idea to these people. You are merely soliciting their reactions. If they all react the same way — for instance, if they all say the ending isn't satisfying, or they all feel they need more backstory about your characters in order to understand who they are — then you should consider how to address this universal point of confusion for your audience. On the other hand, if they each have different ideas about what they like or don't like, then you have to decide for yourself whether their suggestions are worth incorporating.

Finally, a word about who you choose to pitch to and get feedback from. Do not choose people who are by nature bitter and critical and derive joy from crushing the spirit of those around them. This does not mean you should pitch only to those who will mindlessly kiss up to you and say what a genius you are. You want honest, thoughtful criticism. But the last thing you need is a committed naysayer who thinks all ideas suck except for his own.

It is also important that you pitch to people who might be part of the intended audience for your pilot. If it is aimed at college students, your 70-year-old neighbor, even if he won several Emmys for his work on a groundbreaking ABC miniseries in the 1970s, may not be the right test audience. So pick several people who enjoy shows like the one you have in mind. They don't even have to be writers or filmmakers. They just need to be people who like watching short-form videos on the Web and fit the basic parameters of the audience you imagine might be interested in your show.

FOR TEACHERS

The pilot story phase is one where many students begin to crash and burn. This is because although they may have great raw ideas, they are often lacking in the craft and skills needed to tell a story, compounded by the fact that this particular form puts such a heavy demand on craft because of its ferocious need for economy.

Guide them gently but firmly through this phase. MAKE THEM PUT THEIR STORY PITCH OR OUTLINE ON PAPER. Then discuss it with them, scene by scene. Give them the benefit of your greater experience here. Point out potential trouble spots. If you are reading an outline of a scene that reads like a four-page scene to you, press them on that point. Ask them how they plan to convey all the action and information the outline suggests in such a limited amount of space.

One other thing here: Don't be afraid to make them start over with their story. If their story just doesn't work, writing the script itself will be a waste of time. Guide them, help them, make sure they have at least the basics of a solid pilot story in place before letting them go to script.

Finally, if, like me, you are well past the YouTube generation in age, you will need to remember that you may not be the target audience for the material your student is pitching. But the rest of the students probably are. So try to gauge not only your own reaction to the material but the class's reaction as well. It's a tricky line to walk — after all, you know more about story structure and character than the students do. But I think it's important for teachers to remember — especially when evaluating pop culture creations aimed at a younger audience — that just because an idea isn't for you doesn't mean it isn't for anybody.

6 THE PILOT SCRIPT

Now that you've got a solid story outline for your pilot episode, it's time to turn that outline into a script — a short screenplay. Whereas an outline is written in standard prose as a narrative comprised of sentences and paragraphs, just like a novel or a magazine article, a script is written in screenplay format. (For a simple tutorial on proper screenplay format, see Appendix 1.)

There are several reasons why screenplays are formatted the way they are. First and foremost, a script is meant to be filmed, so a screenplay is not only a means to conveying a story, it must also serve as a blueprint for shooting a film. That's why it contains elements like this:

```
EXT. PLAYGROUND — DAY

MARIE (early 30s) watches COLE (5) as he blows soap
bubbles into the air by the swing set.
```

The people who plan the filming of the script (in the case of your web series, that means you) need to identify each location (here, a playground), whether it is a day scene or night scene, who's in the scene, what props will be needed, and so on. Screenplay format facilitates the process by which these crucial production elements can be spotted, highlighted, and tracked.

The second benefit of screenplay format is that in a film, the only information the audience can receive is what they see (the actions, movements, and facial expressions of the actors or physical objects) and what they hear (dialogue, sound effects, music). Thus, whereas a prose piece can contain what is known as interior monologue — spelling out what one or more characters are thinking — a screenplay can only communicate a character's internal thoughts through external means, in what he says or does. Thus, a script's primary components aren't paragraphs but segments of action and of dialogue.

Yes, there are many films where we "hear what a character is thinking" via voice over. But in most cases, it is incumbent on the writer and filmmaker to find other ways to give us a sense of what a character is thinking and feeling.

The third reason scripts are written in this special form is that screenplay format helps the reader translate the written word more directly into sounds and images, elements that enable him to "see a movie" — visualize the action and dialogue as they will appear on screen. Consider the following:

```
EXT. HARD BODIES STRIP CLUB — DAY

A jumbo jet on its final approach roars past a sign that
reads "Live Nude Girlz." An aging Volvo station wagon
sputters into the Hard Bodies parking lot. PROFESSOR ROSS
BROWN (50s) steps out of the Volvo, pulls a baseball cap
down low over his eyes, crosses to the club's entrance.
He throws a nervous glance over his shoulder as he slinks
into the club.
```

You see a shot from a movie, right? Several shots, probably: an establishing shot of a strip club near an airport, followed by a shot of a car pulling into the parking lot and a middle-aged man stepping out of the car and entering the club in an uneasy manner. In a novel the same scene might be handled like this:

```
The first thing Professor Brown noticed as he pulled into
the parking lot of Hard Bodies was the sickening stench
of jet fuel. Through the dusty windshield of his aging
```

```
Volvo he watched a jet glide past the "Live Nude Girlz"
sign. He slapped on a baseball cap and prayed that nobody
he knew would spot him as he hurried to the front door
and into the club.
```

Although it conveys the same basic information as the screenplay format version, that description is not suitable for a script. Why not? Because people in a movie theater don't get scratch 'n sniff cards with jet fuel stench on them. Nor can they read the professor's mind to know that he hopes nobody spots him. So make sure in your script that you focus on what we can see or hear. If you want us to know something internal or unseen, such as what a character thinks or feels, then you must do that through dialogue or specific actions that communicate those internal musings to the audience in a visible or audible way.

BUILDING YOUR SCRIPT SCENE BY SCENE

Just as your overall story has a beginning, a middle, and an end, each individual scene is its own mini-story, with the same beginning–middle–end rhythm and structure to it. Your outline tells you *what* the story of each scene is. But now that you are turning that story into a fully realized script, you need to take that scene and decide *how* to tell it, as its own self-contained little story. You will need to decide: How much of the story of the scene will be told through action and how much will be told through dialogue? Which pieces of the story will be revealed in what order? Is there a more effective way to tell the same story? Are there actions that can dramatize the point of the scene more memorably than dialogue? A thousand little decisions go into shaping not just the broad concept of your series and the construction of your pilot story but the crafting and construction of each individual scene.

Let's go back to our scene of Professor Brown pulling into the parking lot of the strip club. I chose to tell that little mini-story by focusing on the setting first:

EXT. HARD BODIES — DAY

A jumbo jet on its final approach roars past a sign that
reads "Live Nude Girlz."

But I could have made another choice: I could have focused the audience's attention not on the setting but on the character, like this:

EXT. PARKING LOT — NIGHT

PROFESSOR ROSS BROWN (50s) nervously eyes his
surroundings. He starts to get out of his aging Volvo,
then stops, grabs a baseball cap, and pulls it down as
far as he can, hiding half his face.

ANOTHER ANGLE

Professor Brown emerges from the car, slinks across the
parking lot into a club called Hard Bodies, whose marquee
reads "Live Nude Girlz."

There is no one answer as to which version is better. It depends in part on intangible elements like personal taste and in part on the context — what came before this scene. Have we already met Professor Brown, or is this our introduction to him? If we've never met him before, I'd probably opt for version 1 — setting the scene, then introducing the person in that scene — because the location tells us at least something about this unknown person we are meeting for the first time. On the other hand, if the previous scene was of Professor Brown teaching a philosophy class, delivering a lecture on morality and personal choices, I'd probably opt for version 2. Why? Because the previous scene, the morality lecture, would prepare the audience for the parking lot scene. We can cut directly to the closer shot of the professor in his car, clearly about to do something that makes him uneasy. We, the audience, have context for his nervousness.

We're already thinking, "He's about to do something he doesn't feel right about, something morally questionable." This creates suspense — we want to know what the professor is about to do — and suspense engages the audience, makes them sit forward in their seats and think, "I wonder what's going to happen next." By holding off the reveal — that he's about to go into a sleazy strip club — the audience is drawn into the character and his situation more effectively than if you showed the club first, then showed the professor's nervousness.

However, you might argue that cutting directly from a lecture on morality to a sign that reads "Live Nude Girlz" will be a great transition as well as a very funny juxtaposition and that the laughter will build from the sign to the next cut of Professor Brown trying to disguise himself somehow in his car. Perfectly valid argument. Creative choices are just that: choices. There are often several effective ways to approach a scene. You, the creator, must decide which path you think is best for your story, characters, and tone.

Notice that this one tiny little scene is less than a quarter of a page in each version, and yet as the writer, you must make a string of important decisions. Should I start with the setting or the character? How will I show that the professor is nervous about being seen? How much of a "disguise" will he use? A moustache? No — too ridiculous. A ski cap? It's July in Los Angeles, so why would he have a ski cap in his car? Even the tiny decision to spell the word *Girlz* on the marquee with a "z" rather than an "s" is a conscious decision, meant to convey the cheesiness of the setting and the character's action.

The point is that in going from outline to screenplay, you are not merely reformatting from prose to screen format. You are also changing storytelling mediums and must now carefully consider the best, most effective way to take a story built from sentences and paragraphs — your outline — and turn it into a story built from sounds and images. This must be done with every scene. How do you go about making this conversion from prose to screenplay? First, you read the scene as it is in your outline. Then, try to imagine it as you'd like to see the scene on a movie screen. What do you see or hear as you imagine it? Don't rush to answer this question. Give your creative mind the chance to take the raw material and work with it. Even though you may think you know exactly what the scene is from your outline, writing is a process where each step— premise, then characters, then story outline, then script — adds and refines. New elements spring into your mind that you hadn't imagined before, elements that modify and strengthen your original thoughts and images. Maybe when you built your outline, your entire description of the scene was "Professor Brown pulls into the parking lot of a sleazy strip club." Simple, clean and effective — perfectly good for an outline. But now, as you sit at your keyboard and imagine the movie version of that scene, your challenge is to give the audience tangible cinematic evidence of *sleazy*, visual cues that characterize the setting for the movie audience the same way the adjective *sleazy* did for the reading audience. Those visual cues, in my script version, are the signs that read "Hard Bodies" and "Live Nude Girlz" and the proximity to the airport.

You must go through this thoughtful process of translating prose into cinematic action and dialogue scene by scene by scene. The devil is in the details, and the details that take the bones of a story (your outline) and turn it into a fleshed-out screenplay (basis for a short movie) take time, thought, and effort. Don't rush. Take your time as you imagine, write, rewrite, and improve your story and turn it into a script.

One other note: Economy is of the essence. You entire story will be perhaps 5 minutes long. You can't spend the first 90 seconds setting up the atmosphere for Scene 1. Chose your details with precision. Give us the key elements, the ones that speak volumes about the character and situation, and then keep the action moving forward.

DEVIATING FROM THE OUTLINE

It's inevitable. No matter how much time you've spent developing your premise, constructing your characters, and working and reworking the story for your pilot, when you sit down and begin to actually write the script, you will want to change some things. New ideas will spring to mind — not just added details but substantive differences. Maybe, in the outline of the story about Professor Brown, you simply imagined the parking lot scene, then figured you'd cut right to the professor having dinner with his wife and children. But now, as you are imagining the parking lot scene and the professor nervously glancing over his shoulder to see whether anyone sees him going into the club, you begin to think about that notion. Wouldn't it be more powerful if someone he knows does see him? And wouldn't it be stronger if he's seen not just in the parking lot but inside the club itself? You start getting excited about this new thought and image and begin to imagine the professor inside the club. Who might see him? In a flash it comes to you: "Oh! Oh! I know — it's one of his students. A guy from the philosophy class. No, wait — better yet, it's a girl... and she's one of the dancers!"

Does this mean you got it wrong in the outline and should have thought of this back then? No, it's just part of the process. And now that you have this new idea about seeing the female student working the pole in the club, you'll naturally want to go back to the classroom scene and make sure you set her up — establish her and her reaction to the morality lecture in that scene so we know who she is in the strip club scene. Maybe you'll want to add dialogue — a question she asks the professor about difficult moral choices — or perhaps you'll merely want to write in a shot of her facial reaction to something the professor says. In either case, your one new idea — adding an interior of the club scene where the professor sees a female student working there and she sees him — necessitates one or more changes to the previous scene. THIS IS ALL GOOD! This is how writing and creativity build on themselves. You start out with a plain cheese and tomato pizza, and ingredient by ingredient you add layers of flavor and texture until your plain old cheese pizza turns into a feast with the works.

To be perfectly honest, as I was writing this chapter, I merely thought I'd use the parking lot scene as a concrete visual example for the previous section, on turning a prose outline into a screenplay. But as I began writing this section, I realized I could get more out of the example by using it for this section as well. That's the creative mind at work. It builds things layer by layer.

Does this mean you should blindly follow your creative mind wherever it wanders? Absolutely not. Sometimes your creative mind is so wildly manic and inventive that it leads you completely off track, away from the core of the story you are telling. When that happens, you must remind your beloved creative mind that not every impulse it has is a good or useful one. But neither should you feel obliged to adhere to your outline rigidly and slavishly. As my colleague professor James Dutcher is fond of saying, it's an outline, not a suicide pact. If, as you write your script, you find an element of the outline that you feel needs to be adjusted or improved, by all means do so.

Every writer must balance creativity with discipline. I always picture this partnership as if I'm wearing a double-sided baseball cap, like a Sherlock Holmes hat with two brims, one in front and one in back. The front of the cap says CREATOR. It's the front because the creator, the one who has the initial inspiration, gets to go first. But then I have to flip the cap around to the other side, the one that says EDITOR. This is the analytical part of my writer self, the one that must honestly assess my raw creative ideas and distinguish the useful ones (the ones that further the story I'm telling, tell it more vividly, or tell the audience more about the characters) from the ideas that either clutter the story, change the characters in a bad way, or are distractions or detours away from my core story.

Sometimes this battle between your creative self and your disciplined, analytical self can be difficult. The creative self runs on adrenaline and pure excitement and tends to see the editor part of your brain as some sort of evil hall monitor bent on enforcing petty rules that spoil all the fun. But you — the complete writer — need both the creator and the editor if you are to do the best possible job on the project all three of you are working on. So remind yourself that all three of you — your creative self, your editorial self, and your complete writer self — have to play nicely together and treat each other with respect. Your editor will save your ass a million times, stopping your hyperactive creator from wandering off into the woods. But your creative self is not subservient to the editor; he is an equal partner. The creator is the only one who can help you rise beyond the ordinary and boring to tell a truly exciting and vivid story.

It can be tricky business, this task of balancing your creative and editorial impulses. But hey, if you want to write and to make movies, then you'd better learn to embrace the tricky and the complex. If you crave simple, then repeat after me: *Would you like fries with that?*

WHAT MAKES GOOD DIALOGUE: THE 4 CS

Great dialogue is an art all its own. At its best, dialogue pushes the story forward, characterizes the speaker and perhaps the person he's talking about, disseminates exposition and facts the audience needs to understand the story, captures a perfect sense of the times and environment of the script, and somehow seems to do all this effortlessly and naturally, as if the lines spoken by the actors are the only ones that could ever have been written.

This effortlessness is an illusion, of course. Dialogue is crafted with the same care and attention to detail that you put into developing your story. It is molded, shaped, reshaped, and refined many times. The trick is making it *seem* natural and effortless. This is a complex task, one that takes a great deal of practice to truly master. But boiled down to its essence, good dialogue must fulfill what I call the 4 Cs. It must be:

- In *character*
- *Concise*
- *Connective*
- *Clear*

Sounds simple enough, right? Yes and no. Let's take a closer look at the process involved in achieving the 4 Cs.

Before you can write good dialogue, you have to know your characters and know them thoroughly: what they think, how they feel, how and where they grew up. They must be three-dimensional people in your mind. As discussed in Chapter Three, simply saying a character is a "waitress" or "cop" isn't nearly enough. Dialogue is often where the rubber meets the road in terms of how well you know your characters. When you know them well, the dialogue feels specific to that individual human being. It feels real, alive. When you don't know your characters or know them only superficially, the dialogue will be bland, generic, and clichéd.

As you sit at the keyboard and imagine how the scene you described in your outline will unfold on the imaginary movie screen hovering in front of you, your characters will begin to speak. Your brain will imagine what they might say. If the character you are writing for is intimately familiar to you — based on someone you know or a combination of people you know or have observed in real life — then this dialogue stands a good chance of being well written. It is grounded in reality and authentic human speech — in other words, it's *in character*. However, if you are simply winging it, writing about a character you don't really know or simply basing this character's speech patterns on similar characters you've seen in movies or on TV, then chances are the dialogue won't be as good.

For instance, let's say you are writing the scene described in your outline as "Professor Brown delivers a lecture on morality and ethics to his class." If you've actually taken a philosophy class, you can base this dialogue on the type of things your professor used to say. If you've never taken a philosophy class, do not assume that you can simply guess what you think a philosophy prof sounds like. You need to do some research if you want the dialogue to sound authentic. You might drive over to a local college and sit in on an actual philosophy class. Or you could just stay at your computer, switch from your word processing program over to your Web browser and search engine, and find some articles written by philosophy profs on the topic of morality. Or maybe you'll go to YouTube or iTunes and find some audio or video podcasts from college profs on morality. You don't need to quote these verbatim (and probably shouldn't), but you'll have a much better chance of capturing the rhythm and professional lingo of a philosophy prof by observing the real thing than by simply pretending you know what these guys sound like. You might also look for quotes from famous philosophers on morality or ethics that the professor could cite.

The same process holds regardless of whether you are writing a football player, a stripper, a homeless person, or whomever. You need to capture the sound, vocabulary, and cadence of a real human being. To accomplish this, you must either know people like your characters or do some research to gain that sort of knowledge and familiarity. (And to those of you who now feel you must head down to the nearest strip club as a homework assignment, you're welcome.)

Though I've called this research, it's really just one aspect of a larger, more important fundamental of good dialogue: All dialogue must be in *character*. That's the first and most important of the four Cs.

For dialogue to be in character — authentic, truthful, and believable — you must consider a variety of questions about that character:

- How does this character speak? Formally or informally? Does she swear like a sailor, or is she prim and reserved enough to say "H-E-double-hockey-sticks" rather than use the actual word?
- Who is this character, both professionally and personally? Is he a highly educated college philosophy professor who quotes Shakespeare and Greek scholars, or is he a high school dropout who has lived most of his life on the streets?
- What does the character want at this particular moment in the story?
- Even more important, how does he plan to go about getting what he wants at this moment? Flattery? Deceit? Bullying?

The second of the 4 Cs — *concise* — reflects the difference between conversation (the way people talk in real life) and dialogue (the way characters talk in a movie). Even though you want your dialogue to be authentic and believable, you don't want it to be real in a literal sense. Real-life conversations ramble; they include unnecessary repetition, irrelevant asides, and mistakes. Real-life conversations are rarely as precise as you want screen dialogue to be. In real life, people often take 5 minutes or 5 hours to express themselves. Dialogue must capture the essence of what a character wants to express and find a way to convey that essence compactly and, if possible, memorably.

Here is one of my favorite examples of effective, concise dialogue from the feature film *Escape from Alcatraz*, starring Clint Eastwood. Eastwood plays a prisoner at this legendary maximum security lockup. The scene is set in the prison exercise yard. Another prisoner introduces himself to

Eastwood and rambles on and on about his personal history, particularly his childhood. On and on and on he goes, with Eastwood simply staring at him. At the end he asks Eastwood, "What kind of childhood did you have?" Eastwood's response, accompanied by his trademark steely glare: "Short."

That's great dialogue. It expresses so much with just one word, because that one word, in the context of the scene, conveys so much subtext. First, of course, it conveys a literal truth: The Eastwood character had a short and probably difficult childhood. But other meanings and implications it captures include "and don't expect me to tell you the details, I don't talk about myself or reveal much, so get out of my face, you're bothering me."

Certainly not every line of dialogue can or should be that brief. In the speech that precedes it — when the other prisoner goes on and on about his upbringing — wordiness is actually the goal. But in general, good dialogue should be as compact as possible.

The two remaining Cs are more intuitive but still merit mention. In addition to being in character and concise, good dialogue is also *connective* and *clear*. By *connective* I mean that each line of dialogue should be a response to the dialogue or action that immediately precedes it — not necessarily a direct response but a response motivated by the previous line, including changing the subject entirely if the previous line somehow makes the character uncomfortable. (The exception is if you are trying to make a point about someone not listening or paying attention to others around him.) *Clear* means the audience should be able to easily understand the meaning of each line of dialogue. This does not mean that dialogue should always be explicit or "on the nose." Quite the opposite. When dialogue is too "on the nose," it sounds clunky and stilted. Nothing is worse than a character saying something like, "Well here we are, little brother, back in the tiny town of three thousand people where we grew up until Dad left us and Mom tragically committed suicide on Christmas." Expository dialogue like that is the hallmark of an amateur. A professional would probably handle it by showing visually the arrival of the characters (in a car or on a train) and showing visually that we are in a small town. The characters need only say something like, "Feels weird to be back, doesn't it?" Even that is a bit too on the nose. Better still would be a shot of our characters arriving in town, followed by a shot of what they see: a man about their age opening up Watson's Diner, followed by dialogue like, "I guess Opie Watson finally took over the joint from the old man." Though that dialogue doesn't tell us anything about our character's parents, it does give us a clear sense that they used to live here and have been away for a long time. The rest of the information can come out in later dialogue.

MAKING YOUR SCRIPT READ VISUALLY

As the saying goes, actions speak louder than words — not just in real life but in film. As cool as it is to write nifty dialogue, films (even short-form Internet episodes) are a visual medium, and the visual is in most cases the more powerful, memorable, and effective way to connect with the audience. You've heard this before, but it is Commandment Number One of screenwriting and merits bold print and capital letters: SHOW, DON'T TELL. Wherever and whenever you can, SHOW us character and situation through the action, events, and visual elements of the scene. Dialogue will add dimension to your character, but always SHOW us who your characters are through what they do. DRAMATIZE them for us by having their actions and choices ILLUSTRATE and ILLUMINATE who they are deep inside.

Consider the feature film *When Harry Met Sally*. Written by Nora Ephron, the film has some of the sharpest, wittiest dialogue this side of Noel Coward. But if I asked 100 people what they remember most about the film, 98 of them would say "the fake orgasm in the deli scene." In the scene, Sally, played by Meg Ryan, tells Harry it's disgusting that he beds women he barely knows then concocts excuses to flee their bedrooms and run back home as fast as he can. Harry, played by Billy Crystal, defends himself, saying, "I think they have a pretty good time," implying the women are sexually satisfied. Sally asks how he knows they're really satisfied, implying they might be faking their orgasms. Harry, cocky, insists he knows the difference. The dialogue between them is fast, spot-on, highly amusing — and utterly overpowered by what happens next. In the middle of a crowded New York deli, Meg Ryan moans, groans, screams, pounds the table, and pretends to have the world's loudest, longest, most mind-blowing orgasm — then calmly sighs, smiles, and munches her cole slaw.

The dialogue that precedes it — and a great deal of the dialogue through-out the movie — is top drawer. But actions are always more memorable than even the best dialogue. Seeing Sally demonstrate how easy it is to fake an orgasm is 10 times as powerful as any dialogue she can muster to argue that case.

Another tool to help your script read visually is using active, vivid, descriptive verbs. Beginners often use bland, neutral verbs, like this:

```
Edward enters through the front door. He is tired. He
sits on the couch.
```

A stronger version of this would be:

```
Edward trudges through the front door, flops on the couch,
exhausted.
```

Why is the second version better? Because *trudges* paints a stronger visual picture in the reader's mind than *enters*; same goes for *flops* com-pared to *sits*. As my eighth grade English teacher used to say, verbs are the action words. So use them to help your reader see precisely the type of action you have in mind.

Another common mistake made by novice writers is that they over-burden their scripts with an endless litany of unnecessary descriptive detail. "Aren't details good?" you might ask. And my answer would be, "Yes, but only the important ones." Students new to screenwriting often set their scenes like this:

```
INT. DAVE'S BEDROOM — DAY
```

```
The early morning light shines through half-open blue
Pottery Barn type curtains. DAVE, a 36-year-old man with
```

curly brown hair and brown eyes, is asleep in his bed.
Clothes hang out of the open drawers of his Ikea blond
wood dresser. There are also piles of dirty clothes on
the floor: some jeans, T-shirts, a gray suit, socks and
underwear, plus Dave's beloved hockey skates and goalie
pads. There is a clock radio on the nightstand, along
with an empty bottle of Jose Cuervo Especial Gold 80
and some mostly eaten slices of pepperoni, mushroom, and
onion pizza. The clock radio flips over from 5:59 to 6:00
and U-2's "She Moves in Mysterious Ways" begins to play.
Dave groans, reaches over, and turns off the clock radio.
He sits up, gets out of bed, and walks into the bathroom.

I'll spare you the even lengthier description of the bathroom that typically follows. But rest assured that it is similarly flooded by a tsunami of
irrelevant details. The job of the screenwriter is to direct the reader's eye
to the details that are absolutely essential and most revealing. Who cares
what color the curtains are, which items of clothing are on the floor, or
what kind of pizza Dave likes? Does it matter what color his eyes are or
that his hair is curly? NO. Here's a better way to handle this scene

INT. DAVE'S BEDROOM — EARLY MORNING

DAVE (36) snores in the middle of a frat-boy mess of
dirty clothes and discarded pizza boxes. Suddenly, the
clock radio BLARES U-2. Dave groans, knocks over what's
left of a bottle of tequila as he slaps at the clock,
then stumbles out of bed and trips over some hockey gear
on the way to the bathroom.

In less than half the words we still get the complete picture — in fact,
a better picture because now the important details, uncluttered by the
trivial ones, stand out. Furthermore, the images resemble a moving picture
rather than a static one because they are revealed through action. The

pigsty environment is revealed as Dave snores (snoring being a more active picture than "is asleep"). The previous night's tequila is revealed not as a "still photo" or snapshot but as a moving image, knocked over when Dave reaches for the clock. Same thing for the hockey gear: It is revealed through action, when Dave trips over it.

In short, use every language tool at your disposal to make your script read like a movie rather than a short story.

YOU'VE GOT A FIRST DRAFT. TIME TO GET TO WORK AGAIN

First drafts are exactly that: a good beginning. Pat yourself on the back for a job well done. Celebrate with your favorite age-appropriate beverage. Smile at yourself in the mirror and give yourself a well-deserved finger gun. You did it! You da (insert gender)!

Okay, celebration over. Now it's time to wipe that smug grin off your face and get back to work. *But you just said I did it! I'm the man/woman/ other!* You are — you're totally awesome. But a first draft is far from a polished final script. You must now take your first draft, read it with a cold, objective eye, assess its strengths and weaknesses. You must read it as if someone else had written it and you were being asked for your honest, no-holds-barred opinion of each and every word.

Your inner creator has accomplished something miraculous: He has delivered a real script, a story with dialogue and action in screenplay form that can serve as a blueprint for a short-form Internet pilot. Bravo! But now, your inner creator must take a step back and let his trusted and valued partner, your inner editor, do his work, too. The inner editor's work begins with "big picture" questions as he reads:

- Is the premise of the series clearly defined based on what is shown in this one script?
- Can you imagine other stories based on this premise — a lot of other stories?
- Is it clear who the main character is?
- Is it clear what the main character wants and what prevents him

from getting what he wants? Can it be made clearer or presented in a more palpable or memorable way?

- Are all the characters clearly defined through their action and dialogue? Are there any places, large or small, where the characters can be more sharply defined?
- Does each scene advance the story?
- Are there people out there who will be interested in this story and these characters?

Your reflexive answer to each of these questions will be, "Of course all these things are clear and as good as they can be. I wrote it and it's perfect." Trust me, it's not perfect. Nobody — not Emmy-winning, Hall of Fame (if there was such a thing) TV writers, not even William Shakespeare himself — ever, ever wrote a first draft that didn't need rewriting. You must discipline yourself to avoid the natural, defensive tendency to deflect all criticism, even if it comes from you, and just want to be done with the damn thing and move on and shoot the sucker.

The key, I think, is looking at the "criticism" your inner editor is dishing out not as a personal attack but more like the way you might feel when your significant other informs you, just as you're about to leave the house, that the seam in your jeans has split and you really should change unless you want people to see all the way to Adventureland when you sit down. You'd thank them for pointing this out, wouldn't you?

When I get valid criticism of my first drafts — whether it comes from me or from someone else — I'm grateful that I've been saved from exposing my less than best effort to the world. Sure, my first reaction to the criticism is "F*&k you, you're an idiot and I hate you and your children are ugly." But experience has taught me to set that defensive, unproductive reaction aside and consider the note being given. Can I improve my characters or my dialogue? Is there a better way to dramatize that point?

If you can approach rewriting not as a chore but as an opportunity to take something good and make it better, not only will your scripts improve, but you'll find the process of rewriting much more enjoyable.

In addition to the list of "big picture" questions, you will also want to examine things on a microscopic, word-by-word level:

- Is every verb in my description and action lines as vivid and active as possible?
- Is each line of dialogue in character? Would this character say "eat dinner," or would he say "dine" or "grab a bite" or "chow down"?
- Is each speech and line of description as concise as possible?

WHEN IS IT READY TO BE SHOT?

Obviously, I'm big on not shooting your first draft. You must rewrite your script, probably several times. But sooner or later you'll need to ask, "How do I know when I'm done?"

It's a fair question. No script is ever perfect, but neither are you writing the script simply to archive your pages. You are writing it because you want to shoot it, edit it, and post it on the Web for people to see, which can't happen if you are eternally stuck in an endless loop of writing and rewriting. So the question isn't "When is your script perfect?" but "When is it ready to be shot?"

Unfortunately, there is no software currently available that can analyze your script and pronounce it worthy of production or not. But if you have gone through the process of developing your pilot concept and characters, writing an outline for your pilot story, writing a first draft, reading and honestly assessing that first draft, rewriting to improve it, then rereading and rewriting those improved drafts several times, then I think you are ready to shoot — or at least have a script that is ready to shoot. Preparing for the actual shoot, also known as preproduction, is the subject of our next chapter.

FOR TEACHERS

The best way to help students grasp the strengths and weaknesses of their scripts — especially their first drafts — is to have them read aloud in class. Assign the parts, including someone other than the writer to read the action descriptions, and give your students the chance to hear their work performed just as it might be in a professional setting at a table reading.

Hearing a script read aloud quickly exposes poorly written dialogue, excessively overwritten description, and other common rookie screen-writing mistakes. It also highlights the places where your students have written good dialogue and effective, economical description. Either way, the quality of the work or lack thereof becomes more palpably apparent when scripts are read aloud than when they are read silently.

One issue teachers must always confront at this stage is finding the line between guiding the student and doing the rewrite for her. Some Socratic academic purists insist that the instructor must never give the student the answer and therefore refuse to offer concrete suggestions for how to improve dialogue, description, character, or structural elements. I find this approach needlessly pedantic. Certainly I won't rewrite a whole scene or even a whole page for a student. But if I think their dialogue needs work, for instance, I try to offer two or three examples of improved versions of their lines.

One other point worth making to the students about reading scripts aloud: Learning opportunities abound not just in hearing your own script being read but in listening carefully and thoughtfully analyzing your classmates' scripts. A big part of growing as a writer is learning how to dissect and analyze screenplays in progress, whether they are your own or a colleague's. Students should be encouraged to offer critiques and analysis of each other's work, a valuable skill not only to improve their own writing but as basic training for entering the professional world, where the ability to discuss and analyze scripts and pitches is a fundamental part of the job. So remind your students that they are to be mentally engaged at all times, whether the script being discussed is their own or someone else's. Even better, call on them when discussing their classmates' work. Force them to voice an opinion and to back up that opinion with specifics.

7 CHOOSING A VISUAL STYLE

The late Brandon Tartikoff, renowned former president of NBC and self-described TV addict, was so obsessed with MTV and the revolution it brought to visual storytelling in the early 1980s that legend has it he scribbled "MTV Cops" on a scrap of paper, handed it to a writer–producer, and said, "That's the show I want." The show he got, based on that two-word scrawl (and some brilliant work by the writers and directors involved), was the breakthrough series *Miami Vice*. Though the show had excellent stories and characters, its greatest impact on TV was its visual style and the way it revolutionized the use of modern "MTV techniques" in telling visual stories on television in the modern era. These techniques included faster-paced editing, nonlinear imagery and juxtaposition, and the liberal use of current popular music as a soundtrack. Tartikoff understood that TV is a visual medium and that visual style is just as important to the appeal and success of shows in the post-MTV era as story, character, premise, or any other content element.

All good TV shows, including shows designed for distribution on the Web, have a specific and thoughtfully designed visual style. Consider the network TV series *24* and *The Office*. Each has a distinctive visual presentation that not only is eye catching but supports and enhances the underlying content and themes. The "spy-cam" shots and direct address to the camera by the actors in *The Office* reinforce the connection between the audience and the show. They emphasize the sense that we, the audience, are merely eavesdropping on real conversations in an actual office just like the ones we all work in. The intimacy of the style — actors addressing the audience directly and the almost "home video" feel to some of the camera work — intensifies the audience's sense that they not only are observing the action but are "insiders" or participants themselves. In other words, the visual presentation of the show enhances the audience bond. The same technique is used for much the same purpose and effect in *Modern Family*.

In the case of *24*, the split screens and superimposed ticking digital clock constantly remind us that our hero, Jack Bauer, has too many problems to juggle and not nearly enough time. The visual elements of *24* are not merely eye candy; they are also vital elements that crank up the underlying tension that propels the show and the story it is telling. Jack Bauer is fighting against a ticking time bomb, and the onscreen graphics constantly remind us of that intense pressure.

In the Internet TV realm, take a look at shows like *Web Therapy* and *We Need Girlfriends*. Much of *Web Therapy* is shot webcam style, reminding us that this is 3-minute Internet therapy, not traditional 50-minute therapy at the doctor's office. It also reinforces, much like the spy-cam in *The Office* and *Modern Family*, the sense that we are somehow privy to confidential conversations, seeing things that were meant to be private but have somehow magically been captured for our enjoyment. And the amateur feel of the webcam angles — as opposed to a finely crafted and framed feature film composition — reinforce the sense that Fiona (Lisa Kudrow) is a less than professional practitioner of therapy.

We Need Girlfriends incorporates shaky, handheld camera, visually emphasizing the sense that these immature slacker slobs have fairly shaky lives.

Although much of the visual distinction of these shows is executed during production and postproduction, it begins with the script. Your pilot script should convey, either explicitly or implicitly, not just what the show is about but what it should look like. A great example of this is the award-winning web series *Script Cops*. It's a spoof on the long-running Fox series *Cops*, only in the web series, we ride along with crewcut-wearing members of law enforcement while they bust people for writing bad scripts or making bad films. The very premise demands a certain visual style, namely a knock-off of the cinema verité style of the original series. Among the techniques are handheld subjective camera shots that look as if we, the audience, are pursuing the perps; pixelated blurring of breasts or other nudity when someone rushes out of a trailer park home to confront the script cops; and bleeping of profanity.

The mandate to have a distinctive visual style does not — repeat, DOES NOT — mean you should attempt to "direct" the script on the page. You would NOT want to write a scene for *Web Therapy* like this:

```
INT. FIONA'S OFFICE — DAY


Fiona conducts a "web therapy" session with a client. The
CAMERA, with a wide-angle, 14mm lens, is placed low, as
if on her desk.
```

As soon as you begin talking about cameras and lenses, the reader stops visualizing a scene unfolding on his mental movie screen and begins seeing a film shoot, complete with lights and cameras and a grip drinking coffee in a Styrofoam cup while he scratches his hairy butt with a hammer. This takes the reader out of the movie, breaks the spell — the magical, dreamlike continuity of a story being told — and instead connects your reader with the nuts and bolts and sweat and tedium of filmmaking. While you want to convey a sense of the visual, you want to keep your reader connected to what he sees on the screen, not how it is accomplished. A better approach would be this:

```
INT. FIONA'S OFFICE — DAY


Fiona conducts a "web therapy" session with a client,
speaking directly into the webcam embedded in the laptop
on her desk.
```

The reader knows very well what that looks like and can now enjoy the story as it unfolds as they are clearly able to "see" it.

THE MARRIAGE OF STYLE AND CONTENT

As outlined in this chapter, visual style is not something random, something glued onto your show merely because it looks cool. The visual style you choose and develop for your series should be seamlessly intertwined with the content, theme, and world of your story and characters.

Is your show quiet and intimate? If so, the visuals should reflect this — not just in the choice of camera angles and the pace of editing but in the production design and choice of locations. *Intimacy* implies private settings, close-ups, shots of small details that reveal the inner thoughts and feelings of the characters. Your script should reflect these intimate choices, which will then be enhanced and emphasized by the camera choices during production.

Or maybe your script is about a stressed-out mom trying to juggle kids, a career, and a marriage or dating life. In that case, you'll want the writing to embody the overloaded, multitasking nature of your main character's life. Maybe you'll want to borrow from *24* and use split screens showing her negotiating a deal on her cell phone while she bathes her infant on one screen, talking to her 6-year-old on the phone while her lover undresses her on another, eating and writing a memo on a third screen, and writing a grocery list while she pees on a fourth screen. Short, quick scenes might also be called for, and frenetic montage.

There are infinite variations and infinite choices, but the one choice you should not make is to ignore the visual. You are writing not just for the page but for the screen. Content without style and style without content are equally unacceptable. You must have both, and they should be inextricably interwoven.

BEGINNINGS, ENDINGS, AND TRANSITIONS

One of the most effective ways to give your series a distinctive visual or aural signature is through the parts of the show that bind it together: the main title, the end credits, and the transitions between scenes. Think of the main title for *24*: the number "24," in digital readout typeface, jumping closer and closer to you, each jump reinforced by the loud, echoing countdown sound, as if a bomb were about to explode. You're tense already, right? Or consider the opening title of *The Guild* and its lighthearted animation and upbeat but ironic music. It sends the message that this show, in part, is about people who participate in a fantasy world and that this is a comedy, not a drama.

Transitions — how your series moves from scene to scene — can also enhance the visual signature and identity of your show. *Law & Order* is a classic example of how important and valuable transitions can be. I'd venture to say that if you mentioned that classic TV series to most viewers, the first two things about the show that would spring to mind are the music from the main title and the *dun-dun* sound effect they use to transition from one scene to the next. That sound effect, simple as it is, adds a great deal to the show. Coupled with the usual onscreen printout setting time and place, it conveys a sense of drama, of realism, and of the gritty world of law enforcement. And it does this in less than 2 seconds, and it is so memorable that it can legitimately be considered an invaluable part of the show's brand identity.

The CBS comedy *The Big Bang Theory* also has wonderful transitions — animated sequences of planetary activity or subatomic collisions. They are both intellectual and offbeat, just like the characters in the series.

Finally, we come to the end credits. All shows have them, either because they employ high-budget, union cast and crew and are contractually bound to include the names on screen or because they are low-budget or no-budget productions, and giving credit to those who worked so hard to make your show is the least you can do to thank them. In either case, just rolling a list of the names of staff and crew against a black background in silence is not only boring, it is a wasted opportunity. If you are doing a comedy, make your end credits comedic. Network sitcoms commonly use a short comedic scene or tag as the background for the end credit sequence. Or they might use outtakes — humorous mistakes and screw-ups recorded during production — as the background. The feature film *Airplane!* embedded jokes in the endless text of the end title crawl. The chief assistant to the key grip or lighting gaffer on a film is known as the best boy. So Jerry Zucker, David Zucker, and Jim Abrahms included the following in their end credit crawl:

Best Boy... Joe Schmo
Worst Boy... Adolph Hitler

They also spiced up the litany of credits for makeup artists, visual effects supervisors, and the like with occasional credits like these:

Thirteenth President of the United States... Millard Fillmore

Or this:

Foreez... The Jolly Good Fellow

They even found a way to get humor out of the densely worded legalese about copyright law at the end, like this:

This Motion Picture Is Protected Under The Laws Of The United States And Other Countries. Unauthorized Duplication, Distribution, Or Exhibition May Result In Civil Liability And Criminal Prosecution, So There.

Another great example of a creative approach to what could have been merely a mechanical sequence comes from my students' web series *The Ex Couple*. In the series pilot, recently divorced Felicia and Oliver show up simultaneously at the home that belonged to Felicia's mother, Dora, who just passed away. Felicia and Oliver each have a copy of Dora's will — one copy saying the home goes to Felicia, one saying the home goes to Oliver. Dora's lawyer tells them they'll just have to live together until this can be sorted out. We the cut from the angry exes to a TV control room with live images of the now battling exes on the monitors. Dora is in the control room — very much alive — and she says, "And there you have your show, gentlemen. I'm thinking Wednesdays at 8."

Obviously, the premise demands that some of the camera angles in the house imply hidden cameras. Done. But where Mark Liu, the creator of the show, got very clever is in designing the "recap" of the pilot at the top of Episode 2. Rather than just slapping together a standard "previously on *The Ex Couple*" sequence, Mark proposed beginning Episode 2 with a faux trailer for the series within the series. It was a brilliant idea because it took the ordinary — a recap of the previous episode — and turned it into not only information but comedy and entertainment value. And, of course, it demanded that they shoot and edit the faux trailer in a visual style appropriate for cheesy reality show trailers, complete with a booming announcer: "Two exes — one house — thirty hidden cameras — only on Spy TV!"

The point is that nothing should be taken for granted. Every second of your show, every frame, is a creative opportunity. The more the obligatory (credits, recaps) can contribute to the content, tone, and branding of your series, the better.

FOR TEACHERS

As this chapter indicates, visual considerations are not an afterthought and should not be segregated from the script process or reserved for production only. Talk to your students about the importance of the visual while they are developing their scripts. Screen examples for them of effective main titles, transitions, and end credit sequences. If possible, show them script excerpts that demonstrate how the visual style of that show was conceived long before a frame of footage was ever shot — right there on the page. Another valuable exercise is screening a sequence or two from a series or even from a feature film, starting and stopping at various points and asking, "Why is the camera where it is? What do the visuals convey here? How do they support or reinforce the content of the scene?"

Also be sure to make clear to them the difference between writing visually (a good thing, especially the use of strong, active verbs) and obsessively trying to direct the film on paper, which makes the script thoroughly tedious, breaks the spell of the story, and ultimately makes the script unreadable.

A final note: Remind the students that these little touches — clever transitions, engaging and creative main titles and end credits — are part of what separates amateur efforts from professional ones.

8 PRACTICAL CONCERNS: EQUIPMENT AND BUDGET

How much does it cost to make a pilot or an episode of an Internet TV series? That, as the Greatest Generation used to say, is the $64,000 Question, a reference to the name of a popular TV quiz show of the 1950s. Of course, the show began on the radio, during the Depression, when it was simply called *The $64 Question*. So, as you might surmise, the answer to the question "How much does it cost to make an Internet TV series?" is yet another question—in fact, a series of questions:

- How much money do you have?
- What are the production requirements of your script?
- What resources do you already have?
- What resources can you beg, borrow, or steal?
- How creative can you be?

How you answer these questions will determine your budget. The creators of *Sanctuary* had a script that called for elaborate special effects and aspirations to deliver a science fiction epic of feature film length and top-notch production value. They also had extensive credits in the business and were therefore able to obtain financing for their $4.2-million budget. Same goes for the people involved with *H+ The Digital Series*. They had the financial backing and resources of Warner Bros. behind them. At the other end of the financial scale, Rob McElhenney, Glenn Howerton, and Charlie Day, the creators of *It's Always Sunny in Philadelphia*, managed to shoot its half-hour pilot for $75, the cost of the videotape. How were they able to shoot a pilot good enough to attract a major cable network series order on so little money? Through their creativity in using the resources they already had or could get their hands on for nothing. They wrote a script that could be shot in locations they could obtain access to for free, that they could act in themselves, wearing their own clothes, using props they already had lying around, and which could be shot without needing lights or any equipment beyond a simple video camera that they already owned (or perhaps borrowed). The show ran for many seasons on FX and is considered a landmark comedy.

Albert Einstein famously said, "Imagination is more important than knowledge." I'd add to that by saying imagination is also more important than money. If you've got access to financing or have a rich uncle or a nest egg of your own you're willing to tap into, then use your imagination to create whatever big-budget extravaganza your heart desires to see on the screen. However, if you're like most people — long on dreams but short on cash — then get creative. Use your imagination to come up with a premise that can be produced with whatever resources and cash you can scrape together.

You should also be creative about finding ways to barter for things like locations. Professional productions typically pay hundreds or thousands of dollars to the owners of restaurants, gas stations, donut shops, and the like for the privilege of being able to use their physical location (not to mention the inconvenience of having a film crew interrupt the normal flow of business). But there are ways to "pay" for a location without having to actually part with cold, hard cash. Perhaps you could offer to shoot a brief video about the business and to post it online — in other words, free advertising for the location. You could further sweeten the deal by offering an onscreen mention in the end credits of your series or episode. Courtney Zito, creator and star of the award-winning series *Hollywood Girl*, went so far as to design her series to include brief commercials within each episode — commercials she hands out to those who provide free services for her series, such as locations or postproduction sound services.

You can also trade services with your crew to get things you need. You want to add graphics to your main title but are not familiar with the software needed to do that? Find someone who is a graphics whiz, then offer to help them with their weak spot. Trade the use of your time and skill (editing, writing, whatever) for the use of their time and expertise.

EQUIPMENT: FROM THE BARGAIN BASEMENT TO THE PENTHOUSE

Whether you make movies, enjoy fishing or golf, or spend your weekends wailing away on a vintage electric guitar as part of an aging boomer garage band called The Not So Grateful Nearly Dead, there's nothing more mesmerizing than dreaming about just how great you could be if only you could buy primo, top-of-the-line equipment. We all want bigger, better, fancier, more expensive toys, partly because shopping is fun and partly because we all labor under the delusion that we're natural-born superstars just waiting to be discovered — if only we had the money to buy that great new (fill in the blank: titanium Tiger Woods model driver, Eric Clapton signature guitar, or Red One camera). The people who manufacture and market all this high-end gear spend millions of dollars on advertising and marketing in order to perpetuate this grand delusion. It's how they make money, selling you far more than you need or could ever make good use of.

So let's get real. When it comes right down to it, what equipment do you absolutely, positively, really, really need in order to write, shoot, edit, and upload your short-form TV series to the Internet? Here's the list:

A computer. Doesn't have to be the Steve Jobs signature model Mac TurboAirPro 5000 LX Titanium Edition (if there was such a thing). But you will need a basic computer of some sort, with broadband Internet access. Chances are your computer will include another necessary component: *editing software*, which gives you the ability to edit the video you shoot into the most effective sequence of shots. Right now, I'm typing this sentence on a 2-year-old, lower-priced Dell laptop. Even though I didn't specifically request it, it came with Windows Movie Maker, common editing software, installed automatically along with Spider Solitaire. If you own a PC, I'll bet you already have this useful editing software yourself, hidden under *Programs>Accessories>Windows Movie Maker.* If you own a Mac, you'll have iMovie or something similar.

A video camera. Your basic home model will do just fine for most projects and concepts. Your camera will almost certainly include the ability to record *sound*, including a built-in microphone.

That's it, the whole shebang.

Really?

Really. Just ask the guys who made *It's Always Sunny in Philadelphia*.

You won't be able to make something that looks or sounds like *Avatar*, or even like an episode of *Modern Family*. But you will be able to make something as entertaining, engaging, and appealing as your imagination can conjure.

That said, let's be honest. If all you have is a basic video camera, there will be limitations you must take into consideration. If you don't have a tripod, your video will look shaky and handheld—because it will be. The sound you record from the microphone that comes mounted on the camera will be distant and hollow in most situations. Shooting at night or in dark interiors may be difficult or impossible.

In short, your series stands a good chance of having the look and feel of amateur home video. This may be exactly what you want—say if you've created a series that is a video diary of a stoner college student or a heavy metal band on tour. But if your premise demands a more polished or professional feel, you may need to invest some money in obtaining slightly more than the rock-bottom basics.

So for those of you with higher production value goals, and for those of you who, like me, crave more and better toys (my weakness is fancy acoustic guitars), here's the lowdown on more sophisticated, more powerful, and more expensive equipment you may want to know about.

CAMERAS AND CAMERA ACCESSORIES

As I mentioned earlier, one piece of inexpensive equipment that can instantly elevate your camera work from shaky amateur to steady and sure filmmaker is a *tripod*. They run anywhere from about $20 for a bare-bones model to several hundred dollars for something professional. To learn more about tripods (and almost every other aspect of video equipment and filmmaking technique) go to *www.mediacollege.com*. Or you can check out my friend Jay Miles' terrific book *Conquering YouTube*, an excellent comprehensive resource on the and nuts bolts of videography, editing, and sound.

If you don't already own a video camera, the choices nowadays are nearly infinite. A search of the Internet site CNET Reviews under "camcorders" yields a list of more than 300 under $250 (all with zoom lenses). You can buy an HD camcorder starting at around this price point, or get a genuinely professional camera like the Panasonic AF-100 series for several thousand. A fully loaded high-end HD camera with lenses and accessories can easily run over $200,000. But the question isn't "What's the best camera?" but rather "What's the best camera for you and your project, and what do you really need?"

My students at Chapman University have access to a range of video cameras, from basic all the way up to the Alexa and Red One cameras capable of capturing image quality and detail worthy of a big-budget extravaganza at your local multiplex. In the classes I teach on Byte-Sized Television, where they make original web series, when I ask them which camera they want to use, they almost always shout out excitedly, "The Alexa!" or "The Red!" But when I ask them *why* they want to use those cameras, their answers basically boil down to, "Because they're cool." Then I remind them that the audience they're hoping to reach with their series will probably be watching on a laptop computer with, at most, a 17-inch screen. I also remind them that the HD tape cassettes for the high-end cameras cost about $130 each and could easily eat up more than half of their per-episode budget. The more basic cameras, however, use inexpensive SD cards. I usually finish my pitch for the "lesser" cameras by screening some of the best work done the previous year using those "lesser" cameras. The inevitable response from my students is, "That looks pretty darn good."

Another point worth making is that you don't have to buy every single piece of equipment; you can rent. Over the long haul, if you continue to make dozens of episodes, you'll certainly want to own the basic elements you use over and over again, like your camera and tripod. But it may also make a great deal of sense to rent what you need the first few times out, evaluate whether each piece of equipment serves your needs, and how often, and then make a decision about whether to buy it or rent it only when needed.

SOUND EQUIPMENT

Sound and how it will be recorded is commonly the last thing nonprofessionals think about when setting out to make a short video. Unfortunately and unfairly, sound is pretty much taken for granted, unnoticed and underappreciated by audiences — right up until the sound is bad, at which time they complain bitterly. Sound quality is also the very first thing that separates a well-made and engaging web series from — to use a highly technical term — an unwatchable pile of dog crap.

Think back to the home videos your dad shot of you when you were little and he was all geeked about buying his first video camera, circa nineteen eighty-something. You were putting on your Little League uniform or your ballet tutu, or maybe just minding your own business in your room. Dad was about 10 feet away, standing in the doorway, pointing this alien-looking camera thing with a little red light at you. The scene and dialogue no doubt went something like this:

```
INT. BEDROOM — DAY


BRANDON "HOME RUN" STERNE (9), wearing a Little League
Uniform that says "Giants" on the front and "State Farm
Insurance" on the back, double-knots the laces on his
rubber cleats. He is happily daydreaming of circling the
bases in a victorious home run trot when his reverie is
broken by an imposing shadow, the smell of his father's
Polo cologne, and an annoying mechanical whirring noise.
Brandon turns, sees his father DOUG pointing the new
video camera at him.

                    DOUG
              (a little too loud, a little
              too cheery)
          Hey, bud. Whatcha up to?
```

Brandon mumbles something unintelligible into his chest.

                    DOUG
                (even louder)
        What? I couldn't hear you.

Brandon makes a vague attempt to mumble louder. He either says "smoking," "hiking," or "nothing" — impossible to tell because Doug's hollow breathing is right on top of the microphone built into the camera, overpowering any other sound in the room. Doug walks two steps closer and squats down closer to Brandon.

                    DOUG
        Say it again.

                    BRANDON
                (screams into camera)
        NOTHING!!!

You get the idea: an eighties home video classic, probably hauled out for public viewing every other Christmas or so. The audio inevitably sounds like it was recorded inside the trunk of a rusty old Chevy. Though video cameras have come a long way since Madonna sang about being like a virgin, and the built-in mikes are far more capable, there's no avoiding the trademark hollowness of sound recorded by a microphone that is closer to the camera and its operator than to the person speaking. If that's the look and feel you're going for in your series, by all means use that distinctive sound quality to your advantage. I'm serious. Let's say you've created a web series titled *My Parents Are F***ED UP!* The premise is that a teenager interviews his parents, secretly films them when they aren't aware, and then comments on all of it. It would be absolutely WRONG in my opinion to record the sound of the parents speaking using a separate microphone on a boom. The premise and picture demand the hollow, distant sound quality of a home video camera, and the best, fastest, easiest way to create that is by recording the sound using the built-in mike attached to the camera. In this scenario, the filmmaker clearly WANTS to call attention to the filmmaking process. He WANTS the audience to be aware of the camera, and of the microphone, and of the fact that this is being recorded mockumentary style. It's the perfect situation for turning a disadvantage (no money to rent professional equipment and no crew to work with that equipment) into a stylistic advantage and signature technique of your project.

However, if you've got a different sort of premise — one where you just want the story to unfold on screen in a traditional fashion, seamlessly, realistically, without making the audience aware of the equipment and crew — then you'll need to use some of the tools that the pros use to accomplish this. You'll want the camera to be steady (which means using a tripod), and you'll want the sound to be crisp, clean, and even, the way it is in a movie or scripted TV show.

In order to achieve this, you'll need to record the sound using a microphone that can be placed the appropriate distance from the person speaking. This, in turn, may also mean you'll need a boom, an extendable pole with the mike attached to the end of it that can be held above the actors' heads, out of the picture frame, to record the sound from the best possible angle for emphasizing what is being said and de-emphasizing extraneous background noises. If you use a boom, clearly you'll need some crew other than yourself. If you are operating the camera, you'll need someone to hold the boom pole and point the microphone at the actor or actors who are speaking.

Depending on the scene and its requirements, other types of microphones may be needed. For instance, if your scene calls for two people jogging and talking, having a boom operator running alongside them with a pole above his head isn't very practical. In that case, you may choose to use wireless mikes.

As with camera technique, the complete ins and outs of recording production sound are far more complex than can be covered in a few pages. Entire books have been written about the subject. If your webisodes need only the basics, then this brief discussion may be enough. But if you need more detail, consult the list of books and resources in Appendix 2 and get the information that will help you.

LIGHTS

If your script calls for filming in a space without enough available light to allow the audience to see the details you want them to see (e.g., the actor's eyes, or printed words on a note or book), then you will need to use lights. They don't have to be fancy, studio-quality lights. Ordinary household lamps can often work just fine. Michael Buckley lit the simple set of his Internet celebrity dish-fest *What the Buck?!* using a pair of work lights from Home Depot. As of February 2013 the show had accumulated over 350 million hits on YouTube, and to my knowledge, not a single person has commented on the lighting.

The key questions are what you want your images to look like on screen and how you can accomplish it. If you are shooting an interrogation scene and want the effect of a super-bright light being blasted into the suspect's face, then you'll need to find a light with enough firepower to achieve that effect — one ever so much brighter than the rest of the light sources.

By far the most difficult environment in which to mold the lighting into the look you want is the night exterior. Furthermore, the larger the area you want to photograph outside at night, the more lights you will need. And each of those lights will need a power source, which, in turn, may mean you'll need a generator to provide that power. So unless you have easy access to lights and power, or unless you have a substantial budget to work with, you might want to rewrite that panoramic night exterior scene and reset it in an easier location to film — an interior, a park bench, or another small, controllable, easily lit exterior.

EDITING SOFTWARE

No area of filmmaking has benefited more from the digital revolution than editing and postproduction. A veritable smorgasbord of software is available that allows you to upload video to your computer, edit it swiftly and efficiently in a nonlinear manner, and add titles, transitions, sound effects, and narration. Even better news is the fact that a great deal of this software is inexpensive or free, installed at no charge on your computer when you bought it.

The basic, default editing programs that come with your computer are Windows Movie Maker (for PC) and iMovies (Mac). If you have a little money and want to investigate other choices, TopTenReviews rates CyberLink PowerDirector, Corel VideoStudio Pro X5, and Adobe Premiere Elements as its top video editing software choices for 2013. All are available for under $100.

For those who crave greater editing sophistication and capabilities, Apple's line of Final Cut products is the consensus choice. Available for Mac or PC, they range from the $200 Final Cut Express all the way up to Final Cut Studio, a professional-quality product with nearly infinite editing, sound, and graphic tools. It runs about $1,200.

As with the other equipment categories, you don't need to breathlessly rush online to Hardcore Software Junkies R Us and max out your credit card on the biggest, baddest, and best software package available. First check out the stuff you've already got on your computer for free. See how it works and whether it fits your needs. Then, if you bump up against the ceiling of its capabilities, you'll have a much clearer idea whether you need the $200 upgrade or whether you really do want to consider auctioning off your next ovulation on eBay to pay for Final Cut Studio.

LEARNING MORE ABOUT ALL THIS EQUIPMENT AND HOW TO USE IT

For those who consider learning how to upload a photo to Facebook a major technological accomplishment, the thought of learning about digital filmmaking and editing can be overwhelming. To others, navigating the technology is from *The Big Book of Duh*, but you need some help knowing how to use it to capture and edit the elements necessary to tell an effective story or learning about the more subtle and sophisticated tricks of the video trade.

Obviously, the book you hold in your hands right now is a good place to start. But no one book can tell you everything you need to know about making videos from soup to nuts. I have chosen to focus more on the creative process here than on the technical aspects. But the good news is that there are excellent books and instructional resources available that can teach you whatever else you need to learn. Know lots about video capture but zip about how to frame a shot? Or how to storyboard a scene before you shoot it? Or the principles of editing an action scene? Or how to create the best possible soundtrack? Not a problem. Appendix 2 has a list of books that offer in-depth discussions and instruction on all areas of video and audio craft and technology.

FOR TEACHERS

There are many challenges in helping students select and acquire access to the equipment most appropriate and useful to their production. One of the challenges is moderating their natural enthusiasm for stuff that seems cool, like wanting to shoot with the fanciest camera possible when a plain vanilla HD workhorse is really what's called for, or begging for a dolly or crane because they're still buzzing with excitement from seeing the latest Bond film or Michael Bay kinetic epic. While I am a big believer in ultimately letting the students make the final decision (within budget and other limitations) about how they want to shoot their video, I also believe it is the role of the instructor to challenge them to justify their choices. If they have only 10 hours to shoot on one day, and they need to get 20–25 setups in the can, is it really worth spending the hours it will take to set up a dolly shot for the first master, which may be on screen for only 5 or 6 seconds?

At the other end of the spectrum, sometimes students don't see the tools they have at their disposal. A dolly is expensive and time consuming, and if the shot is of two people moving down a hallway talking, borrowing an office chair and rolling the camera operator down the hall in front of the actors might work just fine, giving the audience a sense of motion while still being able to move quickly and not get bogged down laying and leveling dolly track.

When it comes to expenses and equipment, the teacher's role is to provide limits but also to provide imagination and creative ways to get the most bang for your inevitably limited production buck.

9 THE PILOT: PREPRODUCTION

"Failure to prepare is preparing to fail."
— John Wooden, Hall of Fame basketball coach

"Every battle is won before it is fought."
— Sun-Tzu, *The Art of War*

Coach Wooden and Sun-Tzu could just as well have been talking about shooting a pilot. You can't just show up with your camera and wing it. You must prepare thoughtfully and thoroughly if you want your production days — and, in turn, your pilot — to be successful.

In a sense, you've been in preproduction all along as you conceptualized your series and characters and developed your script. You've already created a blueprint for what the finished product will look like on screen. The characters you'll need, the settings, the crucial props and wardrobe are all no doubt delineated in your script. But now you must take the next step and turn those words and images in your script into a physical reality that can be captured on video. The characters you dreamed up have to be played by actors. The settings you imagined must become actual locations found in real life, and you'll need to get permission from the owners of these locations. The scenes you created on paper must now be captured shot by shot, and you'll need to plan each of those shots ahead of time, visualize them in your mind before you show up to shoot, because that's the only way to make sure you have all the tools to execute your vision.

Preproduction requires discipline, attention to every detail of your proposed shoot, and the ability to adapt the creative vision you hold in your mind to the physical and financial realities of the world. Just as carefully developing your story and outline were crucial to the eventual success of your script, the time and effort you put into preproduction can make or break your pilot. Sloppy and half-hearted preproduction inevitably leads to a chaotic, frustrating, and often disastrous shoot. But careful, thoughtful, and thorough preproduction leads to maximum creative freedom and productivity when the camera is rolling and the actors are performing.

So don't take shortcuts. Put your best focused effort into each of the following phases of preproduction.

CASTING: FINDING TALENTED ACTORS WHEN YOU HAVE NO BUDGET

Anybody can put together a great cast when they've got a multi-million-dollar budget. You hire a casting director; she puts the word out to the major talent agencies that represent all the best-known actors. Scripts are e-mailed, phone calls are exchanged, lunch is done, the spa cuisine is ordered, and offers are made. If you've got that kind of budget and contacts, my guess is you don't need this book to tell you how it's done.

But what about the other 99.99999% of the world — those of us not plugged into the Hollywood power elite? How on Earth can we find good actors to perform in our projects when we've barely got enough money to buy bagels and soft drinks for the skeleton crew working for free?

The first logical question is "Why not act in it yourself or get your friends to act in your pilot?" The answer to that question may be that you and your friends aren't actors. If your premise is reality-based — say, a series about your family — then this approach might work. The guys who created *It's Always Sunny in Philadelphia* not only used themselves as the cast for their $75 pilot but continued to appear as the main cast of the show (along with Danny DeVito and Caitlin Olsen) even after they had a substantial budget and a contract with FX. But in many instances, your premise and script will require finding skilled actors who can perform at a professional level but are still willing to work for little or no money.

There are several ways to find experienced and extremely capable actors like this. If you live in or near a major city, there will no doubt be online sites where you can post the specifics of the roles you are looking to cast. Actors will then contact you, and you can set up auditions. Examples of this type of site are Now Casting Inc. in Los Angeles and Auditions Free in Atlanta. I found out about the latter simply by typing "free casting Atlanta" in a Google search box. I got several promising listings, including Auditions Free. So do the same for the city near you and see what you find.

Whether or not you live near a major urban center, there is almost certainly a small theater of some kind somewhere near you that puts on plays. They may have a regular company of actors, or they may search for them on a project-by-project basis, just like you're about to do. In either case, contact them, tell them what you're looking for, and see if they can help by either suggesting actors or sharing how they find talent.

As an example of this, early in my career I worked as an assistant director on an extremely low-budget movie. There were half a dozen small parts — maybe half a dozen lines each — which the producer had not cast but expected me to fill. I knew that I couldn't just throw some inexperienced friends out there in front of the camera; these were speaking parts, and somehow I needed to find a handful of trained actors willing to work for the budgeted sum of $35 per day. So I contacted a small L.A. improv comedy group called The Groundlings. Though they performed in a hole-in-the-wall space themselves at that time, they had been a launching pad for several actors who later made it big. I told them what I was looking for and what it paid, and they got me half a dozen terrific young performers who did a bang-up job for basically gas money. One of these $35-a-day actors was the young Phil Hartman, later a major star on *Saturday Night Live*.

A third widely available resource is the theater department at any nearby university or community college. Young actors are by nature eager to work, willing to do so for the experience even if there isn't any money involved, and they often bring a phenomenal amount of enthusiasm and creative energy to the work. So contact the theater department, or post a notice on their bulletin board, and see what you can find. Not everyone will be great, but I'd almost bet that you'll find more than a few performers who will absolutely blow you away with how good they are.

A fourth resource is word of mouth. The actors you find probably know other actors eager to find work. So if you've found promising actors for parts one and two, ask them if they know anyone who might be right for parts three and four.

One final casting hint: When you post the audition notices, under the space marked "pay" or "salary," don't just put "nothing." At the very least, put "DVDs of all completed episodes." For the cost of burning a DVD, you can make these aspiring actors happy by giving them something of great value to them: material for their reel, which is something they can use to get other work. It sounds like a small courtesy, but you'd be surprised how grateful your cast will be to receive a DVD of their performance.

LOCATIONS: IMAGINATION MEETS REALITY

When you wrote your script, you could no doubt visualize every location you described in precise detail, right down to the little dings in the furniture. You could almost smell the suntan lotion glistening on the perfectly tanned legs of those dancers lounging by the pool of the Bellagio in Vegas or taste the hot dogs and beer your slacker buddy characters were eating in the scene set at Yankee Stadium.

But now that you are not just writing a script but planning an actual shoot, the unlimited potential of your imagination must contend with the litany of limitations that the real world often presents. There's a good chance you may not be allowed to shoot at the Bellagio or Yankee Stadium. And don't even think about trying to shoot at a place like that without obtaining permission. Often you may be able to get permission to film your dream location, only to discover that the price tag for doing so is prohibitive. These types of obstacles can occur not only with grand locations like fancy hotels or ballparks but with almost anyplace other than your own house or apartment. Many stores and businesses find film crews disruptive and want no part of being in a film or TV show. Even open public spaces, like parks, may restrict your ability to shoot that location or may require you to obtain expensive permits and hire park personnel for the day to "supervise" your activity.

If you encounter these roadblocks, does it mean you should just chuck your concept, burn the script, and start over again? Absolutely not. But it may mean you need to get creative and make some adjustments. Maybe your Vegas dancers aren't lounging by the Bellagio pool but rather are gathered around the ordinary pool at one of their modest apartment buildings — because you live in an apartment building in Arizona that looks just like that. Or maybe your slackers are talking not during the game but on the way to the game — because you *can* get permission to shoot on the street near Yankee Stadium, and it looks great in the background.

Another creative approach to overcoming location hurdles is imitating a location rather than shooting at the real thing. For instance, you might be able to shoot an establishing shot of the Bellagio (with a camcorder, out front, just like a tourist), then film two dancers on lounge chairs at some other pool, but keep the shots tight enough that all we see is dancers in lounge chairs with blue water behind them. The audience will *think* it's the Bellagio because of the establishing shot, even though the dancers are really poolside at the Siesta Rate Motel.

PERMITS

The First Amendment guarantees freedom of speech, and of the press, the free exercise of religion, the freedom for citizens to peaceably assemble and to petition the government for a redress of grievances. Unfortunately, it does not guarantee the right to show up wherever you want with a video crew and shoot a TV show without obtaining permission from the rightful owners. In the case of public spaces, like parks, streets, airports, or the Department of Motor Vehicles, this means you have to get permission from the city, county, state, or federal government agency in charge of that location.

Now I know some of you would like to make the case that you as a taxpayer are part-owner of all public things and therefore should be able to use your own property as a location for your project. But trust me: Your friendly local police officer will not share your enlightened vision of communal resources. If he sees you and your actors and crew setting up in the middle of the street or outside the Amtrak station, he's going to ask to see your permit to film there. And if you don't have one to show him, he's going to ask you to leave. Immediately. He might also impound your camera and other equipment. Charm will do you no good. Neither will offering to bring him to the Oscars as your date when you are famous. Offers that involve greater personal sacrifice than that are strictly up to you, but they probably won't work, either.

If you want to film in a public space, especially if you have a crew beyond just you and more than one actor, you will need to get formal permission from the government entity that controls that space.

DEVELOPING A SHOOTING SCHEDULE

If your series consists of a static webcam shot of you at your kitchen table riffing on which celebrity hottie you'd like to get busy with, then you don't really need a shooting schedule. Just sit down, hit RECORD, and spew forth. However, if you've written a script that calls for multiple scenes in various locations, then you need to figure out how long each of those segments will take to set up, light, rehearse, and shoot. An hour? Five hours? Two days? And which hours or days? Are there only certain days or times when you have access to that location? Are certain times of day better or worse to shoot because of sunlight, traffic noise, or any of a dozen other factors? Do any of your actors have time restrictions — you know, like an actual paying job they might have to show up at? Each of these factors must be taken into consideration when determining your shooting schedule.

This may be ridiculously obvious to most of you in this media-savvy age, but it's worth pointing out that the scenes in movies and TV shows are rarely shot in the same order in which they appear in the script and on screen. The scenes are shuffled and regrouped so they can be photographed in the most efficient manner possible. If your script begins and ends in the desert but has a scene by the ocean in between, it wouldn't make sense to drive out to the desert, shoot Scene 1, pack up the equipment and cast, drive to the ocean to shoot Scene 2, then drive back to the desert for Scene 3. You'd group the first and last scenes together and shoot them one right after the other, then pack up and head for the beach — or hit the beach the next day.

So how do you figure out the most efficient way to organize your shoot? The first step is to break your shoot down into its component parts, scene by scene. Though there are professional software programs that Hollywood production managers use to help with this task, it's probably overkill to invest the time and money in elaborate software when you can get the job done just fine with a pencil and some index cards.

At the top of each index card, write the name or "slugline" of each scene, like this:

INT. BEDROOM — NIGHT

Or this:

EXT. BEACH — DAY

Below the slugline, make two lists, side by side. List 1 is the cast members needed for the scene. List 2 is any other crucial factors or components of the scene, such as "location available after 6 p.m. only" or "boa constrictor" or "Eddie in drag." At the bottom of the card, estimate how long you think it will take to shoot the scene. On the back of the card, write a one-sentence description to remind you the essence of the scene, such as "The boa constrictor strangles Eddie at the beach."

Now spread the cards out in front of you and begin to organize them into sensible groups for shooting. What constitutes a sensible group is dictated largely by common sense. For instance, you might start by putting all the scenes that take place at the most frequently seen location in one column — say all the scenes that take place at your main character's home or workplace. Then look at the remaining scenes and see how they group. Just the café and the hardware store? Put them together and make a mental note that you'll need to find these two sites close to each other if possible.

Now look at each of your groups or columns and add up the total of estimated shoot time on each of the cards in that group. If it's your main character's house you might have:

```
INT. BEDROOM — DAY
(3 HOURS)


INT. BEDROOM — NIGHT
(2 HOURS)


EXT. BACKYARD — DAY
(4 HOURS)
```

That's a total of 9 hours estimated. Let's say you're shooting in November in Los Angeles. You know you only have about 9 hours of daylight, so you probably wouldn't want to add any more scenes than this to be shot in one day. And you'd probably want to start first thing in the morning by shooting the exterior scene rather than shooting it last. Why? Because your time estimates for the interiors are just that — estimates. You need sunlight for the backyard scene and don't want to take a chance that the interiors will unexpectedly eat up so much time that you lose the light and end up having to come back to that location an additional day to complete the outside work. On the other hand, if the backyard takes a little longer than expected, no biggie. The last scene you're shooting that day is INT. BEDROOM — NIGHT. If it's dark outside, fine. If not, just tape black cloth over the windows outside. You're good to go either way.

REVISING THE SCRIPT TO FIT THE LOGISTICS

Sometimes, when you put together your shooting schedule, some of the pieces just won't fit properly. You've only got half a day's work at the main house, and the scene that would be perfect to fill that other half day is the lunch scene at the café. Unfortunately the café will only let you shoot on Mondays, when they are closed, and the house is only available on Tuesday, when your parents are out of town and you can film there despite the fact that they said you couldn't.

What's a producer to do?

A good producer runs through all the options and then decides on the optimum choice. Among the options:

- Find a different house or café so they can be shot on the same day.
- Rewrite the café scene to a picnic lunch in the park, because there's a park right near the house that could be shot on Tuesday.
- Convince your parents that the sooner they let you shoot in the house on Monday, the sooner you'll be able to make this pilot and use it to help you get a real paying job, whereupon you can move out of the house, support yourself, and stop being a drain on their retirement savings.

In most cases, hell will freeze over before the third option works. The first option is a possibility but not always easy or available on demand at any given time. The most likely scenario is that at some point during preproduction you will need to make adjustments to the script to accommodate the logistical realities of time, budget, and availability. Even the pros making hundred-million-dollar action films must pay homage to the Gods of Reality and tweak the script a bit here and there to make it more efficient from a production standpoint. So don't let it throw you if your script doesn't instantly and conveniently break down into perfectly organized shooting components. Just get creative again. Ask yourself how the problems can be solved, answer the question in several ways, and then pick the best possible solution. You'll be surprised how many times necessity is the mother of invention and your new idea — new location or other new approach to the scene — turns out to be even better than what you had originally scripted.

MAKING A SHOT LIST

We all know how it goes. A bunch of people are coming over to your place for dinner. You rush out to the grocery store without making a list. After all, it's just spaghetti and salad, so how hard can that be? You grab a cart, the salad fixings, stuff to make that killer sauce you saw what's-his-name whip up on Food Network the other night, and a primo bottle of wine because your friends are bringing over a dead ringer for Halle Berry who saw your picture on Facebook and said, "Hmmm, nice." You grab two more bottles of the wine and speed through the checkout stand with visions of Halle dancing in your head. (Even if you're female and straight, this vision should work for you. We're talking Halle-freaking-Berry.)

You get home and begin madly chopping ingredients only to discover that you forgot to actually buy the spaghetti — and condoms — which doesn't really matter because two seconds later, *ding dong*, Halle and friends show up and find out all you've got is salad (with no avocado — forgot that, too) and sauce, so you order pizza, and the delivery guy turns out to be some buff dude from the gym that Halle is always smiling at, and they laugh and laugh and laugh about finally meeting this way and exchange phone numbers, and she spends the rest of the night talking about how she can't wait to jump his bones and complaining about no avocado in the salad.

The moral of the story is simple: *Only a schmuck fails to make a list.*

The same goes for shooting your pilot. You must make a shot list ahead of time. Failure to do so is a guarantee that you will forget a bunch of really important shots you need and will end up with the video equivalent of an incomplete meal.

Okay, so now you know why need a shot list, and why you will never hook up with someone who looks like Halle Berry. The next question is, "How do you put a shot list together?"

Good news! Your subconscious has been working on this all along, and you didn't even know it. While you were writing your scenes, you were visualizing them, too, on the virtual movie screen in your mind. That picnic lunch scene that you wrote? Look back at the script now, and you'll be amazed at how you'll begin to see the shots you need:

EXT. PARK — DAY

Justin and Ashley share a picnic lunch, spread out on
a blanket on a grassy knoll. A mother plays with her
toddler nearby.

See, right there, right now, you are visualizing a shot or two. Maybe it's a wide shot, establishing the location, then a two-shot of the couple digging into their sandwiches. Maybe the wide shot is taken from up high, on top of the slide, to add drama and interest to the setting. Whatever the case, hit Pause on your mental projector and WRITE THIS STUFF DOWN. NOW. ON A PIECE OF PAPER. I'M SERIOUS. DO IT. TO BEGIN YOUR SHOT LIST, WRITE THIS:

- Establishing shot of park, high angle from atop slide
- Two-shot, Justin and Ashley unpack sandwiches

As you write the second one down, you realize that you'll also want to see that two-shot at various times during the rest of the scene, not just as they unpack their sandwiches. So you go back and amend that second shot to:

- Two-shot, Justin and Ashley (entire scene)

Now release the pause button and let the rest of the scene play out on your mental screen:

JUSTIN

> I put avocado on the sandwiches.

Ashley nods.

JUSTIN

> Want some wine?

Ashley shakes her head no.

JUSTIN

> It's supposed to be really good. This
> guy on the Food Network gave it like 92
> points and said —

ASHLEY

> (blurts it out)
> — I'm pregnant.

```
Justin stops enjoying his lunch. The toddler kicks his
ball into Justin's lap, races over to retrieve it. On
Justin's awkward expression:


CUT TO:
```

It doesn't matter right now what we cut to; we're just working on the shot list for this one scene. And now you have visualized more shots that just the establishing shot and two-shot. I imagine you've seen close-ups of both Justin and Ashley for their dialogue and reactions. Put those on the list, right below the other two shots.

But don't stop with merely writing down what your subconscious throws up onto your mental movie screen. Your conscious artistic mind must also be a part of this process. Your conscious mind might tell you that you need to set up the toddler with the ball earlier in the scene if you want that final moment of Justin, imagining himself as the father of a young child, to pay off. So you add to your list:

- Cutaway — mother and toddler play with ball

But is it just a cutaway, an omniscient, detached shot for the benefit of the audience? Or is it better to make it Ashley looking at the child, smiling wistfully? Yes, that's better. So you cross out the cutaway and replace it with:

- Angle on Ashley, watching mother and toddler
- Ashley's POV: mother and toddler play with ball

Good. Now run through the scene again on your imaginary movie screen. See it shot by shot: the high-angle establishing shot, two-shot of your couple, Ashley smiling at the mom and kid, shot of them with the ball, then back to the close-ups of your two principals and the dialogue. What about the end of the scene? Is the close-up of Justin sufficient to emphasize his reaction? Or do you need other sizes? A push-in to a tighter close-up? Or maybe a looser single to include the kid toddling over to re-trieve his ball from a stunned Justin? Whatever it is, WRITE IT DOWN ON YOUR SHOT LIST.

Do this with every scene in your script. Then go back and look at the index card you wrote up to put together your shooting schedule. Maybe you wrote down:

```
EXT. PARK — DAY
( 1  HOUR )
```

One hour seemed adequate in theory to shoot a simple four-line scene with two people in natural light. But now that you really think about it, you realize you need more time to get the establishing shot, and the cut-away, and the different sizes or angles on Justin and Ashley. So you adjust your shooting schedule accordingly.

```
EXT. PARK — DAY
( 2  HOURS )
```

Now look at the other work you have scheduled for the day you shoot that picnic scene. Does adding an extra hour to that day still work? If not, ask yourself how you can best solve the scheduling problem. Adjust the script? Simplify your shooting plan for one or more scenes? Add an extra day to your shooting schedule?

Your script, shot list, and shooting schedule are all interrelated, and preproduction is where you will constantly revise and adapt each of them to balance the competing demands of creativity versus physical and fi-nancial limitations.

PROPS AND WARDROBE

Props and wardrobe are more than just the items the actors happen to wear or carry. They are windows into each of your characters, externalizations of their internal world, if you will. The way your characters appear on the outside tells us a great deal about who they are on the inside. In the movie *Big*, even though 12-year-old Josh Baskin has been transformed into the adult body of Tom Hanks, he still chooses to furnish his "adult" apartment in Manhattan like the boy he is inside, with a bunk bed, trampoline, and a slew of pre-adolescent toys. In *Little Miss Sunshine*, the dysfunctional family travels to California in a barely functioning VW van that they can start only if they all push it together to get it rolling. Could there be a more apt metaphor for this ragtag collection of misfits who desperately need each other?

This isn't rocket science; it's just common sense in most cases. But props and wardrobe are all too often overlooked by newer filmmakers who squander this rich opportunity to add visual and character value to each scene. So take the time to ask yourself about the visual details for each of your characters. What would they wear? What kind of car would they drive? Or would they take the bus or ride a funky old bike? In most cases, the elements you need can be obtained for free, from your own closet, or the actor's, or at worst for a few dollars at a thrift shop.

SITUATIONS THAT REQUIRE SPECIAL PREPRODUCTION

It would be impossible to detail every situation that may demand preparation for your pilot. Stories and scenes come in all shapes, sizes, and varieties and therefore can have an infinite spectrum of preproduction needs. Nonetheless, these needs must be met and prepared for. So as you go through each scene preparing your shot list, also ask yourself whether there are special elements that demand special preparation.

- Are there any scenes where one or more characters sing or sing to music? If so, you may want to pre-record these to get them just right, then have your characters lip-sync to a playback track when you shoot the scene. By the way, if the song is copyrighted, you'll need to get permission to include it in your video.
- Dance numbers also require significant preparation and rehearsal. If one or more of your characters dance, you will want to rehearse this segment ahead of time.

- Is there any special training called for? Martial arts moves? A fight scene? These types of scenes are choreographed ahead of time, with lots of rehearsal, just like a dance number.

As I said, the variations are endless, but as Sun Tsu said, all battles are won before they are fought. So think ahead and prepare.

FOR TEACHERS

Preproduction class sessions work best as Socratic workshops. Conduct an interrogative with the students. Ask how many days they plan to shoot (unless you are defining or limiting this yourself). Ask whether they plan to do any rehearsal with the actors ahead of time. Most of all, ask them to put their plans down on paper, to prepare a shot list for each scene, then to take this shot list and make a time management budget for each day — a document that takes the shot list and specifies how much time they are budgeting for each scene, for lunch, for company moves, and so on.

This time management budget is a useful tool for discussing whether the students have planned enough time for what they hope to accomplish. Instead of having an abstract discussion about whether they "feel" they can get everything done in the time allotted, the time management budget breaks the question down into smaller, clearly defined chunks to analyze. And because it contains not just the scenes they plan to shoot but their shot list for each of those scenes, it tends to bring the discussion into sharper focus. Instead of asking whether they really think they can shoot Scene 3 in an hour and a half, the question now becomes "Really? You think you can shoot Scene 3 — all 15 shots — in 90 minutes? That's 6 minutes to set up, light, rehearse, and shoot each shot on average. Do you really think you can accomplish that and give the actors and their performances the time and attention they deserve?" Confronted with this sort of evidence in black and white, most students are able to see when they have not planned properly and can make adjustments — schedule more time, condense the shot list, or some combination of the two. Putting the time management budget down on paper helps train the students to previsualize their shooting days and to spot problems more effectively ahead of time. It also serves as a useful guideline on shoot days for judging whether you are staying on schedule or falling behind.

Another helpful preproduction class exercise is guiding the students through one or more production meetings. Teach them how to talk through the production elements of the script, going through it scene by scene, page by page, with the student director leading the discussion and defining her needs (e.g., props, extras, special lighting elements) along the way and urging the other students to chime in and ask questions along the way about their particular area of responsibility (e.g., "How do you see her dressed for this date?" Or perhaps "Are you going to cast the barista who keeps smiling at her, or should I just find a good-looking extra for that?").

The goal, as always, is to get the students to simulate the process that professionals would go through. Even if the script is only two pages long, practicing professional processes trains the students to think and behave like professionals.

10 THE PILOT: PRODUCTION

It's finally here! The day you've been waiting for since that first flash of inspiration for your series popped into your head: the day you arrive on location with the actors and begin shooting your pilot. And because you've put so much time and effort into preparing for this day — writing and rewriting the script until it's exactly what you want, finding the perfect cast, visualizing each scene and building your shot list and time management budget, going over every detail ahead of time — now it practically shoots itself, proceeding exactly as planned without a hiccup, right?

Well, no.

Despite the sage advice of Coach Wooden and Sun-Tzu about the importance of preparation, another bit of timeless wisdom inevitably comes into play when the planning stops and actual production begins. There is dispute about who first codified the wisdom but no argument about its fundamental truth. Written in the original Old English, the advice goes like this: 𝖘𝖍𝖎𝖙 𝕳𝖆𝖕𝖕𝖊𝖓𝖘.

DEALING WITH THE UNEXPECTED

No matter how thoroughly you prepare, you must also be ready to deal with the unexpected. Curveballs that may be thrown your way can include:

- Equipment failure.
- An actor gets a new idea for the scene.
- You get a new idea for the scene.

- When you rehearse the scene, you realize your shot list is flawed and needs to be amended.
- You didn't realize this was the day the city would begin demolition on the street outside your location.
- An intergalactic war breaks out, and the Remulons have landed their battle cruisers right in the middle of your quiet picnic scene in the park.

With the possible exception of the last one, somehow the shoot must go on. No matter what kind of lemons the Video Gods chuck at you, you'll need to stay calm, think clearly, dismiss the urge to curl up in a ball and weep, consider your options, and figure out your best course of action given whatever new circumstances you've been presented. The good news is that making movies is alchemy, so the curveball you're thrown might lead not to disaster but to creative inspiration. As often as not, Plan B turns out to be far superior to Plan A. Best of all, no one watching the final product will ever know that Plan B was pulled out of your ass at the last minute; they'll think you had it figured that way all along.

A prime example of Plan B superiority is the movie *Jaws*, about a super-sized shark that terrorizes a beach town. Since sharks are notoriously bad at performing on cue, the film required the use of a mechanical shark. A bunch of Hollywood special effects wizards built one and nicknamed it Bruce. Alas, Bruce was not a show biz natural and did not perform exactly as planned. The first time they lowered him into the water on location, he promptly sank to the ocean floor. A team of divers retrieved Bruce and made him seaworthy, but the darn thing never quite worked right. Even worse, when it appeared on camera for more than a brief glimpse it looked kind of cheesy. So director Steven Spielberg considered his options and made lemonade out of the lemons he'd been handed. Instead of featuring Bruce prominently on camera, as originally planned, he used subjective camera and put us, the audience, into the shark's point of view, stalking victims from under the water, lying in wait, poised to attack.

It was a brilliant solution. Though at the time this may have seemed like a compromise, it turned out to be the stronger creative choice by far. The scariest moments in this thriller are when we *don't* see the shark. The less we see it, the more frightening the monster is in our minds. We'll never know for sure, but my suspicion is that if the Bruce had worked exactly as planned, and Spielberg showed him to us over and over and over again, the film might have turned out to be a laughable B-movie instead of the classic that it is.

Coping with the unpredictable is an entirely predictable part of the job of making a video. So when the lemon yogurt hits the fan, don't panic. Just smile and deal with it. If you want certainty and guarantees, there's a cubicle right next to Dilbert waiting for you. If you want to make TV shows, get used to the fact that life is what happens while you're making other plans.

BE QUICK BUT DON'T HURRY

This ironic instruction is yet another of Coach Wooden's famous pearls of wisdom. As with many of Wooden's sayings, it applies to far more than just basketball. For instance, it's great advice for anyone shooting an Internet TV pilot on a tight schedule. In a sense, production is game day for filmmakers. The quiet contemplation of preproduction is replaced by the frenzied pressure cooker of actually committing your plans to video while the clock is ticking and sunlight is fading. Maybe you have permission to be at the location for only 2 hours. Or perhaps the actor you cast has to leave for his paying job by 2:00 p.m. Or you've got to finish this scene in the next 30 minutes because that's when the bulldozers start up again in the empty lot next door. Pressure, pressure, pressure.

The only way you'll get the day's work done is by being quick. But the last thing you want to do is hurry. Being quick means being thoughtful but decisive. Hurrying is when you just blurt out any old answer to make the question go away. Being quick means being efficient and staying focused on the task at hand without getting bogged down hemming and hawing about insignificant or extraneous things. Hurrying is careless, unfocused, frenetic activity, which inevitably leads to inefficiency.

A corollary to Be Quick but Don't Hurry might be Have Fun but Stay

Businesslike. Shooting a pilot is tons of fun. You're seeing something you dreamed up become a reality. You're probably working with some of your best friends. If you're shooting a comedy, well, what's not fun about laughing all day long at work? But that last word is key: You're at work. So laugh, joke, have fun, but remember that there's a job to be done. There's a fine line between keeping things loose on the set and letting things fall apart. It's important to have a sense of always staying on the happy but focused and productive side of that line.

GETTING ENOUGH TAKES AND COVERAGE

There are some situations where not only shouldn't you hurry, but you shouldn't worry about being all that quick either. When it comes to making sure you've got all the footage you need before you move on from one shot or one scene to the next, taking a few moments to ask "Do I really have everything I'll need?" is much more important than rushing forward at warp speed. There's nothing worse than getting in the editing room and discovering that you really don't have all the pieces you need to cut a scene together the way you imagined. Well, okay, being eaten alive by a pack of wild hyenas is probably worse. So is an anesthetic-free colonoscopy. But realizing you forgot to get all the shots you need then being forced put the scene together in editing without a key ingredient is its own form of agony.

Even if you've followed your shot list religiously, you must still run the scene on the imaginary flatscreen in your mind and make sure you have everything you need in the can. Funny things happen to the movie in your mind when you shift from the speculative phase of preproduction and shoot the scene with real actors on a real location. The movie can change. Maybe you saw it all in a two-shot in your mind when you drew up your shot list, but now you're seeing close-ups as well. Your shot list didn't call for close-ups to be shot. But now your gut is telling you that you might want them. LISTEN TO YOUR GUT. It's not that you necessarily made a mistake when putting together the shot list. It's just that now you have more information to work with, and this new info is telling you to get more coverage.

You may also find that the movie in your mind flickers or is blurry on certain issues. Sometimes you see a certain moment in a two-shot, sometimes in close-up. So you find yourself uncertain as to whether you really need the close-up or not. My advice is simple: *When in doubt, shoot it.* You're there in the location, you've got the equipment and the actors, and it'll only take a few more minutes. Maybe you won't use it in the end. But having an extra shot or two is a whole lot better than trying to put the jigsaw puzzle together during editing without some crucial pieces.

The same principle applies to evaluating whether you've got enough takes of a given shot. Have you really gotten the performance you wanted? All the way through the scene? Or is there a line the actor always flubbed? Again, better to take a few extra minutes and shoot it again, even if you end up using the first take in the final edit, than to get into the editing room and kick yourself for never shooting a second take.

One final note on this: It's video, so do yourself a favor and play it back and watch it if you're unsure whether you have everything you need. Sometimes what you thought happened on camera isn't what actually happened. This is because our mind tends to see only what it expects to see. For instance, Harvard psychology professor Daniel Simons conducted an experiment where people were asked to watch a video of two teams of basketball players passing a basketball back and forth. One team wore white shirts; the other team wore black shirts. Viewers were asked to count how many times players on one team passed the ball but to ignore the other team. After the viewers finished watching the tape, they were asked questions about how many passes their assigned team had made, plus one other simple question: *When did the gorilla come on screen?* About half the viewers never saw any gorilla and were stunned when the tape was played back and they could plainly see that about halfway through, a person in a gorilla suit walked in front of the camera, beat his chest, then walked off. They never saw the gorilla because they weren't looking for a gorilla. Scientists call this inattentional blindness. Similarly, when you're shooting, you're watching the actors, evaluating their performance. You may not see all kinds of things that have unexpectedly crept into your shot: lights, microphones, passersby staring into the camera, and so on.

You can't always rely on your in-the-moment vision to perceive what shouldn't be in your shot. But the tape doesn't lie. It captures exactly what happened in that moment, even if you missed the gorilla.

The same principle applies to what you hear as well as what you see. You know what the actor is supposed to say, so naturally, that's what you think you heard them say. Unfortunately, the scripted dialogue is not always what the actor actually said. Sometimes he left out a word — a crucial word, one that changes the entire meaning of the line and direction of the story. Sometimes, you think you heard them say the scripted dialogue, and they did — sort of. But they mumbled or garbled the words so even though *you* understand what they said (because you read the script), *the audience hears only a mouthful of unintelligible garbled nonsense.*

So watch and listen carefully during each take. Concentrate on seeing and hearing what they say and do, not what you expect them to say or do. And when in doubt, play back the takes and double check.

By the way, for those of you who are thinking, "How the hell can you not see a freaking gorilla?," just type "Gorillas in Our Midst Daniel Simons" into a search engine, and you can read the study yourself. Even better, go to YouTube and type "selective attention test" in the search box, and you can watch the video. It's the one by Daniel Simons.

Finally, the fact that Professor Simons' study was called "Gorillas in Our Midst" proves that even ivory tower academics know the value of a catchy title.

YOU AREN'T THE ONLY GENIUS ON THE SET

Milton Berle, dubbed Mr. Television in the late 1940s because of the phenomenal success of his variety show, once said, "I know a good joke when I steal one." Amen to that, Brother Berle. Yes, this little pilot you're making is your baby. But everybody else involved can love your baby, too. They are its aunts and uncles and want nothing more than to help your little darling be all he can be. So if anyone, from the star right on down to the guy at the donut shop, has a good idea for something that will add to your project, for God's sake do what any self-respecting artist would do and use that idea.

Among other things, this means you must *listen* to the people around you. It also means you have to create an atmosphere where the cast and crew feel welcome to contribute creatively. If suggestions by the crew are constantly met with an exasperated sigh or steely glare, that tends to be the end of those suggestions ever being floated. And that, my friend, is your loss.

This doesn't mean you have to accept or include every notion thrown your way. But it does mean that the spirit and general attitude on your set should be *Ideas Welcome*. When the mechanical shark failed, coping with the situation by replacing shots of the shark with shots from the shark's POV was an ingenious solution. Does it really matter whether this idea came from Spielberg or from the cinematographer or whomever? The bottom line is Spielberg had the good sense to recognize this as a great idea and to use it in his film.

ACTORS AREN'T PUPPETS

One of the biggest challenges for novice directors, especially those who also wrote the script, is learning how to collaborate effectively with actors. Working with actors is a subject worthy of entire books. In fact, here are two you might want to read in preparation for your shoot:

- *Directing Actors: Creating Memorable Performances for Film and Television* by Judith Weston
- *Respect for Acting* by Uta Hagen, with Haskel Frankel

In the meantime, suffice it to say that actors aren't puppets, and you won't get good performances from them if you treat them as such. You can't manipulate their every vocal inflection or facial tic. As much as you may feel this is your "vision" and you've seen each character's performance on the movie screen in your mind and that's the way it must be, you have to let the actors do their work. This doesn't mean you just sit back and let them veer off in whatever improvised direction they feel like. But it does mean that you can't micromanage their performances.

A good rule is this: Talk with the actors about their goals and motivations in the scene (as in "you're flirting, you want him to like you"), but don't try to tell the actors what specific techniques they should use achieve that goal (as in "bat your eyelashes when you say that, then giggle"). You wouldn't (and shouldn't) try to tell a cinematographer what kind of lights to use or where to put them. Those are his professional choices, based on his expertise. You'd simply say, "I'd like it to be dark and mysterious looking in this scene." Give the actors the same courtesy and professional acknowledgment. Let them do what they are trained to do. This isn't just good manners; it's good filmmaking. You have to allow the actors to own their performances for them to deliver their best, most authentic possible work.

If there are occasions where you feel the need to direct physicality, float the suggestion as an idea, not a directive. For example, you might say, "It feels like you might want to lean closer to him starting in this part of the scene." This gives the actor the freedom to hear what you want but find a way to accomplish that end result in his own way, by either internalizing that suggestion and making it his own or by finding another route to the same destination.

CREW MEMBERS AREN'T SLAVES

Human beings have an amazing capacity to connect and identify personally with the work they do. When the Lakers win the NBA championship, the guy who sells peanuts in the nosebleed section still thinks to himself, "Yeah, baby, we did it, we're number 1!" The part-time barista at Starbucks #5782 thinks of it as *his coffee*, not *their coffee*.

When it comes to the crew of a movie or TV show, you can take that emotional identification and multiply it by 10. Every single person who works on your project will think of it as *her pilot*.

This is a gift from the gods. It means the crew working with you will bust their collective booties to make sure that it's the best pilot it can be. So the very least you can do, whether you are paying your crew or not, is to treat them with the utmost courtesy, respect, consideration, and admiration. Notice what they are doing and say something about it. If somebody contributes a small detail — a lighting effect or a piece of wardrobe or a prop — that adds texture or value to your pilot, then take the 5 seconds to say, "I love that sweater you picked for her. It's *so* perfect for the character."

It's also important to remember that if something is taking longer than you want it to, or if a crew member is struggling with a faulty piece of equipment, they are just as frustrated as you are. Sniping and huffing at the sound mixer as if he caused the mixing deck to go south on purpose is not only a crappy way to act, it's actually counterproductive. Let the guy do his work and fix the problem. The more understanding you are during moments of adversity, the harder the crew will work for you when the problem does get fixed and you're pressed for time because of the delay.

It's a Golden Rule thing: *Do unto others as you would want them to do unto you.* Speaking for myself, I work much harder for people who tell me I'm great than for people who are always critical or indifferent.

The second Golden Rule for treating your cast and crew properly is to always feed them well. No matter how small your budget is or how pressed for funds you are, you've got to make sure that you've got donuts and bagels in the morning, water and soda at all times, and decent meals at the meal break times. If you've got vegetarians, make sure they've got what they need, too. A well-fed crew is a happy crew, and a happy crew is a productive crew.

To paraphrase a well-known ad:

> *Bagels and cream cheese: $10.*
> *Pizza for eight: $22.50.*
> *A loyal crew: priceless.*

THE WORLD IS NOT A SET

Movies and TV have an amazing capacity to make the nonexistent seem real. Watch *Men in Black* and you happily give yourself over to the notion that aliens live among us, and the only reason we're in the dark about it is because of a secret government agency that owns a flashy-thingy device that zaps the memories right out of your brain. Watch *24* and you eagerly buy into the notion that Jack Bauer can single-handedly defeat terrorism while never encountering traffic of any kind in Los Angeles. That's the power of the moving image: Even the wildly improbable seems real.

Ironically, when you're involved in the making of the moving image, you're so immersed in the process of turning fantasy into reality that you tend to forget about actual reality. You start believing that all the world's a set, and all its people merely extras waiting for you to point them in the right direction.

Alas, such is not life. Locations are not just settings to serve your dramatic needs, they are real places where real people will live and work long after you've wrapped. Miraculously, ordinary folks have generously allowed you to disrupt their home or business so you can shoot your scene. Often they have done this for free, out of the goodness of their hearts. The very least you can do is treat their place with courtesy and respect. This means you take care not to damage anything, clean up your trash at the end of the day, and make sure to restore the property to the way it was before you and your crew descended upon it like locusts. This is not only common decency; it's smart business. You may want to come back someday and film this location again. The people who own the location tend to be more open to this request when you haven't burned a hole in their rug.

If you're shooting in a public setting, you will inevitably need to deal with that public. This can be inconvenient; people may stand or wander where you don't want them to, and you'll need to ask them to move. But there's a right way and a wrong way to do this. The right way would be something like, "I'm sorry, folks, but we need to ask you to move over there. Thanks for helping us, we really appreciate it." The wrong way would be, "Okay, you idiots are in my shot and need to move NOW! That means you, fatass!" As a general rule, you want to sound like Mary Poppins, not an angry NFL coach.

Another thing to remember when you're immersed in the make believe of making movies is that the real world still has real physical consequences. Fire is hot. Knives are sharp. The cars and buses in the street are not pretend props from a Looney Tunes cartoon. If you step in front of them, you will not be humorously flattened into a funny pancake version of yourself. You will be maimed or killed.

Always remember that the laws of nature take precedence over the magic of movies. Keep yourself, your cast, and your crew safe at all times. If I sound like your mother here, then you probably had a good mother. Call her once in a while and send her something nice for Mother's Day this year, not that lame e-card at the last minute.

FOR TEACHERS

To be or not to be on the set, that is the central question for teachers during the production phase. Whether 'tis nobler to let them sink or swim entirely on their own, and learn from their mistakes, or to provide guidance in the moment as they work through their production day and help them avoid a sea of troubles. The choice is ultimately yours, and there really isn't a right or wrong answer to the question.

The hands-off advocates make a strong case for allowing the students to make their film, not the teacher's version of the student's film. They also make a valid point that having the teacher present inevitably changes the power dynamic on the set. Instead of the student director or creator being the creative center of gravity, the teacher can't help but draw focus to himself, undercutting the director or creator's obligation and responsibility to be the final word on things, thereby diluting the experience.

On the other hand, my colleague James Gardner is a strong believer that the teacher's presence adds greatly to the learning experience, provided that presence is a Socratic one, one that poses questions that might not have occurred to the students for them to think through and answer. "Why do you think you need this shot?" "Are you sure you have enough coverage?" "We only have time to shoot three of the four remaining shots on your list. Which shots are the most important to you?"

As I said, both approaches have value and pedagogical substance. And you needn't pick one method and stick with it for life. Experiment with both, and use whichever suits you and your particular student population best.

11 THE PILOT: POSTPRODUCTION

Editing has often been called the final rewrite. It's where you find out whether the movie you imagined in your head is the one you shot and whether it works on a real screen as well as it did on the virtual screen in your mind. When it does, it can be thrilling, like pulling off a magic trick. When it doesn't, well, just like in production, necessity is often the mother of invention. You may not be able to assemble the pieces quite the way you imagined, but sometimes that's a good thing. Sometimes you suddenly see a moment or a scene or even the whole story in a new, inspired way and create something different from what you had in mind originally, something even more exciting. Just as with Transformers (the toys, not the movie), the pieces that made a fire truck, when reshuffled, can also form a really cool dragon.

None of this is meant to imply that you should automatically abandon your script and just start improvising during the editing phase. Or that you can now take what you've shot and make whatever movie strikes your fancy, suddenly taking what was meant to be a romantic comedy about a couple in their 20s and somehow twisting that into a sci-fi horror flick about a planet where everyone has three heads: their own, Rush Limbaugh's, and Michael Moore's (how scary is that?). However, it does mean that editing is not a paint-by-number process where you mindlessly assemble your footage exactly as your shot list and script called for. You must take a fresh look at everything and ask yourself whether there might be a better way to organize or present things.

As with cinematography, sound, directing, and other areas we've covered, the art and craft of editing are subjects we can't possibly explore thoroughly in one short chapter. The principles, techniques, and philosophy of editing are subjects worthy of entire books. Fortunately, a bunch have been written. I encourage you to read the ones listed in Appendix 2 if you are new to editing and want a more thorough education on the subject. In fact, even if you aren't new to editing, check them out. They will inspire you and expand your skills and talents as an editor and filmmaker.

But that said, here is a basic overview to help guide you through the process of postproduction.

THE ROUGH CUT: PUTTING IT TOGETHER

Before you even begin to edit, you must watch all the footage you shot to arm yourself with a basic familiarity with what you've got. Yes, I know, you were there when you shot it. But watch everything again, every single shot, every single take, to refresh your memory. Sometimes memory plays funny tricks, and we forget that take where the actor did something really wonderful with that one line, or we forget that other angle we shot. The human mind retains only a tiny fraction of what it is exposed to, and that fraction is even smaller if you drank too much at the wrap party. So be disciplined and watch every frame you shot before making any decisions about how to put it together.

Furthermore, as you watch the raw footage you shot (known as dailies), you should make notes. Every pilot is different, but a typical 3- to 5-minute webisode could easily have 50 or 60 different angles, with multiple takes on each setup. Even the Amazing Kreskin couldn't possibly remember every frame of that. You can save yourself a lot of editing time by jotting down a few reminders for each take. Let's say you shot four takes of the master shot for Scene 1. Using the shorthand "1,1" for "Scene 1, Take 1," your notes might look like this:

1,1 — good performances, mike dips in and out

1,2 — John good, Mary so-so in second half

1,3 — John bobbles "cheesecake" line

1,4 — Mary bobbles last line

Now, when you go to edit Scene 1, and you want to use the master angle for a section for the scene, you have some clues about where to look and where not to look.

After you have watched all the dailies and written notes for yourself, you will begin the process of assembling a rough cut. As the word *rough* indicates, this is not intended to be anything close to a polished, perfected, ready-for-broadcast version of your pilot. Like the first draft of your script, it is a way to put it all together in concrete form so you can evaluate what you have, see what works, and see what needs to be improved or fixed. The rough cut is not the time to obsess over finer points or finesse. That comes later. For now, just cut the scenes together in a way that makes basic sense to you — probably fairly close to the way you imagined it when you put your shot list together. The reason you don't want to spend a lot of time on finesse or polish at this point is that you need to view the rough cut first and get a sense of the big picture. Does the story work? Are the characters clear? Are there places that seem redundant or feel slow? Maybe there are things that need to be edited out, perhaps even entire scenes, which is why you shouldn't polish the editing to a fare-thee-well during the rough cut phase. If you spend hours and hours getting Scene 1 exactly right, frame by frame, then watch your cut and discover that Scene 1 is superfluous and you can really get the whole story moving a lot faster by dropping Scene 1 and beginning with Scene 2, well, you wasted an awful lot of time perfecting something that will never see the light of day with an audience.

In general, you will want to keep the amount of postproduction sound work to a minimum until you have "locked picture," or made the final decisions and edits on the video content. Why spend time fixing the sound on a line of dialogue that may never end up in the final version?

THE ROUGH CUT: ASSESSING WHAT YOU HAVE

Okay, you've watched all the dailies, made your notes, and put together your rough cut. Put it away for at least 24 hours (to gain some distance and perspective), then sit down and watch it all the way through. In my experience, most people, if they are honest with themselves, will have some version of the following reaction to watching their rough cut: "This is a complete freaking mess, utterly beyond repair. I'd like to throw up on my shoes, then burn all this footage so no one will ever see what a no-talent hack I am."

This is a completely normal reaction. Not fun, but normal. Take a deep breath or two and repeat after me: *This is a rough cut. Everybody's rough cut sucks. It's just part of the process.*

When you've stopped dry heaving, do the unthinkable and watch your rough cut all the way through once again. When you've done that, get out your pad of paper and write some big-picture notes. Maybe you want to drop a scene or parts of some scenes. Or maybe the story sags in the middle, but in watching the film twice now, it has suddenly occurred to you that those 2 minutes will work much better as a 30-second montage with music pushing it along than as three flat-footed, bloated dialogue scenes. Again, every project will be different, but for now, write down whatever seems wrong to you and any ideas you have for fixing what seems wrong.

Now watch your rough cut one more time, but this time break it down into smaller pieces; start and stop it wherever something seems off. Ask yourself what seems wrong and what sort of editing adjustments might help. Jot this down, then hit PLAY and keep watching until the next bump in the road.

When you finish this process, even if you haven't figured out quite how to solve all the problems, it's time to leave the rough cut and move on to Cut 2.

One final rough cut note: You may be tempted at this point to screen what you've got for someone, often your significant other. DON'T DO IT. They won't like it, because it's a rough cut and nobody likes rough cuts. I know, I know, your S.O. is dying to see it. And you've been living with it alone for a long time and are dying for someone to see what you've invested all this time and energy on and say, "Wow, that's really great!" DO NOT GIVE IN TO THIS URGE AND SCREEN THE ROUGH CUT FOR AN OUTSIDER. It can only bring you pain and self-doubt. Why? Because no matter how loudly and often you say, "This is just a rough cut," when a person watches something, he can't help but evaluate it as if it's a finished product, like every other video product he's seen at the movies, on TV, and on the Internet. He will react as if you put flour, eggs, tomato sauce, mozzarella and ricotta cheese, ground beef, and spices in front of him and said, "How do you like my lasagna?" He'll look at you in great pain, wanting to be nice, but will only be able to say, "Well, I don't know, I guess it just doesn't look like lasagna to me." Where you see potential, he will only see unassembled, unfinished raw ingredients. And worst of all, his doubt and concern will leap through the air, reach into your chest, and rip the heart right out of you. Lack of enthusiasm is incredibly contagious, and it's the last thing you need right now. What you need is to somehow set aside your burning desire for praise, do your editing work, and wait until you've got a finished product before showing it to your S.O.

REFINING THE CUT

Okay, you've watched your rough cut, made your notes, and had sex with your S.O. because you wisely refrained from screening the rough cut for her and avoided a big fight about her lack of enthusiasm. You're welcome. Now your job is to take the rough cut and start improving it, moving it closer to being a final product.

Notice I said "closer to being a final product," not "all the way there." As with your script, editing demands the patience to go through multiple versions: a second, third, fourth, and fifth cut. It is a painstaking process that requires sustained focus on every detail. The good news is that your spirits will rise with each successive cut. As predictable as it is that you will want to vomit after watching your rough cut, it's also a solid bet that upon screening your second cut you'll quietly say to yourself, "Hey, this isn't half bad. In fact, it's kind of good."

My students go through this emotional roller coaster time and again. I ask them how their shoot went, and they're giddy with excitement — can't wait to see it all cut together. Then we dim the lights and screen the editor's rough cut. When the lights go up, the room is filled with uncomfortable silence. Maybe even shame and humiliation. Their faces say, "I thought it was good, but maybe I just don't have what it takes." I help them through the moment and remind them it's just a rough cut. We screen it again, scene by scene, starting and stopping to discuss how and where improvements are needed. But the nauseous discomfort of the rough cut screening stays with them until our next class session, when the editor screens a revised cut and says, "Hallelujah! It is healed!" Still not perfect, but a gazillion times better than the rough cut. It's actually starting to look like lasagna!

You may be tempted to call it done at this point, eager to slap in a little music and some quick titles and post it on YouTube. After all, you've worked really hard on this pilot, think it's pretty darn good, and want to share it with the world. Don't do it. Not yet. You're not quite done. This is a good time to go back through the books you've read for guidance on editing. Maybe you'll want to review the chapters on editing dialogue, or on pace, or whatever other areas may apply to your pilot. The books obviously won't comment on your particular project, but they will probably stimulate your thinking about it. They can inspire you to take another look at each scene with a fresh eye and can help you bring the quality of the edit — and therefore the quality of the finished product — up another notch or two.

POSTPRODUCTION SOUND

In life, there are certain tasks that always seem to drift to the bottom of the to-do list. Cleaning the bathroom. Going to the dentist. Doing your taxes. For those over 50, getting a colonoscopy. None of these activities are much fun, but all are necessary. Pretending otherwise is simply a recipe for your daily life taking a turn for the worse.

So, too, with postproduction sound. It is among the most thankless, tedious, time-consuming parts of making a film. It is also among the elements that instantly separate a sloppy, amateurish pilot from a polished professional effort. Nothing takes an audience out of a story faster than half-assed sound work. All your hard work creating the premise and characters, writing a witty, well-constructed script, and shooting great performances with brilliant camera angles will be totally lost on the audience if their main reaction to the piece is, "What's wrong with the sound?"

So once you've gone through the process of refining the edit several times and have locked picture — meaning you are totally satisfied with every visual moment of your pilot — it's time to go to work on the audio. Here are some of the main tasks you must tackle:

- **Clarity.** Is every line of dialogue clear and understandable to the audience? Remember: They haven't read the script, so the only way they can understand what is being said is if they can hear it clearly. Sometimes, the actor's best overall performance during a given moment includes a garbled line. You can still use the video performance you want *if* you do one of two things to fix the sound: Steal the audio from a different take or even a different shot of the same moment and "stick it in the actor's mouth" or bring the actor in and have a dialogue replacement or "looping" session.
- **Balance.** You shot a dinner scene between two people. But the sound levels on the two close-ups don't match. One is much louder than the other, even though in the scene, they are speaking at approximately the same level. You need to adjust one or both levels to get them to match.
- **Ambience.** Ambient sound is a key element in establishing and reinforcing a sense of place and time. If your scene is set at a sleazy motel in a bad part of town, you can emphasize this by adding sirens, gunshots, barking dogs, sounds of a couple arguing next door, and so on. All of these can add texture to your scene, though they must also have proper perspective.
- **Perspective.** If the couple next door is arguing, they need to sound muffled, as if there is a wall and distance between them and the camera; they shouldn't sound like they are right there in the room with your actors. Similarly, if you've filmed a scene at a romantic café overlooking the ocean, you might want to add the muted sound of the waves breaking on the beach. But this must be done with perspective, unless you want the audience to think your love-struck couple is in the middle of *The Perfect Storm*.

For specific instruction on techniques for accomplishing any of these tasks, consult one of the sound books in Appendix 2.

ADDING MUSIC

This is the one part of postproduction sound that's actually a ton of fun. Nothing brings a film alive faster than a great soundtrack. That montage of your couple falling in love — the one you were starting to have second thoughts about — suddenly soars with romance when a great song is playing behind it. And the action sequence you shot, the one that never quite seemed to work as well as you imagined, suddenly crackles with heart-pounding excitement when a throbbing music track pulses throughout. We are so conditioned from years of watching movies and TV with great soundtracks that films without any music seem oddly incomplete.

Try to imagine the shark attack scenes in *Jaws* without that haunting *dum-dum dum-dum dum-dum* music underneath. They just wouldn't be as scary. Or imagine a great romantic comedy, building to the climactic moment when our couple finally gets together and kisses — but with no music. They kiss, credits against black, all in silence. I'd venture to say that no music = no emotional payoff = unsatisfied audience.

But where do you get the music from? You probably don't have the budget or contacts to allow you to fire off a quick text message asking Beyoncé whether she'd be willing to write and record something for you. And if you're thinking you can just pull a song off Beyoncé's latest CD and drop it into your soundtrack, well, there's this pesky thing called copyright law that may get in your way. Yes, I know, many people use copyrighted music without permission for their videos on YouTube. But this isn't strictly legal, merely overlooked in most cases because of the sheer volume of material and the fact that most of it isn't posted for commercial purposes. If you want to post on sites beyond YouTube, create your own site, or submit your work to a festival, or if you have any intention of selling your series to someone or sharing in online ad revenue, then you cannot use copyrighted music without obtaining the rights to do so, and those rights typically cost many thousands of dollars.

So where can you obtain affordable music to use for wider, commercial purposes? Several places. First, just as you are an aspiring video maker, hoping to be discovered on the Internet, the Web is filled with aspiring musicians. Surf the Net, find an up-and-comer with a song you'd like to use, and contact that person. Explain what you want, offer a prominent screen credit in exchange for use of the music, and without overselling suggest that perhaps the exposure your pilot and series will garner may also attract new fans and paying customers for the musician's CDs. You may even try offering a nominal fee — say $50 — or offer to buy some of the artist's CDs. If the musician says no, so be it. But one of the unwritten rules of producing low-budget, creative work is that if you ask nicely, they might say yes. But if you don't ask, the answer is always no. (See the interview with Jen Dawson in Chapter Fifteen for one success story on finding great music for free.)

A second way to obtain good music might be to approach a local musician, someone playing in a coffee house or book store, whose musical style fits the needs of your pilot. Again, try to present this as an opportunity for the musician to trade his services and talents for exposure to a wider audience. He's already playing for little or no money, hoping the 50 folks in the coffee house might buy some CDs. Even if your pilot only gets 5,000 hits, incredibly modest for YouTube or other major sites, this would be equivalent exposure to 100 nights of playing live to 50 people.

Finally, let's not ignore the direct route. Perhaps you actually play a musical instrument yourself. You don't have to be Eric Clapton, but if you play well enough and can write a bit of appropriate music, you might be able to fill in the transitions and other short musical needs. One word of caution: Just because you're playing the music (or singing) yourself does not give you the right to cover your favorite hit song and use it for commercial purposes in your pilot. Both the original performance and the writing of the song are covered by copyright law.

CREATING A MAIN TITLE

I used to work for Tom Miller, one of the most successful producers in the history of television. Tom's shows include *Happy Days, Laverne &*

Shirley, *Bosom Buddies*, *Mork & Mindy*, *Perfect Strangers*, *Full House*, *Family Matters*, and the show I helped write and produce, *Step by Step*. Among other gifts, Tom had a fierce passion for main titles. And I bet that if you've seen any of the shows listed above even a few times, you can instantly recall the main title: the smiling cast framed by a spinning 1950s record in *Happy Days*, or Laverne and Shirley hop-skipping to "schlemiel, schlimazel, hasenpfeffer," and so on. On *Step by Step*, it was the family going on the roller coaster ride, at an amusement park right on the shore of Lake Michigan (this amusement park doesn't exist and was created by photographing an inland park and adding the water through visual effects in postproduction). The show ran for 7 years, during which time the number one question I was asked by fans was, "Is there really an amusement park right by the water? I want to go there."

Some people felt that Tom's passion for main titles ran to obsession, that it was a waste of time and money out of step with the changing face of television, where main titles were getting shorter and less elaborate. Even Tom eventually agreed that the longest of the main titles (the original version of the *Step by Step* main title ran well over a minute and a half) could use some tightening. But he refused to do what many shows were beginning to do: reduce the main title to a simple title card, then run the credits for the series stars over the action and dialogue of the beginning of the episode. Why did Tom Miller resist this growing trend? Because he knew that no matter how much TV changed, you only get one chance to make a first impression, and first impressions matter.

The same holds true for your Internet series. Clearly, you can't have a 90-second main title for a show whose episodes will only run 3 to 5 minutes. But this doesn't mean you can't create something short but memorable, a signature beginning that will lure the audience and serve as a quick visual and audio reminder of the tone, flavor, and main thrust of your show. In short, what you want to create is a form of what marketing people call branding for your show, a quick hit that brings a smile to the viewer's face and makes him say, "Oh yeah, I like that show."

Your main title can also help set the table for your series and each individual episode. It can establish the tone of your show, introduce the main character, or even fill in the backstory so people who have not seen the pilot can still understand and enjoy future episodes. Classic examples of this "tell the story of the series in the main title" approach from prime time TV include *Gilligan's Island* and, more recently and more compactly, *My Name Is Earl*. A good prototype of this technique in a web series is the main title for *Mommy XXX* on Crackle. Though the name of the series suggests a great deal about its content, the main title goes further and lets you know it's a comedy, not an actual triple-x-rated series about moms. Accompanied by intentionally hokey visuals and a music track right out of a 1950s family sitcom, the main title voice over is, "Hi, my name is Demi Delia. This is my daughter Brandi, and this is my son Craig. Welcome to my family. Oh, and by the way, I'm a porn star." Then there's more hokey music and little hearts on screen, reminiscent of the *I Love Lucy* main title. It runs just 10 seconds, but it sets the tone and premise, introduces the characters and basic situation, and is funny all by itself, which entices you to watch the show. That's a well-designed main title.

Surf the Net, check out the variety of main titles out there, and ask yourself, "What would make a great main title for my show?" The thought and effort will be paid back tenfold by a good main title that enhances the viewer's enjoyment and connection with your show.

And while we're at it, let's not forget the *end credits* either. In the early 1990s, network television figured out that just running the end credits for a show over a black screen, or even over still frames from the episode, is a waste of airtime. Viewers tune out the second the content on screen stops being worth watching, and there's nothing compelling about watching a bunch of names and credits for the people who supplied the lights or the catering. TV networks could almost hear millions of remote controls turning off the set or switching to another channel the instant the end credits began, meaning millions of viewers weren't watching the next show or next commercial on that station. So the networks finally wised up and urged shows to run original material or humorous outtakes behind the credits.

The same principle holds true for web series. Just as first impressions matter, so do final impressions, so keep them entertained right to the very end. Think of your end credits as an opportunity to make your viewers' final thought be, "I love that show. I've got to watch another episode and tell my friends about it."

My students' show *Red White & Blue* (available at Funny or Die) is a good example of keeping the entertainment going right through to the last crew credit. Each episode took a different approach — some continuing the action from the show, some spoofing other TV shows. But in every case, they found a way to make the end credits entertaining.

FOR TEACHERS

The best piece of advice I can offer on postproduction instruction is this: If at all possible, make sure you have at least one experienced editor in your class. This may mean asking the students who sign up what their skill set is before the semester begins, or on Day One, and doing a little recruiting if nobody raises her hand when you ask whether there are any experienced editors in the group.

Editing is a craft and an art form that is similar to music: Some students have a gift and passion for it, some don't. It requires far more than knowing how to work the software and hit the right buttons. It requires a sense of rhythm within each individual scene and within the piece as a whole. It requires a strong sense of story and character. And it requires more than a little experience to be able to watch a scene, identify ways to re-edit to strengthen it, and have a feel for the dozens of techniques that editors use to maximize the effectiveness and impact of a cut.

That said, you'll also need to involve the entire class during the screenings and discussions of each successive cut. I've found that what works best is to screen the cut without stopping or commenting, then ask for overall or big-picture type notes (e.g., "We need to tighten the opening and get to the story quicker or it drags in the middle" or "We need more reaction shots, not just shots of the person talking"). After the students offer their big-picture observations, you can add any of your own that they haven't covered. Then screen the cut by starting and stopping wherever anyone, including you, has something he wants to discuss or suggest.

Because my classroom is a seminar setup rather than an editing suite, my process is to merely convey the notes to the editor, then let him or her execute them and generate a new cut for the next class session. But I can also imagine value in conducting some sessions in an actual editing suite, where the students can see firsthand the different performance choices from the dailies, or how each individual editing choice can improve the moment and overall quality of the piece.

Finally, the director and the showrunner should spend time in the editing room with the editor polishing the cut — getting the timing just right, making sure the best possible performances are selected for each angle, and making sure that every beat of every scene is put together for maximum effectiveness.

12 BUILDING ON THE PILOT: COMING UP WITH EPISODE IDEAS

A great pilot is a wonderful accomplishment. You've created a world and a set of characters and relationships that have a palpable reality. You've (hopefully) gotten an audience hooked, and now they want more. When you show a pilot, you are making an implicit promise to your audience that there's plenty more where that came from. And (presumably) you had at least a half dozen ideas for future episodes come to mind when you developed the basic premise way back when and asked yourself, "Does this concept have legs?"

So does that mean you should just pick any one of those half-dozen story ideas you cooked up way back when and use it to start developing a script for Episode 2? Maybe. But maybe not. Before you make that decision, you should take a step back and take a fresh look at your pilot. After all, when you came up with that original set of ideas for future episodes, you were flying blind. You hadn't actually written the pilot script. You didn't have a cast, and you hadn't seen the whole thing on film, cut together and in final form.

In short, you've got a boatload of newer, more detailed information than you had when you were first dreaming the whole thing up, and this information must be taken into account in developing your series.

Not only do you have new thoughts, but now would be a good time to get some feedback from others. Unlike when all you had was a rough cut, now you have a finished, polished pilot with a great main title, clean sound, music, and a dynamite ending. It's time to take your baby out for a spin and see how an audience responds to it. You may be surprised which parts of your show the audience relates to the most. Your favorite parts and characters may not be their favorites. They may absolutely love a character or dynamic that you thought was merely incidental and not your strongest asset. This sort of audience feedback is priceless. Despite the fact that you are the show's creator, listening to the audience is vital because they are the ultimate judges of the material in the marketplace.

Time and again, pilots are made with the intention of the series progressing in one direction, only to have the unpredictable alchemy of casting, world events, audience response, and a hundred other factors push the show in a new, unexpected direction. In the pilot of *Happy Days*, the Fonz was a minor character who had all of six lines. But the audience instantly fell in love with that character, as portrayed by Henry Winkler, so the Fonz quickly went from background player to the star of the show. This meant that either new stories needed to be developed focusing on the Fonz, or the Fonz needed to be given a more prominent role in any story previously considered for development.

Same thing for the current CBS comedy *The Big Bang Theory*. By its original design, Leonard, played by Johnny Galecki, is the central role. He's the one with the love interest in the girl across the hall, and Johnny Galecki's credit comes first in the beginning of the show. But those design and contractual decisions were made before the pilot was shot, before episodes aired and the audience was exposed to Jim Parsons, Galecki's co-star, who plays smug, obsessive–compulsive, hyperintellectual, socially clueless Sheldon. Parsons, as Sheldon, consistently scored big with the audience. The more laughs he got, the more material the writers created for him, and the more the show tilted toward Sheldon, who had become, as they say in the TV biz, a breakout character.

Your series is a living organism; it evolves over time, changing, growing, adapting in a Darwinian fashion by emphasizing its strengths and reducing or eliminating its weaknesses. But unlike organisms, which evolve without conscious effort, your series can evolve and grow only if you help it do so. In television, growth must be engineered. From the pilot on, that is the constant job of the series creator: nurturing, adapting, expanding, deepening, and growing the series. The pilot, wonderful as it may be, is only the beginning, a newborn that can reach its full potential only with parental guidance. You've whetted the audience's appetite; now you must fulfill their craving and give them more — not just another helping of the same dish, mind you, but something that gives them new flavors and textures. Think of it as your wedding day, a glorious and memorable celebration, but only Step One in a very long journey with twists and turns and unpredictable developments galore ahead.

GROWING YOUR SERIES

There are a handful of basic ways in which a series can grow. In no particular order, they are:

- New characters
- New relationships between existing characters
- Changes in circumstances for one or more characters
- Deeper exploration of aspects of your characters
- Increased emphasis on one or more formerly minor characters

Let's look at each of these, using the long-running network series *Cheers* as an example of each of these techniques. The *Cheers* pilot is considered masterful. It received an Emmy for Outstanding Writing in a Comedy. But for all its greatness, the series would have languished and disappeared quickly if the writers and producers merely delivered same song, second verse in each subsequent episode. Instead, they took the pilot and built on it, keeping the audience coming back for 272 more installments over 11 award-winning seasons. They consistently grew the series using all of these techniques.

New characters. The series characters presented in the *Cheers* pilot are Sam, Diane, Coach, Carla, and Norm. Cliff, though present in the pilot, was merely a guest star, not a series character as yet. Frasier was added in Season Three as a new love interest for Diane. This was clearly a brilliantly conceived addition, an intellectual counterpoint to Sam's good-time skirt-chasing perspective. Not only did the character help keep *Cheers* fresh and alive for another 9 seasons, but Frasier was spun off into his own series, which lasted another 11 seasons.

When Nicholas Colasanti, the actor who played Coach, died suddenly after Season Three, Woody was added. Also added along the way were Lilith (Frasier's post-Diane love interest and eventual wife) and Rebecca, brought into the series when Shelley Long opted out after Season Five. Each new character brought new dynamics to the series, and each new dynamic brought dozens of new stories and angles to explore.

New relationships. In the case of *Cheers*, evolving relationships were part of the core plan for the series from its conception. In the pilot, Sam and Diane meet for the first time. She's an intellectual snob and he's only looking for a good time, but the sexual tension is there from the moment Diane, alone in the bar for a moment, answers the house phone and takes a message for Sam, who implored her to cover for him in order to avoid speaking to the woman calling for him. As she hangs up, he inquires about the message:

                              SAM
          Well?

                             DIANE
          You're a magnificent pagan beast.

                              SAM
          Thanks. What was the message?

The pilot was merely the beginning of a long, twisting journey for Sam and Diane, and for the series. They were antagonists with a smoldering sexual tension between them for the first season. Then they were lovers with diametrically opposed interests (other than sex) for Season Two. Then they broke up but still had feelings for each other starting in Season Three. Each new permutation in the relationship gave the series a fresh angle to explore, new stories to tell based on this new set of circumstances and character dynamic. You see this all the time on TV, from *Full House* to *House*. The characters enter into new relationships or end old ones to explore the possibilities of new ones. The reason for this is simple: New relationships equal new stories and new growth for the show. *The Big Bang Theory* injected fresh life into the premise and character dynamics after a few seasons by adding more female characters, love interests, for the socially challenged science nerds we'd been following.

Changes in circumstances for your characters. This is really a variation on the new relationship concept. On *Cheers*, the primary new circumstance came in tandem with Kirstie Alley's entrance into the show as Rebecca. Sam was no longer the owner of the bar but was now merely an employee of a large corporation and, more importantly, was now required to answer to an attractive woman, Rebecca, his new boss. In her debut episode, Rebecca explains Sam's new situation to him using a baseball metaphor:

REBECCA
It's the bottom of the ninth, you've
got two outs, two strikes and no balls.

This line is not only a wildly funny joke. It also promises a brand new set of stories and story angles that can now be exploited by the writers.

Family sitcoms have made hay for years by having the sweet, innocent preteen girl suddenly blossom into a young woman with an interest in the opposite sex, instantly generating anxiety and problems for Mom and Dad (and new story ideas for the writing staff). On *Roseanne*, the title character and husband Dan were constantly adapting to new job circumstances, sometimes employed, sometimes unemployed, sometimes working for themselves. Each new circumstance provided a new environment and set of character issues to be explored.

Deeper exploration of your characters. When we pitch and develop a pilot, we tend to reduce the complex humans in the world we create to a one-line description. Sam is a womanizing recovering alcoholic. Diane is an uptight intellectual snob. Norm is an inveterate beer guzzler who spends more time at the bar than at home. But human beings — at least the interesting ones — are multidimensional creatures who often surprise us with new and undiscovered aspects of their personality. So, too, with effective series characters. Yes, of course Norm will make his entrance into the bar each week and sit on that stool sucking his beer until closing time. But the producers and writers were also smart enough to know that there is value (and story material) in taking a closer look at Norm and his inner life. What would happen if a woman suddenly pursued a sexual relationship with Norm? Would he succumb to temptation, or would he be faithful to Vera, his unseen wife on the show? They did an entire episode based on this premise. In the end, Norm remained faithful to Vera, and in the process of exploring this deeper aspect of the character, the audience now had a deeper and stronger bond with the character of Norm. This is the great value of deeper character exploration: It not only gives you a premise for an episode, it increases your audience's connection and devotion to the characters and, in turn, your series.

Increased emphasis on one or more formerly minor characters. We've already seen how this worked with the Fonz and *Happy Days*. And we've mentioned how know-it-all mailman Cliff Claven went from amusing spice to part of the main entrée on *Cheers*. When you go looking for ways to grow and expand your series, you may already have the answer embedded in your pilot or other episodes. Do you have a minor character whom the audience loves? Then maybe that character is ripe for increased emphasis as a recurring character or even a new series regular for your series. On the long-running ABC comedy *Family Matters*, the character of Steve Urkel was originally intended to be a one-shot guest in a single episode. Enter Jaleel White and his portrayal of the hapless nerd. By the end of the taping of this one episode, the audience spontaneously rose to its feet and chanted, "Ur-kel, Ur-kel, Ur-kel!" A series regular and star of the show was born.

GROWING YOUR CHARACTERS

In a television series, the characters must be consistent from week to week, speaking and acting in the manner the audience has come to know and love. And yet, for a series to sustain interest over a long period of time, these same, consistent characters must also grow and change. How can these two seemingly contradictory things be accomplished simultaneously? That, in a nutshell, is one of the most important elements in the art of writing series television.

As the previous section indicates, the principle source of series growth is, essentially, character growth of one kind or another. But TV characters don't — in fact, can't — change the way that characters in a one-shot story, like a movie or a novel, can change. The reason for this is fairly simple: In a one-shot form, the story is over when the piece is over. But in series television, the story goes on, episode after episode. So the characters can grow and change only in incremental ways. And yet, to maintain audience interest, the characters and situation cannot be so static that the audience becomes bored, filled with a sense that they've seen it all exactly this way before and that the series has run out of gas.

What's a writer to do?

One way to look at it might be that rather than shooting for wholesale character changes (as one might in a one-shot movie or novel), the TV writer maintains interest in his main characters by constantly throwing new and greater challenges at them. Take Sam Malone, the devoted skirt-chaser on *Cheers*. When Sam got together with Diane, he was not suddenly transformed into a monogamous Boy Scout, content to look no further than the woman he was with. He was still a womanizer, but now he was a womanizer in a committed relationship *trying* to stay loyal and faithful. This was a source of huge internal conflict for him, and page one of the writer's bible says conflict = story.

The same type of approach was used on the Fox medical drama *House* to keep the title character fresh and the series alive and growing. Dr. House is an unsentimental medical genius who strives for the worst possible bedside manner and the least sympathetic attitude toward his interns and underlings and who pops painkillers like candy, side effects and warnings of the dangers of addiction be damned. If House suddenly became a sober, nurturing mentor with a gentle bedside manner, the audience would abandon the show, stat. He wouldn't be the same character they've come to know and love. But the writers know that complete character inertia can be equally deadly to a show's health. So they turned the heat up on House by presenting him with greater and greater challenges to his curmudgeon demeanor. His formerly timid interns and underlings gain the confidence to push back when House pushes their buttons. His addiction begins to threaten his ability to work — and without work, House would go crazy. So again, these new challenges = conflict = new stories = sustained audience interest.

LEARNING FROM EACH EPISODE YOU SHOOT

Serendipity is an essential component of many great discoveries. Decades ago, a Mrs. Wakefield, owner of the Toll House Inn, was making chocolate cookies but ran out of regular baker's chocolate, so she substituted broken pieces of semisweet chocolate, assuming they would melt and blend into the batter. But they didn't melt, and chocolate chip cookies were the result. Percy LeBaron Spencer of the Raytheon Company was walking past a radar tube and noticed that the candy bar in his pocket melted, leading to the invention of the microwave oven. And in 1992, Welsh scientists were testing a potential new heart drug and accidentally discovered Viagra.

The moral of the story: Sometimes the wonderfully unexpected pops up all by itself. But the unexpected becomes a discovery instead of an annoyance only if you're paying attention. Mrs. Wakefield could have cursed her semisweet chocolate chunks for not melting and thrown the batch in the trash. Mr. Spencer might have pitched his candy bar and maybe his soiled trousers and vowed to be more careful around radar in the future. And the Welsh scientists (and, presumably, the volunteers who took what they assumed was a pill to help their heart only to discover the rise of the unintended side effect) might have perceived their new drug as an embarrassing failure rather than the boon to men's sexual health (and advertising on football games) that Viagra has become.

The law of unintended consequences and random discovery is as potent in television as it is in the kitchen and the laboratory. But you must pay close attention, take note when fate has knocked on your door, and do something to capitalize on your good fortune. If you write a part for a guest star, and the actor you cast hits a home run with the audience and they love him, for God's sake, don't just sit there and smile. Write that part and that actor into your next episode, even if you hadn't planned on it. If you suddenly discover that your main character is hilarious when he goes off on a long-winded political tangent, write another one for him and see whether it works again. Every episode should be viewed as a learning opportunity, another pilot, if you will; it's another chance to add to your series.

In fact, I'll go a step further and make the case that you can't merely wait for luck to show up on its own. You have to go looking for it. For your series to grow, you need to constantly experiment with new combinations of characters and situations and pay attention to the results.

The corollary to this approach, naturally, is knowing when the characters and situations that have been working well for your series have crossed over the fine line between "tried and true" and "Oh God, how many times are they gonna do *that bit* on this show?" Unfortunately, there is no hard and fast rule or battery-powered measuring device that can tell you when a joke or character dynamic has become stale. But if you find yourself getting a bit weary writing the same type of thing over and over, there's a good chance the audience is feeling the same way about watching it ad nauseam. However wonderful that joke or character trait might have been in its day, it's time to let it move on to the great TV afterlife. Thank it for its service, wish it well, but say goodbye. Breaking up is hard to do, but you're a creative person and will find something new to take its place.

HOW MANY EPISODES DO I NEED BEFORE I CAN POST MY SERIES?

Good question — and as with all really good questions, there is no one absolute answer, just more questions. How many episodes are you planning to shoot overall? Six? Sixty? If it's six, you might want to wait until you've got them all in the can ready to go before you post. But if it's sixty, it would be insane to wait that long.

Other questions include:

- How long will it take you to write, shoot, and edit more episodes?
- Are your cast and crew going to bail on you if you don't start posting soon?
- Are you hoping to use the episodes to attract investors or other participants?

Uncertainty aside, let me offer some possible answers to the question at hand. For starters, I'd say that you'd be wise to post more than just the pilot — two or three episodes at a minimum. My reasoning is that you want to get the audience more than a little hooked. If they watch the pilot and can't see Episode 2 for another month, there's a good chance they'll forget all about your pilot and never get around to looking for Episode 2 when you do post it. However, if they've seen the pilot and two more episodes, and they like what they've seen, the chances that they'll come looking for more in a month are much greater. This isn't scientific, but I'd venture a guess that the odds of three episodes remaining close to the surface in a viewer's memory bank are about 20 times greater than if he'd only seen a single episode, the pilot. Again, not scientific, but ask yourself the difference in commitment you have between a show you've seen once and a show that you've seen and enjoyed multiple times.

So three episodes is a good ballpark estimate on when to start posting. It's enough to get the audience fully engaged but not so many that it'll take another year before you can post the next batch of fresh episodes. Even if, because of the nature of your series, you manage to crank out six episodes in a week, it may well be to your strategic advantage to post three, and then post the next three in a week or two. That way, you can constantly be offering your audience something new and fresh rather than giving them six all at once, having them gobble them up, then forget all about you before you post the new stuff a month later.

FOR TEACHERS

In my experience, coming up with story ideas for subsequent episodes is one of the most challenging assignments for students. I believe this is because most students have never been asked to devise more than one story about the same set of characters using the same premise. Because of this lack of experience, plan on being a bit more hands-on in your guidance than you normally are.

First off, require them not only to come in prepared to pitch story ideas for subsequent episodes but to explain how their idea will help the series or characters grow. It may even be valuable to have a class session where you and the students brainstorm and pitch not stories but potential directions and avenues of growth for the series (e.g., "I'd like to know more about how the character got to be the way he is," which might suggest story lines involving his birth family or an ex-girlfriend or wife). This sort of broad, conceptual thinking will ground the students' thinking in the deeper purpose of adding to the palette of the series rather than merely devising some trivial incident around which to base an episode that may not contribute any new dimension to the show.

It may also be useful to ask them to watch a successful pilot and the next two episodes of that series and to then write a brief analysis of how Episodes 2 and 3 helped to grow either the series or one of the characters.

If you find that the students' story pitches are still less than stellar, feel free to jump in yourself, specify a type of series or character growth you'd like to see in Episode 2 or 3, and ask them to pitch new story ideas in the next class session based on these tighter guidelines.

13 MARKETING YOUR SERIES AND YOURSELF

In the movie *Field of Dreams*, a mysterious Voice in the Sky insistently tells Iowa farmer Kevin Costner, "If you build it, they will come." Being a trusting, New Age sort of guy who attended UC Berkeley in the 1960s and believes in peace, love, granola, and the infinite possibilities of the universe, Kevin decides this Voice might be on to something groovy, so he plows under his crops and builds a baseball field. Lo and behold, the universe responds by delivering thousands of baseball fans to Kevin's farm, presumably bringing him fame and fortune, repairing his relationship with his dead father, and solving every other problem in Kevin's life.

Apparently, that's just how the universe rolls: *If you build it, they will come.*

I, too, am a UC Berkeley alum, a big fan of peace, love, and granola, and I think the universe is freaking awesome — my favorite place to live. But although it may be great advice for spiritually inclined, baseball-loving corn farmers, "If you build it, they will come" is a terrible plan of attack for the creator of an Internet TV series. Building it is not nearly enough; if you want to fill the bleachers with fans of your show, you're going to have to be a very non-sixties, business-oriented, 21st-century type and market that sucker 'til it screams. You need to be loud and proud and pimp your show every which way you can. And why not? You've made a great show, now it's time to let as many people as possible know about it and then get them to tell 10 friends, who tell 10 other friends, who tell 10 more friends that they should watch your show.

You've already been Kevin Costner; you've already built it. Well done. Bravo. Far out, man. Take a bow. But now it's time to be the Voice in the Sky and tell everyone you can to point, click, and watch your great new show. Your new, Internet-age mantra should be, "If you SELL IT, they will come."

Right about now, some of you sensitive, creative types might be hearing another Voice in Your Head, one saying, "I'm an artist, not a salesman. I don't do THAT." Kindly thank the Voice in Your Head for its input and remind it that there's a word for artists who refuse to also sell themselves: *anonymous*. Actually, there are a whole bunch of words, like *unknown, unsuccessful, foolish, misguided*, and *self-destructive*. If you want people to know about your work, if you want to have a career in the arts, then you MUST be as serious and dedicated to marketing your work as you were to creating it.

Remember: You're not only marketing your work, you're marketing yourself. Networking, if you will. Building a career, emphasis on the word *building*, which implies care, effort, and commitment over a long period of time. Courtney Zito, star and creator of the successful web series *Hollywood Girl* (see interview with her in Chapter Fifteen), typically puts in about 2 hours a day marketing her show and herself. She checks her *Hollywood Girl* website, posts new clips or news items there and on Facebook, answers e-mail, and develops new marketing material such as trailers for new episodes. My friend Deborah Brevoort, a successful playwright, devotes one full evening a week to submitting and making people aware of her work. Courtney and Deborah are extremely busy women. Courtney has a demanding full-time gig at a TV production company in addition to writing and producing her own web series. Deborah teaches at several universities in addition to writing new plays and maintaining an international travel schedule to attend productions of her plays across the country and around the world. But Courtney and Deb know that no matter how busy they are, they must make marketing a regular part of their work week. Talent is unquestionably a vital component of Courtney and Deborah's success. But so is their dedication to honest self-promotion.

How do you sell or market your video? By using the tools of the medium you're working in: the Internet. These tools include e-mail, Twitter, social networking sites like Facebook, and various avenues to maximize the number of ways your video pops up on search engines like Google and Bing. But before we get to all that, let's start with the single most popular destination for fans of Internet videos: YouTube.

YOUTUBE

Unless you're a multi-billion-dollar media conglomerate with its own dedicated website that already receives millions of unique hits per month, the first place you should post and market your Internet TV show is YouTube. It's simple and free, provides high-quality technology to store and stream your work, attracts a huge, worldwide audience of video fans every day, and can be linked or embedded into dozens of other sites. Best of all, YouTube has a built-in system to help you market your work. The system is known as *tags*.

Tags are keywords that are used to help identify the content and other relevant characteristics of your video. Whenever you upload a video to YouTube, you have the opportunity to enter tags that will help users who might enjoy a show like yours find their way to it. Tags help bring viewers to your show, even if they aren't specifically looking for it but have expressed an interest in one of the tags you have entered.

For example, let's say you've created a web comedy called *Roommates from Hell*. Obviously, your friends and family who go to YouTube and enter *Roommates from Hell* in the search box will find it. But even if you have a thousand Facebook friends and come from a very large Catholic family, your network of personal contacts is but a tiny fraction of your potential worldwide audience. To reach this larger audience — and on YouTube, we're talking about millions of potential viewers — you need to be thorough and creative about the tags you attach to your show. On *Roommates from Hell*, these tags might include:

- Comedy
- Bad roommates
- Dorm life
- College life

- Apartment life
- Pet alligators
- Nose picking

You should also include the names of your cast as tags. After all, they all have friends and family and Facebook buddies who may know there's a video with their friend in it but can't remember the name of the show or what it's about. Also, your cast members may appear in dozens of other videos, and the people watching those other videos may take note of the actor or actress and want to check out their other work.

Right about now, some of you may be thinking, "Hey, what if I slapped a phony tag on my series, one that has nothing to do with my show but will get millions of hits — you know, something like 'free money' or 'Kardashian nude sex tape' or 'Justin Bieber'? Wouldn't that be a great idea?" No, it would NOT be a great idea! Why not? Because although it might bring traffic to your video for an hour or two, that traffic is quickly going to become angry and disappointed traffic, traffic that will complain to YouTube who will, in turn, pull your video.

Coming up with legitimate creative tags for your work as a means of expanding the universe of potential viewers is a worthy goal. Being intentionally deceptive or misleading with your tags is not only pointless, it's self-destructive. Don't do it.

BEYOND YOUTUBE

Although YouTube is the dominant brand name for video hosting (just as Kleenex is for tissues and Levis is for denim jeans), it is far from the only place you can or should post your web series. If you made ketchup, you wouldn't sell it only at one supermarket chain, even if that chain was huge, like Kroger. What about the people who shop at Safeway or Wal-Mart? Wouldn't you want to reach them, too? Of course you would. You'd want to have your product available at every possible retail consumption point that made sense for you and your business plan. And if your product had special features, you'd want to make sure you displayed it at the outlets that best fit those special characteristics. For instance, if your ketchup was organic or health oriented, you'd probably want to display it at a market that attracted health-minded shoppers, say a place like Whole Foods. Or if you made not ketchup but salsa, you'd probably want to display it not only at mainstream chains like Kroger and Safeway but at supermarkets that cater to Spanish-speaking and Latin American clientele.

As I mentioned in Chapter One, there are dozens of sites beyond YouTube to choose from, each with its own pros and cons depending on the specific traits and needs of your project. Some factors to take into consideration when choosing a host site are limitations on video length and limitations on uploading time. Many sites have ceilings on these elements, such as no video longer than 10 minutes or a maximum upload time of 1 hour. If your project is longer than YouTube allows or your upload time exceeds a site's limits, you may need to look elsewhere to find the host site that fits your needs.

Even if your project is short and requires only ordinary support, it behooves you to consider the full spectrum of sites available to you. Stock your product everywhere and anywhere it might attract viewers. Unlike the business world, where Kroger or Safeway may not take your product if you also supply it to the competition, most video sites are nonexclusive. They place no restrictions on the number of host sites where you can post your work.

The only circumstance under which you should consider restricting the number of sites where you post your work is if you think the cumulative number of viewers has to hit a certain threshold in order for you to split ad revenue with the site host. For instance, if a host site will split ad revenue with you once your video receives a minimum of 40,000 unique viewers, and you think you may attract 60,000 total viewers, it makes little sense to post your work 12 different places and get 5,000 viewers here, 6,000 someplace else, and so on. But if your overall objective isn't ad revenue, then cast the net as wide as possible. You've got nothing to lose.

PUBLICIZING AND MARKETING YOUR SERIES

Just throwing your web series up on YouTube and hoping that people find it on their own makes about as much sense as singing in your shower with the window cracked open and hoping a record producer drives by, hears you, and signs you to a multi-million-dollar contract. Not going to happen.

The only way creative work gets discovered is if the creator — perhaps with the help of some partners — puts as much effort into publicizing and marketing his work as he put into creating it. For your creative efforts to attract an audience, the audience has to know the show exists, be drawn to watch it, and know where to find it.

Start with the obvious: your list of personal contacts. Send an e-mail to everyone in your address book asking them to check out your show. Even better, include a link to your video on YouTube so all they have to do is click and watch, right then, while the idea is fresh in their mind. Do the same on Facebook and any other social networking site you belong to: Post a notice about your great new show and include a link to it. In fact, post notices several times, perhaps every other day for a week or two. Some people check Facebook all the time, others only sporadically. You want to reach as many of your contacts as possible. Also, people's lives are busy. They may not have time to click through and watch your video when they read your announcement on a Monday, but they might have time on Wednesday or Saturday afternoon.

Okay, that's Step 1: direct solicitation to the people you already know. Good start, but don't stop there. What about all the people your contacts know beyond your own circle? Maybe you know 200 or 300 people. But each of them may know 200 people. If you could widen the net by having each of your 200 contacts reach out to their 200 contacts, you've just expanded your outreach from 200 potential viewers to 40,000 potential viewers. That's how viral video happens: through the exponential power of 100 people each telling 100 others about a video they liked and then, in turn, each of them telling another 100 people about a video, and so on and so on, until the audience is magically multiplied from hundreds to hundreds of thousands or perhaps even millions.

I don't mean to suggest that by sending out a quick e-mail and one Facebook posting you will instantaneously have a loyal audience of millions for your work. There will be attrition along the way. Not all 200 of your contacts will watch your video, or like it, or serve as volunteer

PR flacks for you by urging all their contacts to watch your show. But you'll get a hell of a lot more viewers by enthusiastically and aggressively touting your show than by sitting on your hands and hoping the world will somehow stumble upon your work.

Are there any other large groups you belong to? Your church, perhaps, or some online hobby group like acoustic guitar players or model airplane enthusiasts? If so, and if they have an online forum or newsletter, then by all means post your link and promo blurb there as well.

It's even worth considering making a flyer about your show, with the YouTube link, and passing it out in front of your local supermarket or coffee house, or even dropping it in the neighbors' mailboxes. What have you got to lose? If you don't ask, you don't get. If you do, well, who knows? Even a dozen new viewers could eventually multiply into hundreds of loyal new fans when they tell their friends who also watch your show, like it, and pass the word along.

In short, do anything and everything you can to spread the word about your show. Felicia Day, creator and star of *The Guild*, made bookmarks hyping her show and left them anywhere she could, including a stack at her dentist's reception desk and several in every public restroom she went into. Leave no stone (or roll of bathroom tissue) unturned.

Finally, it's important to be as disciplined and professional about publicity and marketing as you were during the writing and producing of your series. Just as with your story and script, your marketing and publicity plan should be written down, in black and white, rather than just kept in your head. When you rely on memory or whatever pops into your brain and happens to stick, it's a recipe for sloppiness, forgetfulness, and less than adequate follow-through. However, if you write down exactly how you plan to market your series — a bullet point list is a good way to go — then you not only eliminate the chance of forgetting things, you increase the chance that missing pieces of the plan will become evident to you. You can also share your marketing and publicity plan with fellow video makers or even marketing people you know who may have further suggestions or improvements to offer. By all means, if you know someone who is a marketing expert, take advantage of this contact and her expertise. Show her your plan and ask what she thinks. A simple suggestion from her could mean thousands more viewers for you.

FESTIVALS AND CONTESTS

For the past several decades, the hundreds of film festivals held all over the world have been a tried and true method for independent filmmakers to have their work seen and discovered by film fans and industry professionals alike. Festival exposure, especially for films that won awards at the festival, often led to wider distribution, sometimes by major film studios. This distribution, in turn, led to larger audiences for these award-winning festival films and jump-started the professional careers of the filmmakers.

In recent years, dozens of independent TV festivals have sprung up, hoping to provide the same exposure and advancement opportunities for independent TV artists. These festivals almost always include categories for web TV projects. In fact, some festivals are devoted specifically and entirely to web series. The projects that are nominated for prizes at festivals are commonly scouted by major web video sites and other producers looking for the next hot show. Maybe they'll buy your show, or post it and promote it. Or maybe they're impressed by your voice or your writing and propose working on developing a new series together. In either case, it's a boost for you and your show. (See the interviews with web series creators in Chapter Fifteen for examples of how festival exposure has led to greater opportunities for many creators.)

So research the festival scene (changing and growing by the minute) and submit your pilot or series to any festivals that seem appropriate. Some of the more well-known festivals as of this writing are:

- New York Television Festival: *www.nytvf.com*
- Independent Television & Film Festival: *www.itvf.org*
- LAWEBFEST: *www.lawebfest.com*
- New Media Film Festival: *www.newmediafilmfestival.com*
- Marseille Web Fest: *www.marseillewebfest.com*

- Hollyweb Web Series Festival: *www.hollywebfestival.com*
- Celebrate the Web: *www.celebratetheweb.com*
- First Glance Film Festival: *www.firstglancefilms.com*
- Melbourne WebFest: *www.melbournewebfest.com*

And by the time you read this, there could well be dozens more festivals featuring content made for the Web. So fire up your search engine, type in "web series festivals," and submit away.

SHOULD YOU CREATE YOUR OWN WEBSITE?

In most cases, you and your show are better served by posting it on You-Tube and other established video hosting sites. They have established audiences of devoted video fans, sophisticated search engines designed to help prospective viewers find your show, and an experienced staff dedicated to handling all technical problems 24/7 at no cost to you. Unlike trying to decide whether to own your own car or rely on public transportation, this would be more like deciding between owning, maintaining, and paying for your own car versus having someone drive you wherever you want to go, whenever you want to go, in a really nice car, for free. It's a no-brainer. There's absolutely no reason for you to go to the expense and trouble of creating, maintaining, and promoting your own website dedicated to just your little Internet TV series. Unless…

Well, there are several circumstances where it might make sense to have your own dedicated website. For instance, if your show is interactive or solicits viewer suggestions for where the story might go next, then you would need to create a website for the series that could also handle that sort of regular communication process. Or if your series aspires to have a social networking aspect to it (like *Quarterlife* or *Showbizzle*), then obviously you would need to create a site that accommodated both video hosting and the infrastructure to serve the desired social networking functions. Also, if your series had any unusual technical requirements that aren't available on one of the existing video hosting sites — extremely high resolution needs, say, or specific animation software, that type of thing — then you'd need to build a site to order with the required technical specs in order to fully serve your series. Finally, if your web series is connected to a product or service and is intended to promote that business, then it might make great sense to connect the web series to the website for the business.

But in most cases, putting time, money, and aggravation into building a site merely to exhibit your short-form Internet series is unnecessary and unwise. Point, click, upload, sit back, relax, and let YouTube do the driving while you put all your time, money, and effort into creating more episodes or your next series.

SELLING AND MARKETING YOURSELF

You've made a cool web series and want people to watch it. This is only natural: You've created something you're proud of and want others to see it. But building an audience for this one show is only a fraction of the big picture. You're also trying to build something more permanent and ongoing: a career. Well, good news. Having created this web series means you now have an important and useful tool for building that career. Because when you ask people to watch the show, you're also asking them to check out your various skills.

Think of it as a general audition. Let's say you send a link or DVD of your series to a cable network executive. They watch it and like it, but they send you an e-mail saying that much as they liked the show, it's not what they are in the market to buy right now. Naturally, you'll be disappointed. I would be. All of us, when we show our work to someone, basically want one response: "You are a freakin' genius, and this is the greatest thing I've ever seen." Unfortunately, that sort of unrestrained praise happens about never. In fact, in the arts, you hear "no" at least a hundred times for every time you hear "yes." But getting rejected doesn't mean those hundred submissions were a waste of time. They're just part of the process, a bump along the road to "yes." But more important, there are times when "no" truly does just mean "not now but maybe later." The cable exec who turned down your work might be in a start-up situation where the first material he buys needs to have stars or well-known producers — it's what his investors expect and demand. Alas, your show has no stars, and you are an unknown. You and your show are, to use a technical term, shit out of luck. The exec turns you down. But maybe a year from now, his channel launched, his financial backers feeling more confident about his creative choices, he's ready to take a chance on some shows from unknowns and remembers how much he liked your show. Or maybe he buys several shows from established players and needs one more show to fill out the half-hour or hour, and he remembers your show. Or maybe he gets pitched an idea by a known actor who isn't a writer, the exec loves the idea and the actor, and he thinks back to how much he loved the writing in your show and hires you to create something for this actor.

Building a career is a marathon, not a sprint. It happens small increment by small increment, over decades, not weeks. Slow and steady wins the race. Behind almost every Hollywood headline about overnight success lies a story of years of training, hard work, and preparation. It's true for writers, directors, actors — everybody. So rather than cursing the length of the journey, you'll have a much better time — and probably more success — if you embrace it as the trip of a lifetime and enjoy the scenery and ups and downs along the way.

It's also important to point out that dedicated self-promotion does not mean *relentless* self-promotion. If the only reason you ever contact anyone is when you want something from them, well, that gets really annoying over time. You are now part of a community: the creative community in general and the web series community in particular. And, to paraphrase President John F. Kennedy, "Ask not what your community can do for you, ask what you can do for your community." Some of the time you devote to marketing should be spent giving to others. In addition to writing e-mails and Facebook posts asking people to watch your shows, spend a little time promoting someone else's show that you admire. Maybe you know the person, maybe you don't. It doesn't matter. You're paying it forward, building good karma, doing what's right for another artist.

Or let's say you've submitted your series to one of those festivals I mentioned, but the show didn't get into the festival. Go to the festival anyway. Watch the shows that did get in. Some you won't like, and you'll find yourself howling, "They took that piece of crap but didn't take mine?!" Get over it. It's part of show biz — part of life, for that matter. Sometimes praise and riches will be heaped on the unworthy. Others at the festival will be raving about something you think is garbage. It'll drive you crazy, and you'll curse the festival judges and perhaps even the human race, I promise. But so what? You'll also see some work that will knock you out, that will inspire you and stimulate new creative ideas of your own. And you'll get the chance to meet creators who inspire you. Go up to them, introduce yourself, tell them how much you liked their work. They will thank you. Give them your card and say if they ever need help on a project, you'd be happy to offer it. For free — just because you admire their work. Trust me, you'll get far more value out of the experience than if you got a bit of cash. You'll expand your creative network. You'll learn from people more experienced than you. And the part of me that went to Berkeley in the seventies still believes that the more you give to the universe, the more it gives back. Is that a crazy idea? Maybe. But no more crazy than believing we can create whole worlds in our mind and turn them into web series.

FOR TEACHERS

The natural place to begin is by demonstrating how to upload a video to YouTube, with particular emphasis on maximizing potential viewer outreach by being thoughtful and creative when assigning tags. Next, take an online tour of the various sites with the students to give them a sense of which ones have special features such as high resolution capability, longer running time, or larger total file size limits.

When it comes to social networking and its utility as a marketing and publicity tool, some of your students may actually be able to teach you (and the rest of the class) a thing or two. In addition to your own presentation, it's definitely worth going around the room and asking the students to share creative ways they or their friends have used Facebook, Twitter, or other technologies to network and publicize their work and accomplishments. Social networking is growing explosively and changing by the minute, and students are often among the early adopters on the cutting edge of this revolution.

This is also a topic where inviting a guest speaker — someone whose expertise is marketing and publicity — can make great sense. You are probably a filmmaker, not a marketing person. But just like your students, you must embrace the reality that today's film auteur must also be a film entrepreneur. You can model for the students the notion of reaching out to other experts by inviting them to visit your classroom.

Convincing the students that building a career is a long-term endeavor is always tricky. Their natural enthusiasm and passion make them want to succeed NOW. I once told my students that to become a film or TV director, a writer or producer on a network TV show, a senior studio or network executive, or other highly accomplished creative person, they should expect it to take about 15 to 20 years. "Fifteen years?!" they exclaimed with great horror and indignation. I thought they were going to throw the furniture at me. It's the blissful and, in many ways, useful ignorance of youth. They have no idea how long and difficult a journey they are embarking on, and this is good. It gives them the courage to jump in the pool and start swimming. And the more effort they invest, the more committed they'll be to making it to the finish.

14 BUSINESS USES OF WEB SERIES

To paraphrase Charles Dickens, it is the best of times and the worst of times in the world of television. If you're a viewer, it's definitely the best of times. Never have there been more programming choices. Whatever type of show you crave, there's a channel for it — in fact, several channels, some on cable, some on the Internet. And the wireless world means you have access to this infinite universe of entertainment choices wherever and whenever you want, on your laptop, your tablet, or even your phone. And the cherry on top of all this is the fact that DVRs and other technology now make it easier than ever to zip right past those annoying commercials — which is, of course, what makes it the worst of times for advertisers, who have spent the past 75 years relying on television as the best way to reach a mass audience and persuade consumers to buy their products. For the business community and their barkers on Madison Avenue, the growing ability of consumers to avoid their messages is Excedrin Headache 1.

But the folks who created slogans like "Fly the Friendly Skies" and "Just Do It" aren't going away any time soon. They've just got a bit of a problem, and they know that the best way to solve any problem is with a little ingenuity and a catchphrase, so they've adopted the mantra, "If you can't beat 'em, join 'em." Welcome to the brave new world of branded entertainment, or "advertainment," where the commercial message is no longer an interruption but is part of the actual program content itself, seamlessly blended into the comedy or drama.

This isn't really a new phenomenon. As with all things TV, everything "new" is really just a fresh twist on an old idea. Some point to BMW's acclaimed series of short Internet films *The Hire* — featuring top-notch Hollywood production values, Clive Owen as "The Driver," and, of course, lots of gleaming Beemers — as the official beginning of the branded entertainment trend, but branded entertainment has been part of television since the very beginning. In the 1940s and 1950s, the sponsor's name was often right there in the title of the show: *Gillette Cavalcade of Sports*, or *Philco Television Playhouse*, or the first breakout hit on TV, *The Milton Berle Show*, otherwise known as *Texaco Star Theater*, where every episode began with four actors dressed as Texaco service station attendants singing about the glories of Texaco gas.

From the sponsor's perspective, it was only right that their product should be featured up front and showcased throughout the program. After all, the sponsor was footing the bill for the production. Viewers just sat back in their living rooms, flipped on their sets, and got to watch the show for free. Well, sort of for free. They did have to sit through the commercial messages, including those embedded in the entertainment product itself. Nowadays, however, this once captive audience can hop, zap, or fast forward its way right around the commercials. So if advertisers want their messages heard (and believe me, they do, as they annually spend hundreds of billions of dollars on ads and airtime, with the biggest chunk going to TV), then they'll have to find new and better ways to get viewers to *watch ads voluntarily* and perhaps even *seek them out* as their own form of entertainment.

If you find yourself saying that's crazy, nobody would go out of his way to watch commercials if he didn't have to, then I have two words for you: Super Bowl. Time and again, the Big Game is the highest-rated TV show of the year, and people spend just as much time watching and talking about the ads as they do the football game. For some non–football fans, the only reason to watch the broadcast is the commercials. And, as an added bonus, the ads get viral reruns on the Internet and on dozens of shows devoted to ranking (and giving fresh exposure to) these commercial messages.

"But that's different," you may cry. "Those ads are good — they're clever and entertaining."

Exactly! Give the people ads they want to watch — ads that entertain, that give the viewer a return for his time instead of just abusing it — and not only will they watch ads, they'll talk about them, repost them on Facebook, and serve as an unpaid sales and marketing force on your behalf. This is easier said than done. But why should it be any easier to make a hit commercial than a hit TV show?

It's also worth noting that businesses can promote themselves and their products without making ads per se. Pure entertainment made for the Web can also work well. Sponsoring one or more shows designed to appeal to your customers can work. The small business insurance company Hiscox sponsored the web series *Leap Year*, which featured fictional tech start-ups competing for funding from a mystery investor. The first season's 10 episodes drew 5 million views, enough to convince Hiscox to pony up for Season Two.

Another approach is to create web series that naturally provide a platform to display or demonstrate a product or service within the story. Maybe the characters always meet at the same pizza joint to discuss their problems — and maybe that pizza joint is willing to put up a few bucks in exchange for an establishing shot of their place in every episode. Or maybe they'll just provide the locations for free in exchange for promotional mention. Courtney Zito, star, producer, and creator of the award-winning web series *Hollywood Girl*, has been brilliant in obtaining locations, music, and other production necessities at no cost in exchange for promotional mention of the vendors. (See Chapter Fifteen for an interview with Courtney Zito.)

One of the most creative business uses of a web series was cooked up by Ric Viers, owner of the Detroit Chop Shop, a producer of sound effects for the film, TV, radio, and video gaming industry. Ric created the reality series *Detroit Chop Shop Video Diary*, a behind-the-scenes look at the work his interns do in recording and creating sound effects. Ric's found a way to take what might be a mundane task — recording sound effects — and has turned it into something not only informative but entertaining. In one episode they go to a shooting range to record gunshot sounds, and for some of the interns, this is the first time they've ever fired a gun. Watching as a young woman feels the kickback from a .44 magnum for the first time is great reality TV — and a great way for Ric to recruit future interns and to grow his business. Season One brought in enough new customers that Ric dove right into making Season Two and then Season Three.

CAN YOU SELL AND ENTERTAIN AT THE SAME TIME?

Of course you can. We see examples of this all the time on traditional TV. Some of my favorites are the Old Spice commercials with buff, shirtless, baritone-voiced Isaiah Mustafa: "Hello, ladies. Look at your man. Now back to me. Now back at your man—now back to me. Sadly, he isn't me. But if he stopped using lady-scented body wash and switched to Old Spice, he could smell like me." I'm not alone in my admiration of these spots. The original, which began on traditional TV, has over 41 million YouTube views as of this writing. Its Internet-only Old Spice ad cousins have attracted many more millions of views.

You may have other favorites. Maybe you're a fan of those e-Trade ads with the talking baby. Or maybe you're tickled by the GEICO gecko. The point is, making ads that people clamor to watch is clearly possible. But we also know it's more rare than common.

So what makes these ads entertaining? What qualities do they have that compel audiences to watch them and feel entertained rather than harangued by a used car salesman? Just as with full-length TV shows (and movies and novels and popular songs), there isn't a simple formula or precise recipe that guarantees success. But I think there are certain principles and common traits that entertaining ads share, and those traits are worth examining.

HUMOR SELLS

Especially on the Internet. Just check your own inbox or Facebook news feed: The number one thing that people seem to share virally is something that makes them laugh. Take, for instance, two extremely popular Internet video ads: the Isaiah Mustafa Old Spice spots and the "Uncle Drew" ad for Pepsi, featuring NBA sensation Kyrie Irving. The core value that catapulted each to the rank of viral all-star is humor. Both spots are just flat-out, laugh-out-loud funny. Do they have other values? Sure. Kyrie Irving is a major basketball star, and his athleticism is plainly on display in the ad. And the Old Spice ads have some mega-cool visual effects that seamlessly transport Mr. Mustafa from the shower to a boat to a horse. Not to mention the fact that Mr. Mustafa is a good-looking dude with the body of a Greek god. But the main value in each case is still undeniably laughter. And although there is no such thing as a guaranteed formula for success, "yuks = bucks" comes pretty close.

CHARACTERS THAT CONNECT WITH CUSTOMERS

In Chapter Three we discussed the vital importance of compelling characters — especially a compelling central character — to the success of a web series. Well, that principle doesn't go away just because the story you're telling also has the goal of selling a product. The audience still must connect with the character if you want them to go along with the story and invest in it emotionally. In his book *StoryBranding: Creating Stand-Out Brands through the Power of Story*, advertising guru Jim Signorelli outlines what he calls the six Cs of connecting an audience with your brand. The first C is Collecting the Backstory: doing the basic research on the market for your product. But the next two Cs are all about character: Characterize the Brand and Characterize the Prospect. Let's focus on the first. When you create a central character for your advertainment video or branded web series, you are, in essence, characterizing your brand. Isaiah Mustafa's Old Spice Guy conveys these character traits: appealing, confident, friendly, good sense of humor, young, outgoing, sexy. You could probably add another half-dozen adjectives to the list, but you get the idea. He's the very definition of a man desirable to women, and, by implication, you will be, too, if you just slap on some Old Spice products.

Character is also the best way to employ the adage "Show, don't tell." Seeing is believing, and when we see Mr. Mustafa as the embodiment of sexy self-confidence with an appealing side of self-deprecating humor — well, let's just say it makes a far more compelling case for the benefits of using Old Spice body wash than any list of adjectives ever could.

TELL A REAL STORY

Just because you have only a short amount of time doesn't mean you can't tell a real story. One of my favorite examples of a complete story in 30 seconds is a commercial for Internet service provider AOL. It features a dad trying to deal with his 18-month-old son, who is crying his head off. First, Dad tries to distract the boy with toys, but the kid just keeps bawling. Dad flips open his laptop and tries showing the kid a cartoon. Still no success. Then, in desperation, he types "Supermodels in Swimwear" into the search box. A red-hot, bikini-clad babe pops onto the screen, and the young boy instantly stops crying. He and Dad are mesmerized, grinning at the hottie on the screen. Suddenly, the front door to the apartment swings open and the bikini babe walks in, flashing a welcoming smile, making the men even giddier. Just when you think this is the most sexist ad you've ever seen, the bikini babe smiles back and announces, "Mommy's home." And now it all makes perfect sense. The kid isn't a junior horndog. He just misses his mommy.

It's a perfect three-act story with an inciting incident, central problem, rising action with escalating complications, and, finally, a climax and resolution. Not to mention the fact that it makes great use of humor. And all this happens in just 30 seconds.

Giving the audience a complete story isn't just an abstract goal, a box to check off because some stuffy academic makes you do it. Giving the audience a complete story is part of the implicit bargain you made with them when you asked them to click on your video. You asked them for their time; the very least you can do is leave them satisfied with how they spent their time. It's good filmmaking, and it's good business. And it leaves your audience with a positive feeling not only about how they spent their time but about your brand or product.

GIVE THE CUSTOMER VALUE FOR HIS TIME

One of the most effective ways for advertisers and businesses to connect with prospective customers is by letting those customers know that you share similar sensibilities. Your sense of humor strikes them as funny as well. You know what entertains them, what compels them to click through and spend time on the Internet. Web series are an outstanding way to communicate that message, especially if they are soft sell, that is, they emphasize entertainment rather than a commercial or sales message. Think of it as romancing your customers, dating them, if you will, by building a relationship with them first. Through an entertaining web series, you and your prospective customer get to spend some time together and see whether you enjoy each other's company. Then, after you've established that common bond of shared sensibility, then, perhaps, your prospect might be willing to take the relationship to the next level and become an actual customer.

Even though people continue to spend more and more time each day on the Internet, there are still only 24 hours in a day, some of which must be spent sleeping, eating, working, cursing how slow your browser is today, playing Angry Birds, and so on. So if you want folks to spend time watching your commercial message, you've got to make it worth their while. As discussed earlier, humor is one way to accomplish this. But there are others, such as providing useful information or giving the viewer an inside look at a world he's not normally part of. The Kyrie Irving "Uncle Drew" spots are a great example of this. Not only do they entertain us with the story of senior citizen Uncle Drew taking on all the young studs at the local playground basketball court and kicking their butts, but the spots also take us behind the scenes and show us exactly how the makeup artists used Hollywood magic and skills to turn 20-year-old Kyrie into a convincing version of 60-something Uncle Drew. Usually, the magician never reveals how he did the trick. So when he does take you behind the curtain, it's fascinating. When I watched the video for the first time, I felt like I got two for one: an entertaining short video about an old guy who can still soar above the rim and dunk over the cocky young punks, plus an Inside Hollywood video extra on makeup secrets and magic. I felt like I got my time's worth for the 5 minutes I invested. And I don't mean that facetiously. In today's world, if you want 5 minutes of someone's time, you better be holding up your end of things by providing real entertainment and real value.

By the way, for an up-to-the-minute look at which videos are connecting with audiences, go to *www.visiblemeasures.com/adage*, which lists the most popular ads from the previous week.

EVEN IF YOU'RE NOT A BUSINESS

What if you're not a business? Should you just skip this chapter? No way! Can business uses of web video still be of use to you if your interests are creative rather than commercial? You bet! And the reasons connect back to the reasons for creating for the web that we discussed way back in Chapter One: *opportunity*.

Business uses of web series are growing exponentially. This means that employment and creative opportunities in the field are growing exponentially as well, and this is great news for aspiring filmmakers.

Maybe you're burning with desire to write and direct but just don't have the funds to make even a micro-budget web series. Well, perhaps the answer to your financial problem is to get a business to fund your efforts by offering to create branded entertainment for them. Notice I said "for them." What I'm suggesting is a business proposition, not a plea for funding of your own detached creative effort. You are offering to take your creative talents and energies and put them toward creating a video or web series designed to drive customers toward a business. In exchange, the business will bankroll the effort, but only if you can show them how this effort can be to *their* advantage. So do some research. How have videos been used in your area to help increase business opportunities? The local angle on this is crucial, especially if you're approaching a local business. Telling your local sushi place how Pepsi's national campaign went viral and increased sales by 13% is irrelevant. The sushi place isn't national. But if you can show how video on local food or restaurant blogs is X% more effective than just print reviews, then you've got a reasonable sales pitch and a reasonable business plan for the sushi place.

That's Job One: making it clear what the financial backer will get out of the video. But what will you, the filmmaker and creator, get out of it? If you find yourself thinking, "Yeah, what the hell good will it do me to make some dumb local ad," then you're not seeing the big picture. For the creative person, applying your talents to videos intended for business provides at least four distinct opportunities for you:

- **It's a chance to show your stuff,** to demonstrate your ability to write for the screen and to tell a story visually. You're building a reel, establishing your bona fides as a director and a film professional. You're not just talking about it, you're doing it.
- **It's a chance to practice and improve your craft.** In his book *Outliers*, Malcolm Gladwell examines the common traits among people who achieved extraordinary success in their chosen field — people like the Beatles. One absolute constant is that they had all put in at least 10,000 hours practicing, developing and honing their skills by constantly performing their craft. The Beatles spent years playing 6- to 8-hour gigs at obscure clubs in Germany, getting a tiny, tiny bit better each night and learning thousands of invaluable lessons along the way. By the time they broke through, they were seasoned professionals. They were *ready* for prime time on a world stage. Will you be *ready* when your time comes? Only if you practice. My friend Neil Landau, a wonderful writer and teacher, says you have to get lucky to succeed in show business. But he defines luck as preparedness plus opportunity. When you're starting out, your job is to prepare — that is, to practice your craft as many hours a day as you can. If you can do this and build a reel at the same time — and maybe even get paid to do it — then you'd be a fool not to take advantage of that opportunity.
- **Work breeds other work.** Most jobs happen as a result of personal referral. While you're practicing, you won't be alone. You'll come in contact with dozens of other people: the crew, the client, the actors, on and on. They'll see firsthand what you can do. They'll get a sense of what it's like to work with you. And someday — you never know when or how — they may need someone to do some video work for them, and they'll think of you. Maybe somebody's brother is part of an up-and-coming indie band that wants to make

a music video, and they'll think of you. Or maybe the actress wants to make her own web series to showcase her talents but doesn't want to direct. All kinds of connections can happen, but only if you put yourself out there and show what you can do.

- **You might actually get paid to do what you love.** Okay, so making advertainment or even straight commercials isn't your dream job. But you've got to pay the bills somehow, right? If you have a chance to do that (or even just to supplement your income a bit to maybe fund that cool new web series you've got in mind), then I say that's a win–win. Nobody gets hired to direct anything because they're a charming barista. They get hired because they've proven they can direct, and they've got the reel and the pay stub to prove they've done it professionally.

FOR TEACHERS

If your primary area is business-related — marketing, advertising, public relations, or business communications — then I think the main value of this chapter (and this book as a whole) for your students is in expanding their understanding of the fundamentals of storytelling, especially visual storytelling. Your students will need to learn how to use the screenwriter's tool kit — things like character, conflict, basic story and scene structure, dialogue, and so on — and to put these tools to use in service of their marketing and sales objectives. Their command of these tools will need to be both analytical and practical. They will need to be able to articulate the principles of effective storytelling so that they can analyze and assess both finished work and work in progress. To that end, I suggest giving them both types of exercises.

- Exercise 1: Ask your students to write an analysis of a piece of online branded entertainment. Ask them to be specific in assessing how the storytelling elements like character, humor, and obstacles to the character attaining his goal serve the branding and sales goals.

- Exercise 2: Have your students create a script for a piece of branded entertainment. Then, perhaps, the class can discuss each script and analyze the elements that are most effective and least effective.

If, rather than marketing or sales, your primary area is film or video instruction, then I think your task is in communicating to your students the wisdom of embracing this burgeoning new area as a legitimate way to begin pursuing their dreams of becoming a film or TV professional. One way is to go through the reasons outlined at the end of this chapter. But I'd also encourage you to consider including a business-oriented writing or production assignment in the mix. Some students may find this a detour from what they really care about: pure fictional storytelling. But others may find this an eye-opening and horizon-expanding experience. Film and TV students tend to have a somewhat narrow view of the possibilities for their future: "I'm going to be the next George Lucas or Wes Anderson or Michael Bay." That's a fine dream, but given the hundreds of film programs across the country and the millions of film dreamers, well, do the math. Only a tiny, tiny fraction of students will ever attain that sort of success. But a substantial percentage can and do find a way to make a living via their creative filmmaking skills. And a substantial percentage of those will do it not at a Hollywood studio or major TV network but in the everyday business world.

15 INTERVIEWS WITH CREATORS IN THE WEB SERIES WORLD

The people I've interviewed come from a variety of backgrounds. Some have extensive Hollywood writing resumes and have sought to expand their career opportunities by creating for the Internet. Others have had a touch of success as actors and are looking to promote their acting careers while they grow their creative skills by writing, producing, directing, or all three. Some have self-funded their projects. Some have gotten the backing of major production companies. But all have two things in common. One, they have created original, compelling content for the Web. Two, in the process of creating for the Web, they have expanded their career horizons and invigorated themselves creatively.

These creators have a treasure trove of valuable experiences and insights to share and have been generous and forthcoming in doing so. They've rolled up their sleeves and wrestled with the challenges of creating for the Internet: creative, financial, and marketing challenges. Nike would love these people because despite all the challenges and hurdles, they just did it. I urge you to read the interviews and learn from them — and to pay back the favor by going online and checking out their work.

Read, learn, and enjoy!

BILL ROSENTHAL
TV Pro Finds a New Market for His Skills

Bill Rosenthal is a veteran TV writer and producer whose credits span several decades, from
the 1980s hit *Head of the Class* through *Sabrina
the Teenage Witch* right on up to the acclaimed
Showtime series *Nurse Jackie*. But the Internet and web series offered him something he
couldn't find in traditional television, even on
premium pay cable like Showtime. It offered
him the chance to tell a story in a new and
exciting form. And he just happened to have
been thinking about a story that was a perfect
fit for this new form.

BILL ROSENTHAL

Greetings from Home is the story of how one
military family copes with the fact that Mom is
thousands of miles away, stationed in the Middle East. It's told entirely in the
form of videos sent to Mom by her husband, their teenage children, and their
friends and relatives. It's a story filled with heart and humor — by turns both
moving and hilarious. And it's a story perfectly suited to the Internet because
it's about communicating in the Internet age.

ROSS BROWN: Tell us about *Greetings from Home*. What is it, and how did it
    come about?

BILL ROSENTHAL: Conceptually, there are two aspects of *Greetings from Home*
    that explain the series: The first is the premise, and the second is the
    device for how we tell our stories. Both are equally important. First, the
    basic premise: Our story is about the Griffins, a multigenerational military
    family. We open the day Pete, the husband and father, returns home to
    his family and civilian life after being injured while serving in Iraq. But
    Pete arrives to a big surprise — his wife, Patty, an Army nurse, has just
    been deployed — and the two actually miss one another. So here's this
    career tough-ass Army guy, injured, left to raise his two teenage children
    and contend with Patty's four outspoken and overly intrusive Army Wife
    neighbors. So imagine, if you will, Lieutenant James from *The Hurt Locker*
    confined to American suburbia, and you've got our premise. Now to our
    device: The webisodes (or called chapters) are seen through the eyes of
    Pete's wife, Patty, an Army nurse who's serving in Afghanistan 7,000 miles

away from her family and friends. They communicate by sending her on-line greetings or updates about the ins and outs of their daily lives. These greetings are then edited together in approximately 7-minute segments, each with their own story lines, that Patty watches on her laptop from a barracks on her base. And while the stories are seen through Patty's point of view, the audience never actually sees her. We're watching the series — and the events of the life she's left behind — along with her.

ROSS BROWN: Cool. Where did the idea first take root? Was it on the Internet or in another form?

BILL ROSENTHAL: The project was initially conceived as a half-hour television comedy that my co-creator, Bill Masters, and I wrote on spec and subsequently sold to 20th Century Fox. In our original conception, the family would make a 30-minute movie and send it to Mom, and Mom would watch it. Our feeling was we needed to tell this story — to acknowledge the American military family and maybe make a statement about the many costs of war, the way that $M^*A^*S^*H$ did in the seventies. By the way, my comparison to $M^*A^*S^*H$ is not to suggest that our script and Internet series ever got close to the quality of that fabled series, but rather as an illustration of our goal, lofty as it is. The script went through what I would describe as the typical development process, and by the time of our final draft, it resembled more of an old-school sitcom than something that reflected the times both in terms of content and style. As is the case with most scripts, this one faded away as well. But there was always something to the original idea that intrigued me, not to mention that the country was involved with two military conflicts — Iraq and Afghanistan — and there was essentially no mention of it anywhere on American television. For us, these were stories that needed to be told, especially if the country was ever going to engage in a dialogue about it. Around the same time, the evening newscasts and daily newspapers were filled with stories about how the use of technology was changing the way families communicated with their loved ones serving. All of a sudden there was Skype and iChat and everyone had smartphones that were recording everything about their lives and with these changes, *Greetings from Home* began to transition to something new and exciting.

ROSS BROWN: That's interesting. So in a sense, new technology created a new avenue for these stories — not just a new way to capture the story but a new way to tell the story, using video snippets as sort of the modern filmmaking equivalent to the epistolary novel, a novel comprised of a series of letters or other correspondence.

BILL ROSENTHAL: That's exactly right. What was so much fun about conceptualizing this was the content and the form meshed perfectly. Here we were, able to use all of the attributes of online communication to tell a story, and our conceit became the compiling of our character's messages or greetings into a narrative. This all looked great in our minds, but somehow we needed to get it on the screen. In this case, the computer screen, not the TV.

ROSS BROWN: Interesting. How did the show make it to the Internet?

BILL ROSENTHAL: Bill and I wrote a sample of what we were seeing and then shot a demo of it, with the goal being to show it around town with the hope that someone would want to make more. So, in the summer of 2010, we spent 4 days with an incredible cast and crew and made our sample. We felt great, charged up to make lots more of them. It wasn't particularly expensive; most of the cast and crew did it for free. And then we saw the first cut, and all that excitement went out the same window I quite frankly wanted to leap out of. It was awful.

ROSS BROWN: That's almost always the way it is with rough cuts — you almost always hate them. One of the things I say in the book about postproduction, to people who are new to the process, is that when you see the rough cut, your first instinct will be to throw up on your shoes.

BILL ROSENTHAL: And this one was no exception. Fortunately, the other Bill put his money into the thing so I could still afford a new pair.

ROSS BROWN: That's the nature of rough cuts. No matter how experienced you are, no matter how many times you remind yourself "it's just a rough cut," you always hate it because it's not finished work yet, and your brain can't help itself — it wants to see finished work.

BILL ROSENTHAL: And that's an important lesson I've experienced many times while working in traditional television but needed to relearn for this project. We worked on the edit for several months, trying all sorts of different paths, until all of a sudden it got, dare I say, pretty damn good. We found ourselves with a compelling demo and armed with a lot of ideas — by this point, we had been working on the thing on and off for a few years — now if we could just find someone to talk to. And this is where luck played a big role. Bill's wife is the "Berman" of BermanBraun, a television production company that was also establishing itself as an online supplier too. Their head of TV, Gene Stein, who had been a fan of the original television versions of the script, was very encouraging about what we were doing and passed it around the company. Before long, BermanBraun was doing a meet and greet with Larry Tanz, the president of Vuguru (Michael Eisner's Internet company), that's quickly blossomed into a leader in the world of webisodes. Tanz liked what he saw and wanted to talk about where we saw the project going.

ROSS BROWN: Okay. So now, you have a production company plus an Internet production company interested, and somehow between them, they funded the development of the script into, I believe, 12 chapters.

BILL ROSENTHAL: Yes.

ROSS BROWN: And each chapter is approximately 10 pages long or so.

BILL ROSENTHAL: Right. Yeah. Twelve chapters. Ten pages each. One hundred twenty pages to write, with some very specific budgetary limitations to keep in mind while doing so.

ROSS BROWN: How long did the writing process take?

BILL ROSENTHAL: From the time Vuguru and BermanBraun worked out their agreement to the first day of shooting was about 9 months. The process was identical to the television world. We started with some very general thoughts that had to be approved, wrote detailed outlines and then the scripts, some of which went through several drafts.

ROSS BROWN: Part of Vuguru's business model is to create modular projects so that each chapter can fit into a larger whole that they can potentially market as a movie, but that's not how your project really works.

BILL ROSENTHAL: We had heard that was their model, but *Greetings* didn't really fit that paradigm, and we were very honest about that from the outset. Not only did they ultimately agree, but [they] were very supportive throughout the process.

ROSS BROWN: What's different about writing for the Web than writing for half-hour television?

BILL ROSENTHAL: Well, first, the similarities. The story still has to start very fast. We did two story lines, sometimes three in each of our chapters. But with only 10 minutes per episode, there's even more urgency to make every moment count. Our jokes and story points had to land. With such time constraints, there is little room for error. I think it helped all of us become better writers.

ROSS BROWN: So short-form web series demand an extreme economy of storytelling.

BILL ROSENTHAL: Exactly.

ROSS BROWN: I want to ask you about the visual design for *Greetings from Home*. Because the central concept is that we're seeing the videos sent to Mom in Afghanistan, everything has to be from the perspective of one of the other character's cameras. There are no omniscient camera angles.

BILL ROSENTHAL: That's essentially the hook of the series.

ROSS BROWN: Why did you make that decision, and has it been limiting?

BILL ROSENTHAL: It's the part of the show that gave it the distinctive visual style we have. It's designed to have an authentic look. We wanted it to look like this could really be something that was being sent to a loved one. The cons of the device are it made every shot more of a challenge. One of the more demanding parts for Jared Drake, our director, was finding ways to give it a visual complexity that would also be believable as something shot by someone without the benefit of years of directing experience. Not the easiest task in the world. Additionally, our performers had to be on their game to hold the interest of the audience. Finally, and perhaps the most important trick we relied on, was our use of cutting to mine the comedy and keep the story moving forward.

ROSS BROWN: I thought one of the other assets of the style was it really reinforced the sense of the family's isolation from Mom and her separation from the family. As funny as the video messages are, there's also a constant sense that Mom is 7,000 miles away, and she misses her family and her family misses her. The visuals constantly remind us of that.

BILL ROSENTHAL: Yes, the series is (hopefully) funny. But equally important was that sense of heartbreak and longing of the situation. We watched a lot online series that were funny but didn't have much in the way of character depth. Our belief is in order for the audience to come back 12 times, we needed to give them a reason to care about the characters and their plight.

ROSS BROWN: I think that's one of the great successes of the show, that it effectively combines humor and genuine emotion. It's really heartening for me as an Internet television consumer because so much of Internet television is effectively sketch comedy, funny up to a point but a bit shallow. But because you managed to combine comedy and heart, it enriches the storytelling, and I think that's a real asset of the project and also a great sign for the future of Internet television.

BILL ROSENTHAL: I hope so.

ROSS BROWN: Having worked in standard television for so long, network half-hour television, what do you find attractive about working for the Web? You mentioned creative freedom, the willingness and ability to preserve your vision with fewer influences and pressures.

BILL ROSENTHAL: There was a lot of creative freedom that I personally hadn't experienced in several years. And I loved that we were making something we wanted to make. There was also a bit of a surprise in that the small budget made us think even more creatively than had we been working within the usual money of a TV show. We were also very lucky to have BermanBraun as our production partner on this. They gave us the kind of support writers usually only dream of. And Vuguru had our backs throughout the process.

ROSS BROWN: That's great. Last area I want to touch on is marketing, and I don't know if you've had these conversations with Vuguru and BermanBraun, but that is another huge challenge of the Internet. There is so much product out there, how do you make the audience aware of your project and get them to sample it? Do you know what some of the plans are for that?

BILL ROSENTHAL: That's the big question mark for the webisode form going forward. *Greetings* is being webcasted (is that the correct usage?) on AOL, and one of the frustrations is being one of literally hundreds of headlines, clips, etcetera, that appear on their home page. It's my series, yet I have a hard time finding it. We've been told success is determined by the number of combined streams, with 4 million being the target number. I don't know how we get there if the product is difficult to find. That's the big obstacle for the immediate future. We can hope for word of mouth, but I'm not sure that's a particularly realistic form of marketing in today's digital world.

ROSS BROWN: One of the things that happened in spring 2012 that has never happened before is that many of the major Internet TV outlets launched their upcoming season with a big presentation to advertisers in New York, just like the major broadcast networks have done for decades. Each May, the broadcast networks have what's called the upfronts to present their fall schedule and new shows to the advertising community. This year, for the first time, the online community had what they called the new fronts, and they did it in April, a month ahead of the broadcast networks. So that could be in your future.

BILL ROSENTHAL: The finances of this are fascinating, with great potential as the marriage between TV and Internet becomes more established. But it's still a tough road — look at the problems Facebook is having convincing advertisers their site is valuable. I'm assuming it's going to be; after all, where else do you have a billion eyeballs? But for the moment the profits are still in the future.

ROSS BROWN: Are you hoping *Greetings from Home* is a transition to a great new area of creativity for you: Internet television?

BILL ROSENTHAL: It's funny. There's been some talk of bringing it to television, which is of course where it started in script form, but it's such a perfect project for the Internet. My hope is the audience discovers it online, and we can make more. It was creatively inspiring. Now if only it could also be a bit more financially inspiring as well.

ROSS BROWN: Well, that's the hope of all Internet television creators: that there can be a viable business model.

CARY OKMIN
Branded Content: Part Ad, Part Web Series, All Creative

CARY OKMIN

In the late 1990s, Cary Okmin was just hitting his groove as a writer. After putting in several years as a production assistant and writer's assistant to sitcom writing staffs and honing his craft writing spec script after spec script, he'd broken through and landed a coveted spot on the writing staff of a prime-time network series. All systems were go. The future seemed bright. He'd stepped onto the success escalator and was ready to ride it to the top — the top being a chance to create his own successful sitcom someday. But as they say, life is what happens when you're making other plans. Suddenly, as the nineties headed toward the new millennium, sitcoms were out of vogue. Where a few years earlier there had been 80 sitcoms on the five broadcast networks, now there were only 20. Even scarcer were the type of family-oriented shows that formed the centerpiece of Okmin's resume. Like hundreds of other professional comedy writers, Okmin had to find another way to make a living.

But "another way" didn't mean giving up writing altogether. Because while the door to a career in network sitcoms was closing, a new career portal was opening: creating content for the Web. Okmin found his way to Disney's online enterprise and has worked steadily ever since, now finding himself on the cutting edge of the exciting new world of branded entertainment and content.

ROSS BROWN: Tell us about Toybox Entertainment and what you do here.

CARY OKMIN: Toybox Entertainment was originally a company that cut trailers for feature films and television shows. They're now looking to move into the branded entertainment and original content world, and that's why I was brought over from the Walt Disney Company to kind of spearhead that department and try and move them forward in that arena.

ROSS BROWN: I was going to say you also worked at Disney online and created a branded entertainment web series called *CeReality*, an online reality series designed to promote breakfast products. You made 100 episodes. Tell us about that show. How did it come about, and how did it evolve?

CARY OKMIN: That came about when I was at Disney (and Toybox was the production company, which led to my being here now). The ad sales team came to us at Disney Online and said they wanted to develop original content to promote both Kellogg's and Milk. It was a dual sponsorship, and they were looking to do something that wasn't overt product integration. They wanted something that was entertaining. They wanted to show the insanity that happens from the time a family wakes up to the time they get out the door to school and work. At first, the idea was to shoot a reality show: Find a real family and film them. But we quickly realized that might not be terribly compelling, and we'd be better off scripting the series.

ROSS BROWN: Right.

CARY OKMIN: So *CeReality* — a name I've never been crazy about — focuses on five different families, with about 20 episodes for each family. Each family's group of episodes had a unified style; one was soap opera, one horror, etcetera. Originally, we wanted to make each group of episodes serialized, so you'd have to watch them all to get the complete story. But in the end it was a mix: Some episodes were serialized, some stand alone.

ROSS BROWN: And where were they displayed?

CARY OKMIN: I believe Disneyfamily.com had the exclusive run of them, and then Milk and Kellogg's both run them on their sites. That's always one of the challenges of branded entertainment, deciding what platforms are best to promote the content that you have. Is it truly content? Is it a commercial?

ROSS BROWN: Well, that leads to my next question: How is branded entertainment different from traditional advertising?

CARY OKMIN: It varies. With *CeReality*, we went the sponsorship route. The Kellogg's name and logo were on the title card. They put up the money and the product itself. But the content itself was designed as entertainment, not a hardcore ad.

ROSS BROWN: Soft sell, so to speak.

CARY OKMIN: Clearly we were featuring families and breakfast products while still being as entertaining as possible. So, it becomes kind of a hybrid: part ad, part webisode.

ROSS BROWN: And there's range of branded entertainment. Some of it is very product focused, blatantly selling the product. But in other cases, the product is intentionally backgrounded so that the entertainment value is primary thing.

CARY OKMIN: At Disney Online, we always said that we wanted to be the tail wagging the dog. We wanted to create great content and let that quality sell the product. But different clients had different ideas about what they wanted.

ROSS BROWN: There's always a balancing act with branded entertainment between the entertainment desires and the marketing desires. Do you see your job as a creative person within this environment as trying to maximize the entertainment value in the name of then serving the marketing needs of the client?

CARY OKMIN: Yes. I'm relatively new to branded entertainment. I suppose everybody is for the most part. I think we all started out saying, "Oh, no, it's pure entertainment. We're not going to have any commercialism in this." And then, as you go along, you evolve and you realize a little salesmanship is not such a bad thing, and you figure out ways to maximize the entertainment while still being mindful of the business objectives of the client.

ROSS BROWN: Well, there's nothing worse for an advertiser than having someone say, "There was this fantastic commercial with this guy and a dog and this ball he's chasing." And then somebody asks, "What was the commercial for?" And the answer is, "I don't really know."

CARY OKMIN: Yep, not good.

ROSS BROWN: For branded entertainment to be effective, it must succeed on both fronts: entertainment and marketing.

CARY OKMIN: That's brings up a good point. The other day we were talking about the Kyrie Irving Pepsi video "Uncle Drew" (where young NBA star Kyrie Irving plays a sixty-something old man looking for a pickup basketball game at the park). It's really smart — funny, great production elements. Doesn't feel like an ad at all. I think that's the beauty of the Internet: You post great content, let it go viral based on its entertainment value. It may be weeks before someone figures out, hey, that's a total Pepsi commercial. But by that time, millions have seen it and are reposting it.

ROSS BROWN: Effective marketing has a lot in common with effective storytelling in general. It engages the viewer, makes him ask curious questions like "What's this for?" And if you're engaged, then you might actually remember the answer to that question. "Oh, it's for Pepsi, it's for McDonald's, it's for United Airlines," whatever it is.

CARY OKMIN: Yeah. Absolutely.

ROSS BROWN: Clearly branded entertainment is going to be a huge part of the marketing and advertising future as more and more people have DVRs and ways to avoid traditional advertising messages. The advertisers are still going to want to get the messages out there.

CARY OKMIN: It's not just branded entertainment, it's all marketing and advertising. In today's world, you have to make it compelling and entertaining, or the audience will move on. The good news is that when you succeed in making it entertaining, the audience will watch even though they know it's a commercial. Take the Jack in the Box spots with that offbeat character representing the company. I know they're ads, but they're funny, so I watch.

ROSS BROWN: Well, that's a core storytelling principle. You've got to have a compelling character at the center of the piece. We follow traditional television series because we relate to the characters, or we find them amusing. And so, if you think the Jack in the Box guy is interesting or the Burger King king or the GEICO lizard or whatever it is, then you'll watch.

CARY OKMIN: I agree.

ROSS BROWN: What sort of things are different for you as a branded entertainment writer? Not only writing from the marketing perspective but just having a much shorter time frame to tell the story?

CARY OKMIN: The story is always the most important thing. Whether it's a feature film or a 10-second spot, story always comes first.

ROSS BROWN: One of the examples that I use with my students of great three-act storytelling in a 30-second commercial is a spot for AOL. The commercial is about a dad trying to deal with his crying toddler son. First Dad tries to distract him with toys — no success. Then Dad goes to the computer and tries a cartoon — still no success. Finally, in desperation, Dad types "supermodels in swimsuits" into the search box, and this gorgeous bikini-clad woman fills the screen — and the boy instantly stops crying and smiles at the screen, transfixed. Dad is smiling, too. And then, the front door of the apartment opens up and the model walks in, smiles, and says, "Mommy's home." It's wonderful storytelling. You thought it was about male bonding over a swimsuit model, but it was really about a kid who missed his mother. It was a complete, funny, and compelling story in 30 seconds.

CARY OKMIN: And you were entertained — and remembered the name of the product.

ROSS BROWN: When you work in branded entertainment, what types of crews do you have? Do they work both in advertising and branded entertainment and then sometimes, they're over at a feature film or TV show?

CARY OKMIN: Branded is different only in terms of what the message is. The filmmaking skills and requirements are still the same: composition, lighting, editing, production design, all intended to convey and reinforce the story. Obviously the budget is different on a big studio feature, and branded entertainment crews may be nonunion rather than union, but it's still visual storytelling.

ROSS BROWN: And the quality of the HD video image has improved by leaps and bounds. It used to be if you were shooting video, you were probably doing a bad local car commercial. But now, I mean, David Fincher used digital HD on *The Girl with the Dragon Tattoo*.

CARY OKMIN: One of the luxury car companies — I think it was Porsche — did a contest where they challenged film students to shoot a commercial entirely on their iPhone. The results were really beautiful, and the crew is probably two people, one person that drove the car.

ROSS BROWN: I preach to my students that while branded entertainment might not be their ultimate dream job, it's an opportunity and entry point for them. Especially for cinematographers or any of the craft positions, you're far more likely to get a job as a DP in branded entertainment than you are on a feature film or a TV series.

CARY OKMIN: If I'm 24 years old and want to work on a feature film, I'll probably have to be a PA. But on a low-budget commercial, well, they might say, "Grab the camera, we need help doing this; we need your hands on." I'd taking that hands-on camera job every time.

ROSS BROWN: You began in network television. How did you make the transition to writing for the Internet?

CARY OKMIN: I have no idea how I got here. I was on a Nickelodeon show, and I think that went down, and I interviewed with Disney to be a writer for their Parks and Resorts Online division. From there I moved over to Disney.com, and my creative director over there knew writing, and we tried to figure out how to best utilize both of our backgrounds and our talents. We started developing content, experimenting and also checking out what other people were trying. A great example is this one young lady. Somebody had sent me a video she'd made. She'd taken the audio track for *Ocean's Eleven* and mashed it with *The Great Muppet Caper* and created this great trailer. So we contacted her and did this great piece with her called *Muppet Treasure Island*. Then we created something with the Muppets and *High School Musical*. Disney brought her out from Parsons School of Design.

ROSS BROWN: And how old was she?

CARY OKMIN: At that time, she was a college student. I love that story because it just shows how the Internet really is about opportunity. And if you take the creative initiative and put something out there that's got quality to it, it opens doors for you in the business. And if you make great branded entertainment content, they'll hire you to write or direct other things.

ROSS BROWN: How has writing for branded entertainment helped you grow as a writer in general?

CARY OKMIN: Certainly, being forced to write economically has helped. But I also think being forced to collaborate with clients has helped, too. If you're a writer, you're always going to get notes from somebody, whether it's a client or a network or studio executive. You have to learn how to be collaborative and creative at the same time.

ROSS BROWN: It must also be exciting to be a part of something new (branded entertainment) where there aren't so many rules and people are still trying to define what it is, how to do it, and so on. Sort of like the early days of live television where no one knew what it was supposed to be. You get to be part of the group of pioneers finding out what it can be.

CARY OKMIN: It can also be kind of scary because it's mostly uncharted territory. But it is a lot of fun and it is exciting, as long as you can embrace the notion that failure isn't a disaster, it's just an opportunity to learn and improve.

ROSS BROWN: You can't be afraid to fail if you're going to be working in a creative area. What do you do to stay current in a field that's changing so rapidly? What sort of tools do you use to keep yourself fresh and aware of the latest trends out there?

CARY OKMIN: I subscribe to a whole bunch of newsletters from — there's one called Cynopsis, which is great, and then I have one for sports, one for media, one for the Internet. The best thing to do is just jump on YouTube and wander around.

ROSS BROWN: Of course. I mean, if you were an art student, you'd go to art museums and see what the great masters have done there. I think if you're going to be an Internet artist, you have to see what the Internet artists are doing.

CARY OKMIN: I can't tell you the amount of creative inspiration I've gotten just because someone sent me a link or I saw something posted on Facebook. Even something as simple as that can trigger an idea, help you solve a creative problem you're working on. Something will inspire you on some level.

ROSS BROWN: You also have a young teenage son. Do you use him for inspiration or pay attention to what he's viewing in online entertainment?

CARY OKMIN: All the time. I might sit back and watch him and his friends as they talk about videos they like.

ROSS BROWN: I have a 4-year-old grandson who said something that would delight advertisers and marketers all over the world recently. His parents announced they were all going to Costco, and the 4-year-old said, "Can we buy stuff we don't need?"

CARY OKMIN: That's the thing about kids: They're born consumers.

ROSS BROWN: Thank you for your time and insights. I really appreciate it.

CARY OKMIN: You're welcome.

COURTNEY ZITO
Hollywood Girl Moves Behind the Camera

Courtney Zito knows that being a working actress means you have to work all the time — auditioning, honing your craft, taking whatever parts you can get as you build your resume. She also knows that being a smart working actress means expanding your horizons, skills, and connections by working behind the camera as well as in front of it. So while she was acting in a recurring role on the Nickelodeon series *True Jackson, VP* she also worked on the show in several production capacities, such as audience PA and production secretary. And she loved it — loved it so much she realized she was born not only to act but to be a producer. She combined the two by creating her own web series, *Hollywood Girl*, based on her experiences as an actress trying to make it even though she

COURTNEY ZITO
Photo courtesy of Erzen Design
(*www.erzendesign.com*).

doesn't fit into the stick-thin blonde starlet mold. Her award-winning web series is now in its third season, and Zito's career is on the rise, both behind the camera and in front of it. And most of all, it has invigorated her creatively. She's written her first feature film screenplay, has her own production company, La Dolce Zito Productions, all while working a full-time gig at a busy TV production company and continuing to write, produce, and star in *Hollywood Girl*.

If doing all these things at once sounds impossible, well you haven't met Courtney Zito. She's passionate, driven, upbeat, and a geyser of creative energy. In short, you can tell right away that the future is very bright for this Hollywood girl.

ROSS BROWN: Tell us how *Hollywood Girl* came about.

COURTNEY ZITO: I had been paying my dues for about 10 years when I began working on a show with Andy Gordon called *True Jackson, VP*. I had been doing freelance work as a PA, so I started as an audience PA and somehow ended up filling in on a temp basis for their production secretary. Then, when the job ended, they wanted to keep me around, so they used me on camera as a recurring background player. One thing led to another, and they used me every week and would write me into little bits. I even did some stand-in work for them. It was great. I've always loved sitcoms. I'm a big TV junkie, and I just started absorbing as much as I could. It was multicamera, and I was getting the opportunity to work with people like director Gary Halverson. It was just amazing to watch these pros at work.

ROSS BROWN: The guys from my generation of sitcom writers and directors.

COURTNEY ZITO: Exactly. I was like a sponge essentially, always listening and watching, just trying to learn everything I could because I thought, well, this will make me a better actress. Then, the show got canceled.

ROSS BROWN: Right.

COURTNEY ZITO: It was sad, because I loved working on the show. But around that time, I started thinking I want to do a project of my own. But I'd never directed. I'd never written anything. I had no idea where to even start. First I thought I'd write a book about my dating exploits in L.A. And then, I kept having all these crazy things happen in my life. I don't know if you ever saw the pilot episode, but that's like an actual day in my life.

ROSS BROWN: Losing your ATM card —

COURTNEY ZITO: And then forgetting to pump the gas —

ROSS BROWN: Right.

COURTNEY ZITO: I remember writing about that day on Facebook, and everybody was just like, "This is crazy. Your life is so funny. Your life is like a sitcom." So I decided to start a web series. I didn't know exactly what that meant. I just knew it was something I could do myself and air it on YouTube. I wrote a pilot and I shot it, and I aired it to kind of see if there was an interest, if people would like it, and everyone went crazy and thought it was so cute and everything. So I kept writing and made more episodes.

ROSS BROWN: *Hollywood Girl* has had a lot of success, winning numerous awards at festivals. Has that led to other opportunities for you, either in front of or behind the camera?

COURTNEY ZITO: Both. I've gotten several roles because people saw *Hollywood Girl*. But it also has led to a lot of stuff behind the camera, additional projects of mine. I did a Doritos spec commercial for their contest, and it went viral on YouTube, which was cool. And then we actually won best spec commercial at the International Television Festival in July. And I just finished my first feature screenplay.

ROSS BROWN: So this is invigorating you creatively.

COURTNEY ZITO: Absolutely. I have always been a creative person, but producing the web series has given me the confidence to know that I can have my own projects. So I've started a little production company, La Dolce Zito Productions.

ROSS BROWN: It's a great name — very clever. Do you feel that doing these other jobs — writing, editing, and so on — has made you a better actress?

COURTNEY ZITO: Absolutely, absolutely. Especially editing. You just see things from a totally different perspective. It's made me a better actress and a better writer.

ROSS BROWN: Two-part question: One, how much of Quinn, the main character of *Hollywood Girl*, is you, Courtney? And two, do you now find yourself when you're out there in the world, auditioning, going on dates, living your life, saying, "Hmm, I wonder how I can use this in the show?"

COURTNEY ZITO: I say all the time that making a show about my life has made me take myself less seriously — in a really good way. The day of the ATM machine and driving away without the gas, I was screaming, and I was so mad at myself, and now, when stuff happens, I'm just like, "Oh, that would be a great episode." I really am like Quinn in so many ways. She's my alter ego. She's a little more exaggerated for the sake of comedy, but pretty much everything that you see in an episode is drawn from my real life in some way. In Season Two, the first three episodes are about Quinn's journey trying to fit into the "skinny girl" Hollywood mold when that's not realistic for her, and that's a very real experience for me.

ROSS BROWN: I wanted to ask you about that because that's one of the things that I think is really compelling about the series is that aspect of Quinn's character, that she doesn't fit the unrealistic body image that Hollywood has for women to be super thin, that she's got real curves and —

COURTNEY ZITO: Right.

ROSS BROWN: And all those things. Do you feel a responsibility? I mean not just to tell your own story but to sort of send the message to other women about this?

COURTNEY ZITO: Absolutely, absolutely. I have a young fan base; they're like 16, 17 years old, and I want to be a positive role model for these young girls. They'll send me messages on Facebook: "You're so beautiful." And I'm like, "But you're beautiful, too. Everybody is beautiful." And I always say to them, "Beauty is on the inside. Never forget that." I have a niece who's 12 years old, and I think a lot about the images she's bombarded with.

ROSS BROWN: It's a lot of pressure on teenagers.

COURTNEY ZITO: Yeah. And when I was growing up, I felt all that pressure and all that. And it's 10 times worse now. And so I thought it was really an important message to send to these young girls that you don't have to fit in that mold. Everybody is different. You need to learn to love yourself and accept yourself and bring what you have to the table.

ROSS BROWN: Well, it's a great message to send out there. I wanted to talk to

Courtney the producer, to ask you a couple of questions. How do you get your crew? Do you pay them? Do you barter with them? Are they friends of friends?

COURTNEY ZITO: All of the above. I've always paid a DP because they come with equipment, they come with experience, and things like that. In Season One we did the audio ourselves, and it wasn't ideal. So in Season Two I hired a sound guy. I also bought a camera in Season Two to try to avoid having to hire a DP, but I really can't handle that job and act and direct and produce, so I'll probably go back to paying a DP. Everyone else on the show works for free because they believe in the project.

ROSS BROWN: What about in postproduction?

COURTNEY ZITO: I edit.

ROSS BROWN: Wow. Had you edited before?

COURTNEY ZITO: No.

ROSS BROWN: You just learned on the job?

COURTNEY ZITO: I learned on the job. I had just started using iMovie right before *Hollywood Girl*, and a friend was kind enough to give me a version of Final Cut Express, which made a huge difference. In the beginning my friend helped me learn the program. Then one night we were editing an episode, and he said, "I'm going to bed. You finish the episode." And I was like, "But I don't know what I'm doing." He said, "Learn." He was totally right.

ROSS BROWN: That's really impressive that you became so skilled at editing so quickly.

COURTNEY ZITO: I had to; I couldn't afford to pay an editor. And there was a learning curve, for sure. I was a little shaky at first but got a little bit better with each episode. I think you can see that on screen; the editing gets better as Season One goes on. And even in Season Two, I'm trying new things and getting better, and the cuts are getting tighter.

ROSS BROWN: Well, I think the editing room is where you really learn about stories, and it makes you a better writer and a better actor.

COURTNEY ZITO: Absolutely. And I also feel editing is an extension of directing, part of shaping the way the story gets told. With me being the director and the editor, I can make sure to really get my point across.

ROSS BROWN: Absolutely. Now, once you've shot and edited it, how do you market the show? What sort of social media tools do you use? What other tools do you use to get people to watch you? Because you can't just stick it on YouTube and hope. You've got to bring people there somehow.

COURTNEY ZITO: Exactly. As an actress, I have always been very Web-savvy; I've had a website for 10 years, and I started on Facebook early on. If I saw a movie and I really liked it, I'd watch the credits to see who's involved with the movie, and I would stalk them on Facebook. So, I started building this network. I have 5,500 friends on my first profile. And then I have an acting page with about a thousand, and then I had to start a second profile because I couldn't add any more friends. And that was all pretty much already in place when I started *Hollywood Girl*. So I just used that platform to get the word out about *Hollywood Girl*.

ROSS BROWN: How much of your week do you spend on marketing and promoting your series?

COURTNEY ZITO: I would say a couple hours every day. I wake up, and I check on my pages, and I respond, and I post.

ROSS BROWN: That sounds about right. I really try to convey to my students that marketing your work has got to be part of your job.

COURTNEY ZITO: I wake up, and that's the first thing I do. I heard somewhere with regard to acting that you should be doing something every day for your acting career. And so I just got into the habit of jumping on the computer first thing and networking. It's a way of life now.

ROSS BROWN: Well, it feeds on itself. It grows as you make more connections.

COURTNEY ZITO: Exactly.

ROSS BROWN: And it grows exponentially then.

COURTNEY ZITO: I go on YouTube and try to find other web series and cross-market with them and things like that. And of course I enter the show in festivals, which is where our biggest jump in fans and viewers has come from. *Hollywood Girl* has been in six festivals in the past year, and I've met all these producers who have now become friends and fans and vice versa. It's really opened up this whole new networking group for me.

ROSS BROWN: The web series community is really like this kind of extended family. The people who make web series and really seem to help each other out and cross-market their websites or Facebook pages, all of those things.

COURTNEY ZITO: Festivals devoted entirely to web series — like the LAWEB-FEST — are especially great. I've met some amazing creative people, and I've made some very good friends where we really understand the challenges we all face. If I'm having a bad day working on the show, I can call them up, or vice versa. We just lift each other up. I feel very lucky that they've accepted me into this fantastic community.

ROSS BROWN: Let's talk about episode length. Most web series are in the 2- to 5-minute per episode range. Yours are two to three times that length. Can you share what your thinking is behind that?

COURTNEY ZITO: I just felt like I couldn't tell enough of the story in 2 minutes.

I originally wanted each episode to be 22 minutes, like traditional TV comedies, but the logistics of doing that for me are just too hard.

ROSS BROWN: Right.

COURTNEY ZITO: But I still want to do real stories with real character development, and I just didn't feel like less than 10 minutes was enough time to accomplish that. I've tried to write less than 10 pages, and I can't do it. I just can't do it. And I have a co-writer now who's amazing, Kelsey Scott. And we run into this problem all the time where we'll have this amazing episode and it'll be up to 16 pages.

ROSS BROWN: When you're excited about the material, you always want to write more, no matter whether it's a webisode or a feature film script.

COURTNEY ZITO: You get so into the story line and everything, and you're like, "Oh, we could do this and we could do this." So it keeps growing.

ROSS BROWN: And I think it's part of the first draft, discovery process, to not censor yourself at first. Later, when you revise, you can edit it and shape and condense and make other choices.

COURTNEY ZITO: Sometimes I wait until I'm in the editing process to make those choices. Episode 2 and Episode 3 of Season Two were originally shot as one episode. When I went into post, I was like, "Oh, I'm only halfway through the cut and I'm already at 9 minutes." So we decided to cut it into two episodes. But I hear from my audience all the time that they like longer, more complex episodes. They want the 22-minute episode. And I'm like, "Yeah, maybe someday." That's a lot of work, guys.

ROSS BROWN: I notice when I'm watching the show that you trade promotion in the show for locations, for music, and maybe other things that I just don't remember.

COURTNEY ZITO: Yeah. Those are the two biggies. I mean, when you don't have the money, you barter. And so, I was like, "Okay, I need the location. I'm going to go talk to the owner, and I'm going to tell him that I'll give him a commercial in the episode." And so, for the life of my show, as long as it's on air, he's going to have a little plug in there. And the same thing with the music. I mean, I started saying, "Hey, anybody want to get me some music for the show and I'll put a link to your website in the credits and you'll get a nice little plug" And it just kind of spiraled from there. I think I've paid for one location in two seasons. But, other than that, I've gotten everything else for free, location-wise and music-wise.

ROSS BROWN: Are you interested in taking *Hollywood Girl* and trying to sell it as a half-hour show to a cable network?

COURTNEY ZITO: I would love to. I mean, that ultimately was the goal and the dream all along. But the show is already happening as a web series, I'm having fun, and I have creative control.

ROSS BROWN: Web series are a perfectly valid form all their own, and I think, in order to make the leap from being a web series to being a half-hour series, you either have to be a huge phenomenon or have star power, like the Lisa Kudrow series *Web Therapy*.

COURTNEY ZITO: Right.

ROSS BROWN: Final question: What are your long-range career goals?

COURTNEY ZITO: You know, it was always acting, but now, because of *Hollywood Girl*, I have lots of goals. I really love producing, and I've come to love directing. So I'm kind of just letting life take me where it's going to take me right now. I think I would always miss acting if I didn't do it. Some people have told me I need to focus on producing or directing, to just put the acting aside, and I can't do it yet. I think it's something that, in some form, I'm going to have to always have in my life. But I'm going to just go where the journey takes me and not fight it. If an opportunity presents itself, I'm going to go for it and just kind of see what happens.

ROSS BROWN: I think that's really smart. Even though you may have started out of doing this web series as a way to further your acting career —

COURTNEY ZITO: It's gotten so much bigger than I originally anticipated.

JEN DAWSON
Party Girl Has Some Serious Game

They say that life is what happens while you're making other plans. They might also say the same about creating your own web series, especially if you're Jen Dawson. There she was, just living her life as a young actress and keeping a diary about the ups, downs, and just plain moments of weirdness of her post-divorce dating life. Then one day, she started telling someone some of the anecdotes she had chronicled, and it became apparent that her diary might be much more than just a personal confessional. It might be the very firm basis of a great web series.

JEN DAWSON

As she developed and produced the series, Jen's next revelation was that her talents extended well beyond acting. She was a smart writer, a clever and resourceful producer, and most surprising of all, an outstanding editor — so good that now she gets offered paying gigs editing other web series.

Jen's journey is all about self-discovery — learning that she's way more than a party girl and way more than just a pretty face in front of the camera.

ROSS BROWN: So *Party Girl* is based on your dating diary?

JEN DAWSON: Loosely based. It started from a conversation about using my diary as a stand-up schtick. Stand-up wasn't quite for me, but I knew my diary had an episodic feel to it — a new entry, a new guy, a new episode. So I explored ways to tell episodic stories. Of course, originally I thought of doing a half-hour television series, but I knew actually getting that done was out of my hands, so I kept digging. During that time, the web series world was just taking off because of *lonelygirl15*, so I immersed myself in the world of web stories, which are now known as web series or webisodes.

ROSS BROWN: *Lonelygirl15* was one of the first big web series hits. So, you started working on the web series in 2006 or 2007, something like that?

JEN DAWSON: Yeah, 2006.

ROSS BROWN: Wow. That's a lot of nurturing — a long development period.

JEN DAWSON: Yeah, with all the research of how to tell a story on the Web, the format, how long to make it or how short to keep your audience interested and then dissecting my diary to see where the stories were and how to shape those into episodes and a series, yeah, absolutely.

ROSS BROWN: Your training is as an actress?

JEN DAWSON: Yes.

ROSS BROWN: But you wear all these other hats on the show: You direct and you write and you edit the show yourself?

JEN DAWSON: Only out of necessity. You have to understand when you produce anything with no money, if someone — whether it's your DP, editor, or actor — gets a paying gig, you have to have a Plan B in place. And for the record, over the course of producing 11 episodes I have lost at least one or the other. But I have always been hands-on with the whole project, so after shadowing, if you will, the director or the editor for a few episodes I felt totally comfortable picking up and doing it myself. Of course it took me a bit longer, but I had time on my side since it was my series.

ROSS BROWN: Do you edit it on Final Cut?

JEN DAWSON: Yes.

ROSS BROWN: And you're just self-taught on that?

JEN DAWSON: Yes. At first I'd use iMovie, this simple editing software that came with my Mac. I'd do storyboards off the footage and give that to the editor, and then he would build the episode on Final Cut. One episode in particular, the editor actually liked the cut I put together, so I had to sit with him and rebuild it in Final Cut. After that, I never went back to iMovie.

ROSS BROWN: Well, you're a very good learner then because the show has a very nice visual style to it there. You have a very good instinct for where to put the camera, and the show also has great visual effects in it from time to time. For instance, the episode where you date the flight attendant and he compares your private parts to a landing strip, and suddenly we hear the cockpit conversation as if a plane is coming in for a landing and there are landing strip lights running up and down your thighs. I thought that was brilliantly funny. Was that visual effect written into the script ahead of time, or was it something you came up with in postproduction?

JEN DAWSON: The landing strip lights and the cockpit sounds were totally the editor's ideas. The editor and I had always talked about adding quirky effects à la Ally McBeal, so that gave him the freedom to play around and find those moments. He also had a friend who was just learning an aftereffects program, so between the two of them, they made it happen. When he showed me the first cut, all I could say was, "Brilliant." I work with all kinds of talented, creative people, so I tell them, "Even though this is my story, please do what you want to do as an artist." And they always bring something to the table that I would never have thought of. *Party Girl Plus One* is a much better series because of their creative contributions.

ROSS BROWN: It's really smart of you to create that kind of collaborative creative atmosphere on the set. Sometimes, there's a temptation when it's your baby to be too controlling. But creating an open creative atmosphere is a much better way to go. You're going to get credit for it anyway because it's your series, but good ideas are good ideas no matter where they come from.

JEN DAWSON: Exactly.

ROSS BROWN: Because the show is based on your dating diary, do you find yourself out on dates thinking, "Would this be a good episode?" or thinking, "Gee, this date is going really well, this is terrible, it's not going to be any good for comedy and my series?"

JEN DAWSON: Well first, I started writing in my diary 4 years before I even started the series. I had no idea it would actually be read or for that matter shown to anyone. The diary was really for myself. I stopped writing in my diary about a year before I started making the series. Second, when I was actually making the series, I didn't date much because I had no life or time to date. Finally, if you've dated enough, you realize you start recycling the same type of guy, so there really was no need to continue writing anyway.

ROSS BROWN: How many different — are there like 12 prototypes of guys?

JEN DAWSON: I'm sure there are books on prototypes of guys. I found there are all kinds of characters out there, so when I was keeping my diary, I would name each entry — you know, "Sir Smells-a-Lot" or "Black Card" or "Jolly Green Giant." It helped me remember the situation and the guy.

ROSS BROWN: I think the fact that it was a diary just for yourself and wasn't intended to be the source material for a series is a real plus. It's what makes the series feel so authentic; these were just your honest experiences and feelings.

JEN DAWSON: Exactly.

ROSS BROWN: How do you balance all these different jobs when you're on the set? How do you focus on acting when you're also thinking as a director and a producer? Do you have to compartmentalize depending on what you're doing at any given moment?

JEN DAWSON: I do a lot of prep work. And because the material is so close to me, I'm ready to go when we shoot. I mean, it takes a lot of multitasking, and I definitely had to learn how to focus my energy when I'm on camera and behind the camera.

ROSS BROWN: How long did it take to shoot the 11 episodes?

JEN DAWSON: It took a little bit over a year. I shot episode to episode — in other words, one at a time. Most people will shoot everything at once and then edit everything. I would shoot an episode, edit, post it, then I'd shoot the next one, edit, post it. Before you know it, I had four episodes and then five. It was addictive, and the more I did it the easier it became. It took a little over a year to produce 11 episodes for the first season. And then I started on the trailers and electronic press kits and promotional material. I was having fun.

ROSS BROWN: Is it all self-funded, or did you get sponsors?

JEN DAWSON: It was self-funded.

ROSS BROWN: And so with your crew and cast, it's all barter?

JEN DAWSON: Deferred payment. All the actors are SAG. And SAG has a new media agreement where the actors can be paid a negotiated rate on a deferred basis. My DP and editors were also on deferred. There were a few occasions where my DP got a paying gig on the day we were set to shoot, so I'd pay him something since I didn't want him to lose money. I'd also take care of my crew. Although they liked helping out, I wanted them to know I appreciated their time and dedication to the show.

ROSS BROWN: What about marketing and promoting the show: How have you gone about doing that?

JEN DAWSON: I have to say, marketing is probably the hardest part and not the area I'm very good at. It's also probably the most time-consuming without being as much fun. I'd rather be writing and producing the show. Unfortunately, marketing is essential. That's why brands pay big dollars to get their products out there. I feel lucky to get the views I have with no money. I played around with different ways to promote the show and get it out there, but I'm still trying to figure it out, and it's been 3 years.

ROSS BROWN: You've gotten a lot of festival recognition at LAWEBFEST and other festivals, the Marseille Web Fest also, I believe.

JEN DAWSON: Yes.

ROSS BROWN: Has that helped the audience for the show? Has that been its own promotional tool?

JEN DAWSON: It really helps other filmmakers appreciate your show.

ROSS BROWN: What about music? How do you get the rights to music for your show? Do you know composers, or do you barter for that as well?

JEN DAWSON: When I started the series, I didn't think about music because the first cut had no voice over and no music. It was just straight storytelling, and it sucked. I sat on the footage for a few months. One day when I was playing around with it on my iMovie, I added a voice over and music from my iTunes, stuff like ABBA, stuff that I didn't have the rights to.

I immediately knew this was where the show needed to be, but I also knew I probably couldn't get the rights from ABBA.

ROSS BROWN: And it costs thousands and thousands of dollars to buy those rights.

JEN DAWSON: Right. So then I went to Myspace, which at the time was still known as a promotional site for unsigned and unknown musicians. I got a huge response from musicians all over the world, and the general consensus was, "Yes! Use my music. Get my music out there." I'd feature them on my site and do a write-up on them.

ROSS BROWN: I think that's a great example of how you have to be entrepreneurial, inventive, and take some risk and ask people if they can help you, and you'll be surprised how many creative people will say, "Yes, let's cross-promote. I want to get my music heard." By the way, the music is very good in the show. I wouldn't have guessed that these were unknown musicians.

JEN DAWSON: These are all independent artists — incredibly talented. Finding music has been one of my favorite parts of putting the series together. Listening to songs and having that "ah ha" moment — this song says exactly what I am trying to say. You realize you're not alone in some experiences.

ROSS BROWN: And when you put your show on YouTube, you can tag it with the musicians' names, so their fans who might be looking for just their music will find your web series as well.

JEN DAWSON: That's right. My audience gets to check out their music, and their audience gets exposed to my series.

ROSS BROWN: Right.

JEN DAWSON: And we're talking great music, I mean, some of these people are just amazing.

ROSS BROWN: You don't have to be famous to be talented.

JEN DAWSON: Exactly, and it was cool to actually exchange e-mails and information and sometimes meet them in person. People I would've never met otherwise. One guy from New York came out, I met him at the Viper Room. He was just cool to hang out with, and we talked about the marketing issues that we both share as artists.

ROSS BROWN: I really admire the fact that you looked at the early cut of your series and said, "Okay, this isn't working," and then found a way to improve it. I think too many times, whether it's the script or the finished film, people just put their first draft out there and say, "Well that's it." I think art has to get shaped over time.

JEN DAWSON: My show would have been dead in the water with that first cut.

ROSS BROWN: I say this to my students all the time about first cuts: "Here's what's going to happen: You're going to work very hard, you're going to be really excited about what you shot, and you're going to so want to love the first cut, but when you see it, you're going to want to throw up on your shoes because you hate it. Because no matter how many times you tell yourself, 'It's just a rough cut,' your brain expects to see finished material. So when it doesn't have finished sound and it doesn't have transitions and it doesn't have music and all of that stuff, you go, 'That sucks.'"

JEN DAWSON: When I saw the first cut, it actually was a blessing in disguise. Every first cut after that, for every episode, I knew it was just a baseline and could only get better.

ROSS BROWN: Do you think you improved as a writer, improved as a director, improved as an editor over the course of doing the show?

JEN DAWSON: Absolutely. I learned something with every episode. For instance, after seeing how much adding the voice overs and the musical transitions helped the early episodes, I realized I needed to write the scripts with those elements in mind. I'd actually write with a rhythm I didn't start with when I began the show.

ROSS BROWN: I think the voice over connects us to Jen's character and to her thoughts and her point of view. After all, the show is based on a diary, and that's what a diary is, a written record of your thoughts.

JEN DAWSON: Well, it's interesting because the voice over was never there initially, and actually, it is what makes the show.

ROSS BROWN: I agree. It makes us care about Jen emotionally and lets us know that her quest to find her "plus one" is important to her. It's not just, "Okay, I went out on a date and it turned out badly." She went out on a date and was hoping that this maybe could be the permanent plus one.

JEN DAWSON: Right.

ROSS BROWN: You're taking the show around now, at least the concept and the webisodes that you have, and trying to find partners who are interested in making it into a half-hour series?

JEN DAWSON: Yes.

ROSS BROWN: How is that going?

JEN DAWSON: I'm excited because I feel like I'm not only passionate about the material but now I'm comfortable with selling it. Me doing the selling, which is crucial because I am the show, and my experiences with life and dating are such an important part of what I'm selling.

ROSS BROWN: I think that's very astute. Having somebody else try to sell this series — an agent or a lawyer or whatever — will never be as effective as you being in the room and selling it.

JEN DAWSON: Right.

ROSS BROWN: Has the series led to other opportunities for you in any aspect of your professional life, either other acting opportunities or production opportunities that wouldn't have occurred without the series?

JEN DAWSON: The series landed me a really great manager who got me auditions for a bunch of pilots during pilot season. Branding a "Jen Dawson" type, if you will. That was kind of cool. I've also been contacted to direct and edit for other people because they liked my work.

ROSS BROWN: That's really interesting because this is something that you had no training and no experience, and you're totally self-taught, and now people want to hire you to edit.

JEN DAWSON: Yeah.

ROSS BROWN: I think that's one of the most exciting things about the do-it-yourself nature of web series. You develop a broader set of skills and ways to market yourself, ways to make a living, ways to connect with people creatively other than just, "Hi, I'm Jen, I'm an actress."

JEN DAWSON: I have to say, it was the best experience and was the best thing I ever did because I did learn how to deal with people and negotiate things and ask for things. I learned skills I had no idea I had. I realized what was inside of me and that sometimes I needed to push myself, including creatively. Doing the show helped me grow and take chances in front of the camera and behind the camera because editing gives you so much insight as an actor. I think every actor should sit down with an editor and shadow them for a week because you learn so much about how performances come across on camera.

ROSS BROWN: I think that's a really great point. I feel the same thing about writers, that you learn so much when you actually see something you've written get shot and get into the editing room and see how the story and the performances get built and structured moment by moment in the editing process. It really expands your knowledge and teaches you to visualize the film when you write, to take into consideration what this is going to look like on camera and what this is going to look like edited together and how important just a small reaction can be as part of the rhythm of the scene.

JEN DAWSON: In editing, you realize how much as a writer you overwrite and as an actor you overact. You learn that most of the time less is more in film.

ROSS BROWN: The most important moments in the show, in terms of our connecting with Jen, are not when she's talking but when she's listening to what the guy she's dating is saying or doing and seeing her reaction—when the date is going off the rails and we're seeing your face just frozen there going, "Uh-oh, it was going so well and now it has turned to crap."

JEN DAWSON: I remember one episode in particular where we had shot me saying whatever my line was about four different ways — flirty, funny, straight, you know — and what we ended up using was the moment *before* the line, because it said more than the line did.

ROSS BROWN: I can really hear from your voice and see in your body language how enriching this experience has been creatively for you. Whether or not it gets monetized, there is no replacing that kind of creative invigoration in your life and expansion of your creative horizons.

JEN DAWSON: Absolutely.

MICHAEL AJAKWE
Writer, Producer, Director, and Web Series Festival Promoter

In his 20-plus years as a writer, producer, and director, Michael Ajakwe, a first-generation Nigerian American, has had a rich and productive career spanning theater, television, and film. In theater he has worked with renowned performers like Glynn Turman, Debbie Allen, and Tracee Ellis Ross. As a TV and film writer he's worked with dozens of household names including Martin Lawrence, Greg Kinnear, Sherman Helmsley, and Tracy Morgan. He continues to maintain a busy schedule as a writer, producer, and director in all three areas.

MICHAEL AJAKWE

In 2010, Ajakwe added another impressive credit to his already stellar resume: founder and creator of the world's first all–web series festival, the LAWEBFEST. The festival has grown by leaps and bounds, both in the number of submissions and in their quality. Because of this great success, the festival is expanding from 3 days to 4 in 2013.

Michael Ajakwe is living proof that if you've got talent, dreams, and the willingness to work tirelessly to achieve those dreams, then there are no limits to what you can accomplish. And that's what the Internet and Internet TV are all about: no limits.

ROSS BROWN: So you're a writer, producer, director, and the creator of the LAWEBFEST, the first of its kind festival just for web series, is that correct?

MICHAEL AJAKWE: That's correct.

ROSS BROWN: When did the LAWEBFEST begin?

MICHAEL AJAKWE: The idea came in December of 2009; we launched in March 2010.

ROSS BROWN: So you've had three and coming up on the fourth webfest in 2013?

MICHAEL AJAKWE: Yes.

ROSS BROWN: That's great.

MICHAEL AJAKWE: March 28 through the 31st of 2013, we've expanded by 1 day this year — 4 days instead of 3.

ROSS BROWN: What made you decide to create the festival?

MICHAEL AJAKWE: I did a web series myself and found it interesting and fun. I come out of traditional television like you.

ROSS BROWN: Right.

MICHAEL AJAKWE: And I was watching these little things and I said, "Man, this is a different animal. Wouldn't it be cool if we came together to showcase them on a big screen?" We network and encourage each other and exchange ideas. And I'm thinking it was an LA, New York thing. I didn't realize it was happening all over the country and then all over the world. It just blew me away.

ROSS BROWN: How has the festival grown both in quantity and quality over the years that you've been having it?

MICHAEL AJAKWE: We honored and screened 50 web series the first year. The next year we screened 123, the next year we screened 178. We'll probably screen 200 web series in 2013.

ROSS BROWN: Wow.

MICHAEL AJAKWE: There are so many shows out there. There's probably 3,000 web series, maybe more, but at least 3,000.

ROSS BROWN: It's hard to keep track because while you're counting, new ones get posted out there. And that's just what you can find on YouTube and Vimeo, on the sites you know about.

MICHAEL AJAKWE: Right.

ROSS BROWN: That doesn't count the sites you don't know about.

MICHAEL AJAKWE: I met the guy that does the website Slebisodes; it's now called Web Series Today, but it was called Slebisodes. It's a site devoted to chronicling web series, and even he didn't know about many of the shows we had at the festival. It's really exciting how many shows are being created.

ROSS BROWN: What about the quality of the submissions you're getting? Are you seeing it increase as people learn more about the form?

MICHAEL AJAKWE: Yes, I am. Some people think of web series makers are just amateurs picking up a camera and shooting — no script, just amateur improv. But what I found are people who went to school for writing, for filmmaking, and for acting, and they haven't had a chance to express themselves because it's tough to break into the business. So they took a day job and kept trying to get a break. And then here comes this new thing called web series, and suddenly there's a second chance for them to get into the game and use that degree, use that passion inside of them, and tell their stories. These people have talent. Plus the cameras, editing equipment, everything is consumer friendly now, which really helps when you're on a do-it-yourself, low-budget project.

ROSS BROWN: That's one of the things that I've found in interviewing other web series creators, that they, by necessity, had to learn new skills, and in the process they've discovered new creative aspects within themselves that they weren't aware of. People who were actors or actresses suddenly discover they're quite skilled with editing, and now they're getting offered jobs professionally doing that or as production people or producers, and I think that's really exciting because it's expanding people's creative horizons in ways that they just could not have foreseen if it wasn't for this kind of do-it-yourself aspect of the form.

MICHAEL AJAKWE: And a lot of people in television and film, they want a web series credit, so they'll do it for almost nothing just to say "I did a web series" because that's a hot new thing.

ROSS BROWN: The word I always associate with the web series is *opportunity*; there's creative opportunity, growth opportunity, and exposure opportunity. All those things make web series exciting creatively.

MICHAEL AJAKWE: I really believe in the web series, and I believe that it will take its place along with television and film and theater as another entertainment option.

ROSS BROWN: I want to go back to something you said earlier about building networks and communities through web festivals. Do you see these festivals, especially international festivals like LAWEBFEST and the Marseille Web Fest, as tools for increasing international collaboration?

MICHAEL AJAKWE: Oh yes, absolutely. I'm meeting creative people from all over the world because of web series. I've met writers, directors, actors, from Italy, France, New Zealand, Australia, India, Canada. Oh my, Canadians are incredible. It's amazing what they're doing with web series in Canada.

ROSS BROWN: After the LAWEBFEST was launched, you helped launch the Marseille Web Fest along with Jean Michel Albert, who lives in Marseille.

MICHAEL AJAKWE: Yes, Jean Michel contacted me through a mutual friend, Kathie Fong Yoneda. Kathie had been to the LAWEBFEST and said she had a friend who wanted to do something like it in Europe. So we began e-mailing each other for about a year and a half. During that time Jean Michel came to L.A. and observed the LAWEBFEST. The first Marseille Web Fest was in October of 2011, and they're growing just like we are, adding another day to their festival in 2013.

ROSS BROWN: I noticed that several web series were shown at both festivals.

MICHAEL AJAKWE: Jean Michel and I maintain a very open dialogue. We don't see each other as competitors. We share information, resources, and contacts.

ROSS BROWN: That seems to be the collaborative spirit of the web series world.

MICHAEL AJAKWE: Exactly.

ROSS BROWN: How did you first get interested in web series and new media?

MICHAEL AJAKWE: Working on TV shows, working on a show called *Eve*, a sitcom. Traditional. There was a kid, a writer's assistant, and he was working on something, his own thing. And I said, "What are you working on?" He played it for me, it was a little show, a sketch comedy show. I said, "What's that?" He said, "That's a web series." I thought it was cool. So, when I was in between gigs, I decided to start watching web series. I spent a year watching web series, trying to understand the form.

ROSS BROWN: When you watched all the series, what did you observe as the differences between traditional television and web series? Obviously the length is one issue, but what else struck you as different and unique about web series and their form?

MICHAEL AJAKWE: I think, number one, like you said, is the length. But they're still able to tell a story, and there's still character growth in those few minutes, and that amazed me.

ROSS BROWN: Yeah, I've been very impressed, even to the extreme of 5-Second Films. Have you seen 5-Second Films?

MICHAEL AJAKWE: Yes.

ROSS BROWN: Those are really not character-based, they're jokes, but they're still funny, and they do have a beginning and middle and end of a sort. I think that's another great educational thing about web series for aspiring writers: They have to learn how to be economical in their storytelling.

MICHAEL AJAKWE: I always look at it as starting a scene later, or leaving it sooner.

ROSS BROWN: Let's talk about markets. Where do you see the broad-based model for people being able to make money doing this headed? Do you think it's going to be advertising based or subscription based? Or maybe an iTunes type of model?

MICHAEL AJAKWE: I think probably all of the above. I think first people have to get used to watching web series because we don't have a culture where the majority of people do that yet. But very soon, we will.

ROSS BROWN: I think that's an astute point about how these things evolve naturally over time. When I was a kid growing up, there were the three networks and that was it. So when cable TV subscriptions became common, I'd talk about broadcast television versus cable television. But none of my students make that distinction now. In fact, most of them don't really make a distinction between web series and other forms of visual entertainment. It's just all video content, and if it's interesting and entertaining and engaging for them, they'll watch it.

MICHAEL AJAKWE: I'm seeing shows online that you're not seeing on television, shows dealing with every topic, every sector of the population. I've never seen more diversity than I've seen in web series. It's incredible. I think people just have to get used to watching them, starting with web series makers. A lot of web series makers don't watch web series. They watch their shows, their watch their friend's show, but they don't watch things just to check them out, and that's a shame.

ROSS BROWN: Good point. If you were going to be a novelist, you'd read novels.

MICHAEL AJAKWE: If you're a filmmaker, you watch movies. If you're going to be a television writer, you watch TV.

ROSS BROWN: If you're going to be a web series maker, you've got to watch web series.

MICHAEL AJAKWE: You got to watch them and make cool shows so that people watch it and say to their friends, "Oh man, you've got to see this show."

ROSS BROWN: Right.

MICHAEL AJAKWE: I think we have an opportunity, the community, worldwide, to make web series a cool thing, but it starts with us. It starts with making great shows.

ROSS BROWN: Because you've worked in all areas — film, theater, and traditional television — how has your journey through web series both as a creator and as a festival promoter helped you grow? Has it expanded your creativity in the other forms of writing, has it given you new ideas about plays, new ideas about feature films, new ideas about storytelling in general?

MICHAEL AJAKWE: That's a great question, Ross, great question. Yes, it has. I look at the web series no different than the novel or TV show or a movie. It's all content that can be adapted to other media. When someone reads a book and loves it they say, "Oh, this would make a great movie." Or someone reads a magazine article and says, "Oh wow, this is great, this underground dance craze called disco."

ROSS BROWN: And *Saturday Night Fever* gets made. We have a tremendous model in traditional television with *The Simpsons*. *The Simpsons* started out as —

MICHAEL AJAKWE: Interstitials.

ROSS BROWN: Right — short 1- or 2-minute pieces between skits on the Fox variety series *The Tracey Ullman Show*. In effect, these animated shorts could have been a web series if there was such a thing back then. And it's grown from those little shorts into the most successful prime-time series in history.

MICHAEL AJAKWE: Somebody saw those little interstitials and said, "Why don't we expand this into a show?" Imagine if no one thought about that?

ROSS BROWN: I think that's another service that web series provide to the larger creative community: They serve as an incubation lab and a development lab for major content creators and studios and networks. I think that's all to the benefit of the creative community.

MICHAEL AJAKWE: Web series, to me, are a wealth of source material. A person can look at a bunch of web series and say, "Oh, okay, that's cute," and forget about it. Or they can look at it and say, "Oh wow, this could be a good movie, this might be a great TV drama series, comedy series," whatever.

ROSS BROWN: Right.

MICHAEL AJAKWE: Unfortunately, a lot of media executives don't even watch web series. I met with one guy at a major studio who said, "Web series, those are pretty bad." I said, "Really? How many have you watched?" He said, "About two." I said, "Do you know how many web series are out there? There are like 3,000 web series out there."

ROSS BROWN: I know. It's very short-sighted. Are there bad web series? Sure, lots of them. Just like there are bad TV shows, bad movies, and bad books. But that doesn't mean you should stop watching TV, going to the movies, or stop reading. It just means you have to search to find the high-quality stuff.

MICHAEL AJAKWE: Right. And, as they say, beauty is in the eye of the beholder. Not every TV show, movie, or web series can appeal to everyone.

ROSS BROWN: But I think that's another great thing about web series: You don't have to appeal to millions and millions of people the way a broadcast network TV show does. If you've got 100,000 loyal fans for a web series, that's a great success. And I think it's win–win. It's win for the audience, it's win for the creators.

MICHAEL AJAKWE: Exactly.

ROSS BROWN: The same thing is true in the book world. If you sold 100,000 books, that would be a very, very successful book.

MICHAEL AJAKWE: Just because a web series doesn't get millions of hits doesn't mean it's not good. Some web series people are caught up trying to figure out what will go viral, and I feel that's the wrong way to approach it.

ROSS BROWN: Certainly it's the wrong way to create. You can't just focus on guessing what everybody else wants. To be a storyteller, you have to say, "What's the story I want to tell?"

MICHAEL AJAKWE: Right.

ROSS BROWN: What are the most exciting things, in your opinion, about the future of web series?

MICHAEL AJAKWE: I love the democratic nature of it. In television, in film, it can be very prohibitive in terms of who gets in. You need money or access to money to be in the game. Or, oftentimes, the right connections.

ROSS BROWN: Right.

MICHAEL AJAKWE: So think about how many voices that we might never know of, who could have been great filmmakers but they didn't have the resources, they didn't go to film school, they didn't know someone who could lend them money to do a film or whatever. Oftentimes, the people in control just aren't open to new voices, they're not open to diverse voices.

ROSS BROWN: You don't need permission to make a web series.

MICHAEL AJAKWE: I believe the future is very bright for web series. They're going to continue to grow creatively, the audience for them will keep growing, and sooner or later they will find a home, a place on the Internet where people can go to find high-quality web series. That's why our motto this year — every year we have a different motto — our motto for LAWEBFEST 2013 is "The Future Is Now."

ROSS BROWN: That's a good quote for the end.

CHRISTINE LAKIN
In It for the Long Haul

Christine Lakin has been in show business practically her entire life. She began her acting career at the tender age of 7 as the youngest member of the Atlanta Workshop Players. She then starred in dozens of national and regional commercials for top ad agencies before landing her debut film role at age 11 in the TNT Civil War drama *The Rose and the Jackal*. Shortly thereafter she landed the role of Al Lambert on the hit ABC sitcom *Step by Step* (where the author of this book served as head writer and executive producer for 6 years). After the series ended and she entered adulthood, Christine continued to act extensively in independent films, the theater, and guest appearances on TV including *CSI*, *3rd Rock from the Sun*, and *Veronica Mars*.

CHRISTINE LANKIN

Follow Christine Lakin on Twitter
@yolakin
www.hulu.com/lovin-lakin
www.christine-lakin.com

It's an impressive resume, no doubt about it, one that Christine continues to add to all the time. Her latest credit: creator of her own award-winning web series *Lovin' Lakin*. As you'll see in the interview, Christine has gone through a long and difficult labor birthing the series. But pros like Christine know you can't let a few snags keep you from doggedly pursuing your creative goals.

ROSS BROWN: We spoke in the summer of 2010 for the first edition of this book, and at that time, you had just finished production on *Lovin' Lakin* and were in the process of finishing the postproduction and beginning to market and sell the show. Now here we are almost 3 years later, and the show is just getting out to the public, being posted online and in festivals. That's a long time, so I thought you'd have a lot of valuable insights to share about the process of marketing and selling a show. So take us through your journey. When you first finished the show — and I use the term *finished* loosely because I know you've done a lot of tweaking in the intervening time — what happened?

CHRISTINE LAKIN: Well, in mid-2010 we screened the show at the William Morris Agency, who represented the production company that funded the show. William Morris had an agent who handled their alternative media projects. He started shopping the show, which was awesome because it took the burden off of myself and my partner, Dave Mahanes, to figure out where to take the show and all of that.

ROSS BROWN: When you say "shopping," you mean to cable networks?

CHRISTINE LAKIN: To different online outlets, meaning Netflix, Hulu, iTunes. We needed to see what the market value was, where we'd get the best deal and the most exposure. But it was hard to gauge because the whole business process of selling shows to these outlets was still unformed, with no set procedures in place for buying and selling. So it was a slow process. Reeeeeeally slow. Finally things started to solidify a bit; for instance, Hulu started a premium channel, and they were making deals for premium content. But we (and the agents) were still trying to assess what the fair market value of the show was — how much per click, etcetera. So that's pretty much what took so long.

ROSS BROWN: Did you shop it to cable channels as well with an eye toward turning the web series into a half-hour comedy?

CHRISTINE LAKIN: I would have loved to. Unfortunately, at this point, it was out of my control. The production company, Oops Doughnuts Productions, had funded the project, and William Morris represented them, which meant they represented our project. But the production company and William Morris had bigger priorities than my little web series, so their time and energy went toward those bigger priorities, and *Lovin' Lakin* stayed on the back burner. It was so frustrating for me. We'd screen the show, and people would love it and say, "When is it coming out? When is it coming out?" And for a year and a half, 2 years, all I could say was, "I don't know." It was just incredibly frustrating.

ROSS BROWN: It's very hard because there are no rules yet for what the marketplace is, how it operates, and what few rules and guidelines there are change every 3 months. It's a moving target.

CHRISTINE LAKIN: Exactly.

ROSS BROWN: Because of the time lag, were you asked to recut the show?

CHRISTINE LAKIN: Yes and no. We got notes and made some changes, but the real issue was that the production company got busy with other things.

ROSS BROWN: That's the mixed blessing of being funded by a production company. On the plus side, they put up the money. But the downside is you may not be their top priority.

CHRISTINE LAKIN: Not only that, when we finally made our Hulu deal, which was basically the original deal we were going to make anyway, we discovered we had to buy insurance.

ROSS BROWN: Insurance for what?

CHRISTINE LAKIN: Errors and omissions.

ROSS BROWN: Right, okay.

CHRISTINE LAKIN: And that insurance is not cheap. And the lawyers who put the deal together are not cheap. Just the lawyers and the errors and omissions cost more than what the actual content cost. It was absolutely ridiculous, but these were the requirements of formalizing a deal. And then Hulu came back to us and said, "You don't have licensing for the 2-second clip of the *Step by Step* opening theme song you're using."

ROSS BROWN: Of course, of course.

CHRISTINE LAKIN: And to go and get that would have meant going to Warner Bros., and nobody wanted to deal with that. So I then had to hire an editor to come in, go back through the files, and figure out a way to recut the opening because our original editor had moved to South Dakota. All this, of course, took more time.

ROSS BROWN: So at this point were you looking back and thinking you should have just gone to YouTube in the first place?

CHRISTINE LAKIN: Yes. Should have gone to YouTube in the first place.

ROSS BROWN: So now that the show is online, what are you doing to market it?

CHRISTINE LAKIN: Well, the good news about all of this, and there is a silver lining, is that as frustrating as all of this was, the production company, Oops Doughnuts, had a publicity team on retainer. So when we finally did have an airdate, we were able to get some really great press: a piece on *E!*, we were on *Entertainment Tonight*, we did *The Insider*, all kinds of online stuff. It was awesome.

ROSS BROWN: So that's where having a production company behind you was an advantage. Plus the fact that your series has some star power in it, people like Patrick Duffy and yourself and Kristen Bell —

CHRISTINE LAKIN: — and Kristin Chenoweth and Seth MacFarlane. That's helping us a lot.

ROSS BROWN: One thing I've heard quite consistently from actors who have done web series for themselves is how much it has expanded their creative horizons and their awareness of skills they have other than performing in front of the camera. Has that been your experience?

CHRISTINE LAKIN: Absolutely. The whole creative process — from conceiving the show to writing the outlines and scripts to filming it to sitting in the editing room — I had such a good time doing it. I got to do it with some of my best friends, and it was one of the most creatively rewarding processes that I've had. Because of that, I started to write a lot more. I wrote a short script based on a friend's life as a private tutor to families in Los Angeles. My friend gave it to one of her tutoring dads who was a well-known writer–producer named Scott Winant, and he read it and liked my writing. He said we could turn this into an hour-long pilot. So under his mentorship this spring I wrote an hour-long and it went out to the CW yesterday.

ROSS BROWN: I think that's fantastic. It's the single most exciting thing that I'm hearing from creators of web series, this creative blossoming that happens. Because you have to do all kinds of new things — writing, editing, producing — it pushes you outside of your comfort zone.

CHRISTINE LAKIN: Definitely, and I think, more than anything, it took the mystique away from writing and creating something. Before, as an actress, I'd read a script or see a show and say, "God, I just don't know if I'd ever have an idea as good as that. I don't know how they did that." But the web series format, because it's short, isn't as daunting. It gave me the confidence to try, to say, "Who can't write three pages?" Or come up with a concept and say to your friend, "Let's improv this and see what happens."

ROSS BROWN: Right.

CHRISTINE LAKIN: And then you put it together and it becomes this little puzzle, and you have a really good time figuring it out, and it's a joy, it's not a burden. It frees you to say, you know, "I can actually do this. I can write."

ROSS BROWN: Well, it's not surprising to me that you can do this. A lot of the work you do as an actress — understanding motivation and character wants and all of those sorts of things — is the same type of work that writers have to do.

CHRISTINE LAKIN: Yeah.

ROSS BROWN: How has this informed your acting? Do you approach acting with a different perspective now that you've spent time writing and in the editing room, looking at your performance frame by frame by frame?

CHRISTINE LAKIN: Oh my God, time and time again. I think more than anything, it gave me an outlet to do what I feel is my brand of comedy, which I don't always get to do as an actress for hire because not everybody has my particular sensibility and not everybody has written specifically for me. It's just much easier when you write for yourself because you know exactly how you want the line to be delivered.

ROSS BROWN: In addition to writing the 1-hour pilot, have there been other opportunities that have come along for you as a result of doing the web series?

CHRISTINE LAKIN: Yes. I was asked to co-host a show called *Internet Icon*. It's on YouTube. Ryan Higa and I are the stars, the judges. It's a competition show, like a *Project Runway*. Ten contestants each make a video under certain time constraints and rules and have a different theme for every challenge. The worst video of the day goes home, and we whittle it down to the final winner. On the surface it seems easy to make a short video. But it's very difficult to do it and make it entertaining, concise, and tell a real story.

ROSS BROWN: Right.

CHRISTINE LAKIN: I come from a storytelling background. I'm a TV/film person, and Ryan is a YouTube person. So I think our sensibilities were complementary. To make a great 3-minute video it has to be catchy, but it also has to tell a real story if you want to bring the audience back for more episodes.

ROSS BROWN: I think that's a great point because you're right, a web series has to be both, it has to have catchy, pop culture YouTube elements, but storytelling is still the name of the game. If you don't have compelling storytelling, especially compelling characters, it may work for one or two videos, but not for a series.

CHRISTINE LAKIN: On *Internet Icon* there were these two boys, the Fu brothers, who made this beautiful stop-motion video with this little rubber ducky. It was a prop challenge. They wrote a song, recorded it, and made a stop-motion music video all in less than a day. It was so impressive.

ROSS BROWN: The facility with which the younger generation, even younger than you, is able to make web series is astonishing. Thinking visually comes so naturally to them. You're in your early thirties, and for your generation, this is still a new medium. But for kids who have grown up on this, the YouTube generation, it's just like the alphabet.

CHRISTINE LAKIN: Second nature, absolutely.

ROSS BROWN: *Lovin' Lakin* won the Best Web Series award at the New York Television Festival. So congratulations on that.

CHRISTINE LAKIN: Thank you.

ROSS BROWN: What was the festival experience like for you?

CHRISTINE LAKIN: It was so much fun. I was supposed to be there all week going to panels, and meeting people, and networking. But as Murphy's Law would have it, I got an acting job doing an episode of television that same week. So I was literally at NYTVF for 2 days, then had to fly right back to California. But for the couple of days I was there, it was a great experience. In addition to screening pilots and web series, they also have a pitch festival. So you are able to write and submit pitches to tons of networks. I think I pitched five different places with new material and new ideas, had some really good meetings there. And there were a couple of guys from Warner Bros. International who we're talking to now about turning *Lovin' Lakin* into an interstitial for their other shows.

ROSS BROWN: I think that's one of the other really exciting things about web series: The show is more than just a show, it's also a calling card for you, something that displays your talents. An audition piece for something that you may not know you're auditioning for, if you will.

CHRISTINE LAKIN: It was just a great opportunity. I think the more of these festivals that we're able to do now, the better. We're doing LAWEBFEST, and we've entered into the Streamys. To have the chance to network and get recognition for my web series, that's awesome.

ROSS BROWN: Definitely a great validation, especially after such a long wait for launching the show. I want to talk to you about the sense of community in the web series world. One of the things I have observed is the strong sense of community amongst those who are exploring and blazing a trail in the form.

CHRISTINE LAKIN: It's great. You go to these festivals, and you watch other people's stuff. Naturally, you compare yourself to them, and sometimes you're like, "Holy shit, that was really impressive." And sometimes you're like, "Hmm, I don't really know what that was, but that was... interesting."

ROSS BROWN: I think both types of experiences are valuable because it can inspire you or challenge you when you see something that really impresses you. But even if you see something that you don't like or don't get, it helps you take note of what works and what doesn't.

CHRISTINE LAKIN: The festivals are also great platforms for increasing awareness of your show. After the New York Television Festival, I was tweeting about the award, and it got people to jump on YouTube and check out the show.

ROSS BROWN: On a different subject than *Lovin' Lakin*, you've also created some short animated videos using the software available at a site called Xtranormal. The site basically provides an easy-to-use kit for simple animation. You made two very funny shorts — one imagining a conversation with your father and one imagining a conversation with your mother — about your acting career, which they seemed to have no clue about, no idea what you did or why you did it.

CHRISTINE LAKIN: Yeah.

ROSS BROWN: They were about 3 minutes each. How long did it take you to do the actual animation? You wrote the script first obviously and then —

CHRISTINE LAKIN: I didn't.

ROSS BROWN: You didn't write a script first?

CHRISTINE LAKIN: No. Here's what happened: A friend of mine had made an animated short using Xtranormal. I think it was called "A Talk with My Agent" or something like that. He posted it on his Facebook page, and it got reposted on Deadline Hollywood and some other sites. I saw it and I thought it was really funny, and I wondered, "How did he make that?" So I went to the link, and it was simple — just as easy to use as Shutterfly or anything like that. You pick an avatar from some basic choices — a young girl, older woman, young guy, etcetera. Then there are some basic sets, a couple of things you can do angle-wise.

ROSS BROWN: A master, a two-shot, close up…

CHRISTINE LAKIN: Yeah. And you can also make the character look at the camera and pause or blink, you know, for a comedic effect.

ROSS BROWN: Like on *South Park*.

CHRISTINE LAKIN: Exactly. So I just started playing around with it, improvising a chat with my mom. There's a box for dialogue.

ROSS BROWN: So, did you do this over a period of days or all in one evening?

CHRISTINE LAKIN: No, maybe like an hour and a half.

ROSS BROWN: Wow, that's amazing.

CHRISTINE LAKIN: So I just wrote it in the dialogue box, and then I would click Animate, and it would come out — and it made me laugh.

ROSS BROWN: Some of what makes the animated pieces from Xtranormal so funny is the robotic nature of the voices they insert.

CHRISTINE LAKIN: They're hilarious, and you write with those voices in mind. So I'd write it, look at it, then rewrite it and watch it again. And then I just started to add profanity because I thought that was even funnier in those weird robotic voices. It's really cool software because people can have their own animated web series without actually knowing how to animate.

ROSS BROWN: Are you working on any other web series?

CHRISTINE LAKIN: Well, I've shot some experimental improv stuff with a friend. And I actually have an idea for a new web series I'd like to write, but for now I've been focusing on the 1-hour pilot script because if I can actually sell something to make money, that would be —

ROSS BROWN: It's always a good thing to actually get paid for your creative work in addition to just being inspired.

CHRISTINE LAKIN: Yeah. But I have thought very seriously this year about actually buying a big desktop computer and biting the bullet and learning Final Cut because I have this other project, my live show *Worst Audition Ever*, and we do eight, nine shows a year and video every single one of the shows. I figure, why pay somebody to edit these things if I can have the equipment and do it myself? There's a learning curve, but if I want to get serious about creating more shows, I might as well learn Final Cut.

ROSS BROWN: Well, you've always had multiple creative desires and outlets, but it sounds like the web series experience has kind of turbocharged your creativity.

CHRISTINE LAKIN: Oh, definitely. If I can make a living and still have autonomy doing the things that I really want to do that are passion projects and have a good time doing them, then, I mean, that's the best of both worlds.

ROSS BROWN: That's great.

YOU'RE READY — HONEST — SO GO DO IT!

Listen carefully. I suspect you might hear a low roar in the distance. That growling, grumbling sound you hear is the insatiable hunger of the Internet for fresh, entertaining content. Every laptop and desktop computer in the world yearns for it. Mobile devices and tablets demand it. The hunger for new video entertainment is global and grows exponentially 24 hours a day, 365 days a year. And the best news of all is that entry to this world is open not only to established professionals but to anyone with a video camera and some imagination.

Somebody is going to make a great web series and maybe even a great deal of money satisfying this profound hunger. In fact, the desire for short-form video is so enormous that it will take thousands and thousands of creators to feed it.

You can be one of those creators. It will take inspiration and a lot of hard work, but what the heck is there something else you'd rather be doing than creating a little video world of your own and sharing it with millions on the Internet?

There are always so many things I want to tell my students in the final minutes of our final class session. *I hope you learned a lot. I hope you had fun. Write well. Write often. Be bold. Be creative. Believe in yourself. Take chances. Make movies. Make us laugh. Surprise us. Entertain us. Move us. Above all, tell us* your *stories — the ones only you can tell from your unique perspective in your own voice.* It's the last week of class, and I know the students are already thinking about Christmas vacation or about their summer plans. But I'm a teacher, so I desperately want to be wise and inspirational, to send my film and TV students off with a sense of purpose and determination to make their creative mark on the world. I want to leave them with something pithy, something memorable, the perfect few words that will inspire them for decades to come and motivate them to tell great stories and make great shows. But in the end, the truth is that the best advice I can give is this: JUST DO IT!

It is humbling and a bit disquieting to be a supposedly learned college professor and realize that the best wisdom I can impart is an advertising slogan. But it really does boil down to that. Thinking about creating a web series is worthwhile only if you actually sit down, develop the idea and the characters, devise a pilot story, write a script, shoot it, and edit it, and then make more episodes.

This book, I hope, has given you a lot of helpful guidance about the process of making a web series. But process is meaningful only if you also put it into practice. We all have voices of procrastination and doubt in our heads. You know the ones I'm talking about — the ones that tell you not to dream, to second guess every idea you ever have. Set them aside. Believe in yourself. Don't worry about what "they" want out there. Create a show that YOU would want to see and have faith that there are thousands and thousands of others like you out there on the Internet who will also want to see it.

Turn on your computer and surf the Net. Check out a few web series. Nine out of ten times, your reaction will be, "I can do better than that."

Yes, you can. But only if you sit down today and get to work creating. You're ready — honest — so go do it.

I can't wait to see your show.

SCREENPLAY FORMAT TUTORIAL

FADE IN:

EXT. DEADHEAD GUITARS/SAN FRANCISCO — DAY

Each scene has a <u>complete slug line</u> stating whether it
is interior or exterior, giving a reasonably specific
description of the location and indicating day or night,
dusk or dawn.

The first time a location is used, provide the most
detailed description in the heading. Once you've
established that Deadhead Guitars is in San Francisco,
drop the <u>San Francisco</u>.

If it's important for the audience to know immediately
that it's in a specific city, make sure there is some
identifying landmark (e.g., the Golden Gate Bridge) or
else add this line:

TITLE: "SAN FRANCISCO"

after the slug line or somewhere in the text. You can
also use a title to indicate the time period, LIKE THIS:

TITLE: 1966, THE SUMMER OF LOVE

Specifying the time period in the slug line is inappropriate.

EXT. GOLDEN GATE PARK — DAY

When you switch to a new location, use another slug line indicating this. If you're shifting emphasis to a new area within this location, you can use an abbreviated slug line (or, more properly, <u>shot</u>), such as:

ANGLE ON REDWOOD TREE

A squirrel with an acorn in his mouth scurries up the trunk.

Or:

NEAR BANDSTAND

A YOUNG WOMAN dances and sways to music that only she hears.

Generally, avoid explicit camera references — keep them <u>implicit</u>. For example: "A lone tear trickles down her cheek" implies a close-up of the young woman's cheek — you don't have to specify CLOSE-UP or CU of her brow.

On the rare occasions when you <u>absolutely must</u> make a close-up explicit, it works like this:

CLOSE ON — HER CHEEK

as a lone tear trickles down it. Then you follow it up
with:

BACK TO SCENE

She wipes it off and continues dancing.

INT. HAIGHT ASHBURY APARTMENT — DAY

Sometimes you will need a "time cut" within a scene. This
is because every second of screen time must be accounted
for in a script. For example, the following paragraph:

Freedom Jones enters the apartment, rolls a joint, smokes
it, then stares at a blank TV screen as he consumes an
entire bag of Oreos.

is not acceptable screenwriting, since the above may take
an hour or more. Instead, choose moments to cut from and
return to the scene. For example:

Freedom enters, immediately removes his Sears repairman
uniform.

CLOSE ON — A JOINT

as Freedom rolls it with precision.

PULL BACK TO REVEAL

Freedom is now buck naked, sitting on the floor next to a
bag of Oreos, smoking the last of the joint staring at a
blank TV screen.

You can also do a slug line such as:

SAME LOCATION — A SHORT TIME LATER

and then use some visual clue to suggest time passing, such as the bag of Oreos now being empty.

The first time you refer to a character in the description, capitalize the entire name, as when JERRY GARCIA enters the guitar shop and we've not seen him before.

In all subsequent references, such as when Jerry Garcia crosses the room, he's in plain old upper and lower case. However, in dialogue, the character name is always in all caps:

> JERRY GARCIA
> Anyway, it's in all caps in the
> identifying line above.

> BOB WEIR
> Although if I were to call out to Jerry
> Garcia in my dialogue, the name would
> <u>not</u> be in all caps.

> JERRY GARCIA
> Far out.

Sometimes you may want the audience to <u>hear</u> a character before seeing him or her, yet the character is in the scene, for instance, appearing unexpectedly from behind a door. In such a case, put (O.S.) after the name:

                    JERRY GARCIA (O.S.)
         Dig this: O.S. is an abbreviation for
         off-screen.

Sometimes the audience can _hear_ a character's thoughts,
or there is a narrator speaking to us who is not in the
scene. In that case, the use of "V.O." is appropriate:

                    AGING HIPPIE (V.O.)
         This is an abbreviation for Voice Over.
         Whoa, it's kind of like when I hear
         voices in my head.

Important sounds are also in all caps, as when POLICE
SIRENS APPROACH.

Always double space between the scene description and
dialogue but single space within either a continuous
dialogue or a continuous descriptive section.

If your scene description continues on to an entirely
different subject, skip a line between sections. Use the
spacing on the page to your advantage — for emphasis,
pacing, and rhythm. Try to make the experience of reading
as close to the experience of watching a movie as
possible.

Long paragraphs of description are difficult to read. If
your paragraph is more than four or five lines long, edit
it down or break it up into smaller paragraphs.

                         JANIS JOPLIN
              (grinning)
         Hey man, that (grinning) above my
         dialogue is called a parenthetical
         description. Use parentheticals
         sparingly, like when the character's
         manner or expression might change the
         meaning of the line. But don't overuse
         them, that's a drag.
              (drinks some whiskey)
         You can also break up dialogue with
         minor actions, especially those
         referring to the character speaking.
         But never put a parenthetical at the
         end of dialogue (here).

If Janis takes another slug of whiskey — which is always
a possibility — write it below the dialogue in an action
or descriptive line, like this:

                         JANIS JOPLIN
         Got it?

She takes another slug of whiskey.

Also, if the action you need to describe is more
substantial, bring the description fully to the left
margin. If the same character continues to speak after
the action has been described, place a (cont'd) after the
name:

                         JANIS JOPLIN (cont'd)
         Okay?

EXT. FILLMORE WEST — NIGHT

Generally, there is no need to write "CUT TO:" between
scenes. It is assumed that we cut from one scene to
another unless specified otherwise.

There are occasions to give us "FADE OUT:" or "DISSOLVE
TO:" or other specific optical effects. But most optical
effects are chosen in the editing room, so be sparing in
the script stage.

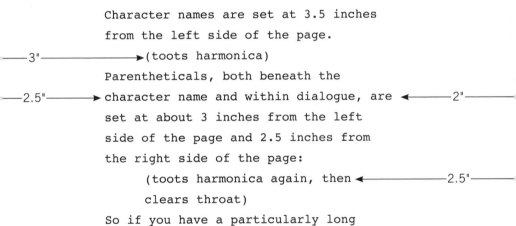

.5"➤ Set your left margin to 1.5 inches, your right margin to
1 inch. Indent dialogue 2.5 inches from the left side of
the page and 2 inches from the right side of the page.

──3.5"──────────────────────➤ BOB DYLAN
                  Character names are set at 3.5 inches
                  from the left side of the page.
──3"────────────────➤ (toots harmonica)
                  Parentheticals, both beneath the
──2.5"──────➤ character name and within dialogue, are ◄────── 2"──────
                  set at about 3 inches from the left
                  side of the page and 2.5 inches from
                  the right side of the page:
                        (toots harmonica again, then ◄──────── 2.5"───────
                        clears throat)
                  So if you have a particularly long
                  parenthetical, it'll look like that.

Top and bottom margins are approximately 1 inch. Skip
two lines between the end of one scene and the slug line
of the next. These are reasonably standard guidelines,
though you can fudge things if your script is running too
long or short.

The typical font is <u>Courier 12 point</u>. This font resembles that of a typewriter. It dates from the time long ago when scripts were actually written on typewriters. There are two good reasons why you should <u>not</u> use one of the more attractive fonts that came with your computer:

- The Courier font is still the standard in Hollywood, so if you don't use it your script will immediately seem odd and, quite likely, amateur.
- It's much easier to judge how long a script will run if it uses the standard font rather than something exotic.

If dialogue breaks across a page, handle it like this:

JERRY GARCIA
Start the dialogue normally, man, then
(MORE)

JERRY GARCIA (cont'd)
when the page breaks, type that "MORE" as indicated, repeat the character name at the top of the next page and put the "cont'd" in. It's not rocket science, man.

One formatting approach to <u>avoid at all costs</u> is <u>centering</u> character names and dialogue, as in:

GINSBERG
I saw the best minds of my generation
destroyed by madness, starving
hysterical naked.

SURFER KID
Gnarly.

INT./EXT. MERRY PRANKSTERS VW VAN — DAY

Some situations aren't quite interior or exterior but
some kind of combination. If we, the audience, are inside
the car with the characters but the car is outside, the
heading would be as above. Just use common sense.

Page numbers are in the upper right corner and do <u>not</u>
have a period after them.

6.   INT. FAIRMONT HOTEL — NIGHT   6

A selling script doesn't have numbered scenes, but a
shooting script does. Scenes should be numbered both left
and right, and the number <u>should</u> have a period after it
to help distinguish it from a page number. When someone
buys your script, put scene numbers in; otherwise, don't
bother.

The major factors in determining a technical scene (one
that needs a new slug line to distinguish it from the
previous scene) are <u>location of camera</u> and <u>time of day</u>.
There is a change in technical scenes if we cut from day
to night at the same location. It is a new scene if we
cut from one room to the next room in continuous time.

There is no change in technical scenes if the camera
stays in one location but can see into another. If we
stay with LENNY BRUCE in the living room while he shouts
to a STRIPPER taking a shower in the bathroom, it's the

same scene. If the camera moves into the bathroom, it is
a new scene.

In terms of style, the basic idea is to give the briefest
complete description possible that emphasizes what
is important and de-emphasizes what is not. Clarity
and economy are crucial, so it is best to limit your
descriptions to what can be <u>seen and heard</u>.

Try to live by the rule: <u>Every sentence is a shot</u>. And
every shot should have a subject—predicate — someone
doing something. Audiences, including readers, will hook
onto action.

For example, instead of listing the contents of a room,
then describing a character enter, try describing the
character entering and reveal the contents of the room
as the character walks through it. We'll follow the
character's action and won't even know the room is being
described.

Scripts are still printed on one side of a piece of paper
rather than double sided.

FADE OUT

RECOMMENDED READING FOR A MORE DETAILED DISCUSSION OF THE CRAFTS

A complete discussion of every skill needed to make a short pilot — writing, directing, cinematography, sound, editing, graphic effects, production management, online marketing strategies, on and on — would take thousands and thousands of pages of text and would defeat the purpose of this book: providing a concise guide to the basic creative issues involved in creating a short-form TV series for the Internet. Still, many of you will want deeper instruction than this one book can offer in one or more specific areas. Fortunately, ample literature and instruction are available on each of the relevant crafts and skills you might need. Here is a short guide to some of the resources filmmakers and film school faculty have found most useful in each of the areas you may want to explore in greater detail.

General Video and Filmmaking
Conquering YouTube: 101 Video Secrets to Take You to the Top by Jay Miles, Michael Wiese Productions, Studio City, CA, 2011
How to Shoot Video That Doesn't Suck by Steve Stockman, Workman Publishing Company, New York, 2011

Directing
Directing Actors by Judith Weston, Michael Wiese Productions, Studio City, CA, 1999

Respect for Acting by Uta Hagan, David Hyde Pierce, and Haskel Frankel, Wiley, Hoboken, NJ, 2008

Cinematography

DSLR Cinema: Crafting the Film Look with Video by Kurt Lancaster, Focal Press, Boston, 2010

Master Shots: 100 Advanced Camera Techniques to Get an Expensive Look on Your Low-Budget Movie by Christopher Kenworthy, Michael Wiese Productions, Studio City, CA, 2009

Sound

The Practical Art of Motion Picture Sound by David Lewis Yewdall, Focal Press, Boston, 2011

Sound Design by David Sonnenschein, Michael Wiese Productions, Studio City, CA, 2002

The Sound Effects Bible by Ric Viers, Michael Wiese Productions, Studio City, CA, 2008

Editing

Cut by Cut: Editing Your Film or Video by Gael Chandler, Michael Wiese Productions, Studio City, CA, 2012

In the Blink of an Eye by Walter Murch, Silman-James Press, Beverly Hills, CA, 2001

The Technique of Film & Video Editing: History, Theory, and Practice by Ken Dancyger, Focal Press, Boston, 2010

Production Planning

Film Production Management 101: Management & Coordination in a Digital Age by Deborah Patz, Michael Wiese Productions, Studio City, CA, 2010

Animation

Animation Unleashed by Ellen Besen and Bryce Hallett, Michael Wiese Productions, Studio City, CA, 2008

The Animator's Survival Kit by Richard Williams, Faber and Faber, London, 2012

SYLLABI AND COURSE OUTLINES FOR TEACHERS

At Dodge College of Film and Media Arts at Chapman University, where I teach, I have developed a two-semester sequence called Byte-Sized Television I and II. In the first semester, each student pitches a concept and characters for a short-form Internet TV series. They receive feedback from me and their classmates, then pitch a pilot story, write a script, and revise it after workshopping it aloud in class. From the 18 or 20 pilot scripts written, I select two to be filmed. I select a director, producer, cinematographer, editor, and so on for each pilot and guide the students through preproduction. Each pilot is then shot on digital video, edited, and refined until it is ready to be posted on the Internet.

During the second semester, the students write and produce three more episodes of each series. We focus not only on finding additional stories within the premise but on expanding and growing the series and characters. The students change jobs on each episode to give them a variety of experiences, although the writer/creator always serves as executive producer and has the final creative word on all decisions, just as is the case in the professional world.

The following syllabi and course outlines are provided to give you a sense of how to organize the courses on a week-to-week basis.

FTV 313/513

BYTE-SIZED TELEVISION I
FALL 2012
Instructor: Ross Brown
Class Hours: Tuesday and Thursday 1:00–2:15 p.m.

Course Description

Prerequisite, FTV 130 or consent of instructor. An exploration of the creative and logistic challenges of creating a narrative episodic television series and generating episodes, including writing a pilot concept, series characters, and a pilot script, and producing television pilots. May be repeated for credit. Fee: $300. (Offered fall semester.) 3 credits.

Course Objectives

Each student will create and write a pilot script for a 3- to 5-minute narrative TV series. Two scripts will go to pilot and be produced by the writer/creator, with other students functioning as crew. Of the two produced pilots, one or both will go to series, with the creator functioning as executive producer and supervising a writing staff in development of several episodic scripts to be shot the following semester in FTV 413. All produced pilots and episodes will be webcast.

Course Requirements

Students must be available Friday, Saturday, and Sunday November 2, 3, and 4 to film the selected pilots.

Class Attendance

Students are permitted two absences (BUT NONE PERMITTED FROM SHOOT DATES); two tardies (or leaving class early) will count as one absence. Three absences will result in loss of half a grade (e.g., A– to a B+); four absences will result in loss of a full grade. Five absences will result in an F.

- Class *participation*. See "Grading" below.
- Professional presentation. Work filled with spelling, grammar, formatting, or typographical errors will be marked down.

Required Text

Brown, Ross. *Create Your Own TV Series for the Internet*. Second edition. Studio City, CA: Michael Wiese Productions, 2014.

Grading

Grading will evaluate creative content, writing skills, grasp of the concepts, and professional presentation of your concept, story, and pilot script. During preproduction, production, and postproduction of the pilots, your grade will be based on your craft skill in your particular job, collaborative contributions and effort, and growth through the semester and willingness to learn new and unfamiliar skills and tasks. The overall grade will be computed as follows:

- Pilot script (divided equally between premise, characters, story, and execution), 30%
- Collaboration and contribution to filming of pilot, 30%
- Quality of peer evaluations you write, 10%
- Quality of series development analysis you write, 20%
- Participation in class critiques and other classwork, 10%

- A: Exceptional
- B: Very good
- C: Satisfactory
- D: Unsatisfactory
- F: Failure

COURSE SCHEDULE, FALL 2012

Week 1, 8/28 & 8/30

Introduction to course

Discuss syllabus and rules and regs of the course

Screen examples of web series pilots

Creating a solid concept that has legs

Creating compelling characters

Creating a strong character landscape

Assignment: Read Preface and Chapters One–Three; Prepare concept and character pitch

Week 2, 9/4 & 9/6

Pitch concept and characters

Assignment: Read Chapters Four–Six; Revise concepts as needed, prepare pilot story pitch

Week 3, 9/11 & 9/13

Revise concept and characters, pitch pilot story

Assignment: Read Chapter Seven; Write first draft

Week 4, 9/18 & 9/20

Workshop first drafts

Assignment: Revise first drafts

Week 5, 9/25 & 9/27

Workshop first drafts

Assignment: Revise first drafts; Read Chapter Nine

Week 6, 10/2 & 10/4

Workshop revised drafts

Instructor selects 2 scripts to go to pilot

Week 7, 10/9 & 10/11

Preproduction and casting planning

Form 2 crews

Assign job responsibilities

Assignment: Read Chapters Ten and Eleven

Week 8, 10/16 & 10/18

Preproduction and casting

Progress reports from each job category:

Location and casting update

Production design report

Camera and sound report

Week 9, 10/23 & 10/25

Preproduction and casting

Formal production meeting on each pilot

Directors present preliminary shot lists

Week 10, 10/30 & 11/1

Final production meeting on each project

Directors present revised shot lists

Main title discussion on each project

*** *Shoot pilots over weekend 11/2 11/3 11/4 (2 crews)*

Week 11, 11/6 & 11/8

Screen dailies

Screen rough cuts

Week 12, 11/13 & 11/15

Fine cuts

Week 13, 11/20

Third cuts; develop main title

No class 11/22: Thanksgiving holiday

Week 14, 11/27 & 11/29

See fourth cuts

Pitch episode ideas

Week 15, 12/4 & 12/6

Workshop first drafts of Episode 2

Week 16 (Finals Week)

Workshop revised first drafts

Screen pilots with main titles

FTV 413/613

BYTE-SIZED TELEVISION II
SPRING 2013
Instructor: Ross Brown
Class Hours: Tuesday and Thursday 2:30–3:50 p.m.

Course Description

Prerequisites: FTV 130. Building on the series pilots created in FTV 313, students will learn about the collaborative writing and production process as practiced in the creation of narrative episodic television series designed for the Internet. May be repeated for credit. Fee: $300. 3 credits.

Course Objectives

Course seeks to give students experience in working collaboratively on a narrative episodic television series designed for the Internet. Students will learn how each craft — writing, directing, on-set production, and postproduction — contributes to the overall vision and success of the series and of each individual episode. Students will also learn how each episode beyond the original pilot both tells a self-contained story and contributes to the ongoing story and growth of the series characters.

NOTE: *Because of its nature as a production course, this class requires a lot of work outside the classroom. Students will be asked to work both individually and collaboratively on several episodes and tasks simultaneously.*

Course Requirements

Students must be available on all *of the following Friday, Saturday, and Sunday shoot dates:*

3/1, 3/2, 3/3, 4/5, 4/6, 4/7, 4/26, 4/27, 4/28

Class Attendance

Students are permitted two absences (BUT NONE PERMITTED FROM SHOOT DATES); two tardies (or leaving class early) will count as one absence. Three absences will result in loss of half a grade (e.g., A– to a B+); four absences will result in loss of a full grade. Five absences will result in an F.

Required Text

Brown, Ross. *Create Your Own TV Series for the Internet*. Second edition. Studio City, CA: Michael Wiese Productions, 2014.

Grading

Grading will evaluate creative content, grasp of the concepts, professional presentation, professional conduct within the classroom and throughout the production, and growth through the semester and be apportioned as follows:

- Written production analyses (Episodes 2 and 3), 10%
- Written final cut analyses (Episodes 2 and 3), 10%
- Craft proficiency in your roles on each episode (includes peer evaluation of your contribution), 60%
- Quality of your peer evaluations of others, 10%
- Participation in class critiques, 10%

- A: Exceptional
- B: Very good
- C: Satisfactory
- D: Unsatisfactory
- F: Failure

COURSE SCHEDULE, SPRING 2013

Week 1, 1/29 & 1/31

Introduction to course; expectations

Production procedures

Screen pilots

Discuss responsibilities of each crew position

Review green light process

Brainstorming session for stories, Episode 2

Week 2, 2/5 & 2/7

Read drafts of Episode 2

Assign crew roles and initial preproduction tasks

Discuss production needs for Episode 2

Rewrite and prep Episode 2

Production meeting 1, Episode 2

Paperwork tutorial

Workshop: Contributing to the overall creative vision

Week 3, 2/12 & 2/14

Rewrite and prep Episode 2

Production update, Episode 2

Week 4, 2/19 & 2/21

Rewrite and prep Episode 2

Production update, Episode 2

Location survey, Episode 2

Story discussion, Episode 3 (assign writers)

Assign crew jobs, Episode 3

Week 5, 2/26 & 2/28

Final prep, Episode 2

Production meeting 2, Episode 2

Read Episode 3

Production meeting 1, Episode 3
Review shot list, Episode 2
Shoot Episode 2, Friday 3/1, Saturday 3/2, Sunday 3/3

Week 6, 3/5 & 3/7

Screen dailies, Episode 2
Production updates, Episode 3
Screen and discuss rough cut, Episode 2
Assignment: Written production analysis of Episode 2 and peer evals

Week 7, 3/12 & 3/14

Screen and discuss 2nd cut, Episode 2
Rewrite and prep Episode 3
Production updates, Episode 3

Week 8, 3/19 & 3/21

Read and prep Episode 3
Screen and discuss 3rd cut, Episode 2
Location survey, Episode 3
Brainstorming session, stories for Episode 4
Assignment: Written final cut analysis of Episode 2

Week 9, 3/26 & 3/28

Spring break

Week 10, 4/2 & 4/4

Final prep, Episode 3
Review shot list, Episode 3
Table read, Episode 4
Production meeting, Episode 4
Assignment: Written production analysis of Episode 3 and peer evals
Shoot Episode 3, Friday 4/5, Saturday 4/6, Sunday 4/7

Week 11, 4/9 & 4/11

Screen dailies, Episode 3

Screen and discuss rough cut, Episode 3

Production meeting, Episode 4

Read revised draft, Episode 4

Week 12, 4/16 & 4/18

Screen and discuss 2nd cut, Episode 3

Read revised draft, Episode 4

Prep Episode 4

Week 13, 4/23 & 4/25

Screen and discuss 3rd cut, Episode 3

Final prep, Episode 4

Review shot list, Episode 4

Location survey, Episode 4

Assignment: Written final cut analysis of Episode 3

Shoot Episode 4, Friday 4/26, Saturday 4/27, Sunday 4/28

Week 14, 4/30 & 5/2

Screen dailies, Episode 4

Screen rough cut, Episode 4

Week 15, 5/7 & 5/9

Screen and discuss cut 2, Episode 4

Finals Week

Screen and discuss final cuts of entire series

Wrap party

ABOUT THE AUTHOR

Ross Brown began his writing career on NBC's award-winning comedy series *The Cosby Show*. He went on to write and produce such hit TV shows as *The Facts of Life*, *Who's the Boss?*, and *Step by Step*. He has created prime-time series for ABC, CBS, and the WB. His play *Hindsight* received two staged readings at the Pasadena Playhouse (Pasadena, California) in July 2007. His short play *Field of Vision* was performed in Chicago at the Appetite Theater's Bruschetta 2008 festival. His play *Trapped* was selected for the 2011 Festival of Appalachian Plays and Playwrights at the historic Barter Theater in Abingdon, Virginia.

He is an assistant professor of film and media arts at Chapman University in Orange, California, where he developed the cutting-edge Byte-Sized Television courses on creating TV series for the Internet.

SAVE THE CAT!®
THE LAST BOOK ON SCREENWRITING YOU'LL EVER NEED!

BLAKE SNYDER

BEST SELLER

He made millions of dollars selling screenplays to Hollywood and here screenwriter Blake Snyder tells all. "Save the Cat!®" is just one of Snyder's many ironclad rules for making your ideas more marketable and your script more satisfying – and saleable, including:
- The four elements of every winning logline.
- The seven immutable laws of screenplay physics.
- The 10 genres and why they're important to your movie.
- Why your Hero must serve your idea.
- Mastering the Beats.
- Mastering the Board to create the Perfect Beast.
- How to get back on track with ironclad and proven rules for script repair.

This ultimate insider's guide reveals the secrets that none dare admit, told by a show biz veteran who's proven that you can sell your script if you can save the cat.

"Imagine what would happen in a town where more writers approached screenwriting the way Blake suggests? My weekend read would dramatically improve, both in sellable/producible content and in discovering new writers who understand the craft of storytelling and can be hired on assignment for ideas we already have in house."
> – From the Foreword by Sheila Hanahan Taylor, Vice President, Development at Zide/Perry Entertainment, whose films include *American Pie, Cats and Dogs, Final Destination*

"One of the most comprehensive and insightful how-to's out there. Save the Cat!® is a must-read for both the novice and the professional screenwriter."
> – Todd Black, Producer, *The Pursuit of Happyness, The Weather Man, S.W.A.T, Alex and Emma, Antwone Fisher*

"Want to know how to be a successful writer in Hollywood? The answers are here. Blake Snyder has written an insider's book that's informative – and funny, too."
> – David Hoberman, Producer, *The Shaggy Dog* (2005), *Raising Helen, Walking Tall, Bringing Down the House, Monk* (TV)

BLAKE SNYDER, besides selling million-dollar scripts to both Disney and Spielberg, was one of Hollywood's most successful spec screenwriters. Blake's vision continues on *www.blakesnyder.com*.

$19.95 · 216 PAGES · ORDER NUMBER 34RLS · ISBN: 9781932907001

24 HOURS | **1.800.833.5738** | **WWW.MWP.COM**

THE WRITER'S JOURNEY - 3RD EDITION
MYTHIC STRUCTURE FOR WRITERS

CHRISTOPHER VOGLER

BEST SELLER

See why this book has become an international best seller and a true classic. *The Writer's Journey* explores the powerful relationship between mythology and storytelling in a clear, concise style that's made it required reading for movie executives, screenwriters, playwrights, scholars, and fans of pop culture all over the world.

Both fiction and nonfiction writers will discover a set of useful myth-inspired storytelling paradigms (i.e., "The Hero's Journey") and step-by-step guidelines to plot and character development. Based on the work of Joseph Campbell, *The Writer's Journey* is a must for all writers interested in further developing their craft.

The updated and revised third edition provides new insights and observations from Vogler's ongoing work on mythology's influence on stories, movies, and man himself.

"This book is like having the smartest person in the story meeting come home with you and whisper what to do in your ear as you write a screenplay. Insight for insight, step for step, Chris Vogler takes us through the process of connecting theme to story and making a script come alive."
> – Lynda Obst, producer, *Sleepless in Seattle, How to Lose a Guy in 10 Days*;
> author, *Hello, He Lied*

"This is a book about the stories we write, and perhaps more importantly, the stories we live. It is the most influential work I have yet encountered on the art, nature, and the very purpose of storytelling."
> – Bruce Joel Rubin, screenwriter, *Stuart Little 2, Deep Impact,*
> *Ghost, Jacob's Ladder*

CHRISTOPHER VOGLER is a veteran story consultant for major Hollywood film companies and a respected teacher of filmmakers and writers around the globe. He has influenced the stories of movies from *The Lion King* to *Fight Club* to *The Thin Red Line* and most recently wrote the first installment of *Ravenskull*, a Japanese-style manga or graphic novel. He is the executive producer of the feature film *P.S. Your Cat is Dead* and writer of the animated feature *Jester Till*.

$26.95 · 448 PAGES · ORDER NUMBER 76RLS · ISBN: 9781932907360

MASTER SHOTS VOL 3
THE DIRECTOR'S VISION 100 SETUPS, SCENES AND MOVES FOR YOUR BREAKTHROUGH MOVIE

CHRISTOPHER KENWORTHY

Master Shots has been one of the most successful filmmaking book series of all time. *Master Shots Vol 1, 2nd edition* and *Master Shots Vol 2* have generated cumulative sales of more than 60,000 copies and critical acclaim throughout the world. In this new volume, Kenworthy helps directors define their vision in every shot. This book provides the techniques to make a breakthrough film.

"Master Shots Vol 3 *offers fabulous insight into the purpose behind each shot. I'm so thankful for this book — it's my new secret weapon!"*

> — Trevor Mayes, Screenwriter/Director

"Finally! Someone has had the cleverness, initiative, and imagination to set down on paper a film language that has been passed down and amalgamated only by word of mouth since the days of Méliès and D. W. Griffith. Like Dr. Johnson's Dictionary of the English Language, *Christopher Kenworthy's* Master Shots *series seeks to make tangible and permanent what otherwise might be gone with the wind."*

> — John Badham, Director, *Saturday Night Fever, WarGames, Short Circuit*;
> Author, *I'll Be in My Trailer* and *John Badham on Directing*; Professor of
> Media Arts, The Dodge School, Chapman University

"A fascinating look at amazingly simple ways to use the camera, making this an essential read for anyone looking to hone the craft of visual storytelling."

> — Erin Corrado, www.onemoviefiveviews.com

CHRISTOPHER KENWORTHY is the creator of a new series of Master Shots e-books (with HD video and audio) including *Master Shots: Action, Master Shots: Suspense,* and *Master Shots: Story.* He's the author of the best-selling *Master Shots Vols 1* and *2*, with *Master Shots Vol 3: The Director's Vision* released in 2013.

$26.95 · 238 PAGES · ORDER NUMBER 196RLS · ISBN: 9781615931545

WRITING THE TV DRAMA SERIES 3RD EDITION

HOW TO SUCCEED AS A PROFESSIONAL WRITER IN TV

PAMELA DOUGLAS

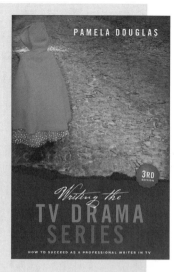

This new edition builds on the book's reputation by bringing the very latest information, insights, and advice from major writers and producers. It is a complete resource for anyone who wants to write and produce for a television drama series or create an original series, as well as for teachers in screenwriting classes and workshops. Offering practical industry information and artistic encouragement, the book is both nuts-and-bolts and inspiration. The Third Edition leads readers into the future and engages provocative issues about the interface between traditional TV and emerging technologies and endless possibilities.

"Right now is the golden age of TV drama and Pamela Douglas' Writing the TV Drama Series *is far and away the best resource I know of for any writer wishing to work in this tremendously challenging and rewarding field."*

> – Daniel Petrie, Jr., president, Writers Guild of America, West and Oscar-nominated writer

"Remarkably comprehensive and up-to-date, Writing the TV Drama Series *is a candid, enthusiastic introduction to the craft and culture of dramatic television."*

> – Jeff Melvoin, executive producer, *Alias, Northern Exposure*

"The breadth and depth of practical advice on real-world writing should enlighten and inspire any aspiring TV drama writer. It should enlighten because it is clear, free of jargon and explains the business and the design of television dramas. The interviews with successful writers makes this book valuable all by themselves, but there's so much more."

> – Diane Carson, Ph.D., editorial VP of University Film & Video Association

PAMELA DOUGLAS is an award-winning screenwriter with numerous credits in television drama. She was honored with the Humanitas Prize and won nominations for Writers Guild Awards and Emmys. Twice her shows also won awards from American Women in Radio and Television. As a developer, she wrote the pilot, bible, and 13 episodes of the acclaimed series *Ghostwriter*. Additional series credits include *Star Trek: The Next Generation, Frank's Place, Paradise, Trapper John, M.D.*, and many others. She has been a member of the Board of Directors of the Writers Guild of America. At the University of Southern California, she is a tenured professor in the School of Cinematic Arts, where she is head of the Television Track in the Screenwriting Division.

$26.95 · 250 PAGES · ORDER NUMBER 172RLS · ISBN: 9781615930586

SELLING YOUR STORY IN 60 SECONDS
THE GUARANTEED WAY TO GET
YOUR SCREENPLAY OR NOVEL READ

MICHAEL HAUGE

BEST SELLER

Best-selling author Michael Hauge reveals:
- How to Design, Practice, and Present the
  60-Second Pitch
- The Cardinal Rule of Pitching
- The 10 Key Components of a Commercial Story
- The 8 Steps to a Powerful Pitch
- Targeting Your Buyers
- Securing Opportunities to Pitch
- Pitching Templates
- And much more, including "The Best Pitch I Ever Heard," an exclusive collection
  from major film executives

"Michael Hauge's principles and methods are so well argued that the mysteries of effective screenwriting can be understood — even by directors."

> — Phillip Noyce, Director, *Patriot Games, Clear and Present Danger,*
> *The Quiet American, Rabbit-Proof Fence*

"... one of the few authentically good teachers out there. Every time I revisit my notes, I learn something new or reinforce something that I need to remember."

> — Jeff Arch, Screenwriter, *Sleepless in Seattle, Iron Will*

"Michael Hauge's method is magic — but unlike most magicians, he shows you how the trick is done."

> — William Link, Screenwriter & Co-Creator, *Columbo*; *Murder, She Wrote*

"By following the formula we learned in Michael Hauge's seminar, we got an agent, optioned our script, and now have a three-picture deal at Disney."

> — Paul Hoppe and David Henry, Screenwriters

MICHAEL HAUGE is the author of *Writing Screenplays That Sell*, now in its 30th printing, and has presented his seminars and lectures to more than 30,000 writers and filmmakers. He has coached hundreds of screenwriters and producers on their screenplays and pitches, and has consulted on projects for Warner Brothers, Disney, New Line, CBS, Lifetime, Julia Roberts, Jennifer Lopez, Kirsten Dunst, and Morgan Freeman.

$12.95 · 150 PAGES · ORDER NUMBER 64RLS · ISBN: 9781932907209

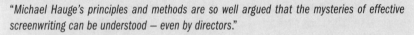

24 HOURS | **1.800.833.5738** | **WWW.MWP.COM**

CINEMATIC STORYTELLING
THE 100 MOST POWERFUL FILM CONVENTIONS
EVERY FILMMAKER MUST KNOW

JENNIFER VAN SIJLL

BEST SELLER

How do directors use screen direction to suggest conflict? How do screenwriters exploit film space to show change? How does editing style determine emotional response?

Many first-time writers and directors do not ask these questions. They forego the huge creative resource of the film medium, defaulting to dialog to tell their screen story. Yet most movies are carried by sound and picture. The industry's most successful writers and directors have mastered the cinematic conventions specific to the medium. They have harnessed non-dialog techniques to create some of the most cinematic moments in movie history.

This book is intended to help writers and directors more fully exploit the medium's inherent storytelling devices. It contains 100 non-dialog techniques that have been used by the industry's top writers and directors. From *Metropolis* and *Citizen Kane* to *Dead Man* and *Kill Bill*, the book illustrates — through 500 frame grabs and 75 script excerpts — how the inherent storytelling devices specific to film were exploited.

You will learn:
· How non-dialog film techniques can advance story.
· How master screenwriters exploit cinematic conventions to create powerful scenarios.

"Cinematic Storytelling *scores a direct hit in terms of concise information and perfectly chosen visuals, and it also searches out... and finds... an emotional core that many books of this nature either miss or are afraid of.*"
— Kirsten Sheridan, Director, *Disco Pigs*; Co-writer, *In America*

"*Here is a uniquely fresh, accessible, and truly original contribution to the field. Jennifer van Sijll takes her readers in a wholly new direction, integrating aspects of screenwriting with all the film crafts in a way I've never before seen. It is essential reading not only for screenwriters but also for filmmakers of every stripe.*"
— Prof. Richard Walter, UCLA Screenwriting Chairman

JENNIFER VAN SIJLL has taught film production, film history, and screenwriting. She is currently on the faculty at San Francisco State's Department of Cinema.

$24.95 · 230 PAGES · ORDER NUMBER 35RLS · ISBN: 9781932907056

THE MYTH OF MWP

In a dark time, a light bringer came along, leading the curious and the frustrated to clarity and empowerment. It took the well-guarded secrets out of the hands of the few and made them available to all. It spread a spirit of openness and creative freedom, and built a storehouse of knowledge dedicated to the betterment of the arts.

The essence of the Michael Wiese Productions (MWP) is empowering people who have the burning desire to express themselves creatively. We help them realize their dreams by putting the tools in their hands. We demystify the sometimes secretive worlds of screenwriting, directing, acting, producing, film financing, and other media crafts.

By doing so, we hope to bring forth a realization of 'conscious media' which we define as being positively charged, emphasizing hope and affirming positive values like trust, cooperation, self-empowerment, freedom, and love. Grounded in the deep roots of myth, it aims to be healing both for those who make the art and those who encounter it. It hopes to be transformative for people, opening doors to new possibilities and pulling back veils to reveal hidden worlds.

MWP has built a storehouse of knowledge unequaled in the world, for no other publisher has so many titles on the media arts. Please visit www.mwp.com where you will find many free resources and a 25% discount on our books. Sign up and become part of the wider creative community!

Onward and upward,

Michael Wiese
Publisher/Filmmaker

INDEPENDENT FILMMAKERS
SCREENWRITERS
MEDIA PROFESSIONALS

MICHAEL WIESE PRODUCTIONS
GIVES YOU
INSTANT ACCESS
TO THE BEST BOOKS
AND INSTRUCTORS
IN THE WORLD

FOR THE LATEST UPDATES
AND DISCOUNTS,
CONNECT WITH US ON
WWW.MWP.COM

JOIN US
ON FACEBOOK

FOLLOW US
ON TWITTER

VIEW US
ON YOUTUBE